SVIATOSLAV RICHTER

SVIATOSLAV RICHTER

pianist

Karl Aage Rasmussen

TRANSLATED BY RUSSELL DEES

NORTHEASTERN UNIVERSITY PRESS
Boston

Published by
UNIVERSITY PRESS OF NEW ENGLAND
Hanover and London

NORTHEASTERN UNIVERSITY PRESS

Published by University Press of New England

One Court Street, Lebanon NH 03766

www.upne.com

© 2010 Karl Aage Rasmussen and Gyldendalske Boghandel,
Nordisk Forlag A/S, Copenhagen 2007. Published by agreement
with the Gyldendal Group Agency

Manufactured in the United States of America

Typeset in Arnhem, The Serif, and The Sans by Passumpsic Publishing

Designed by Eric M. Brooks

University Press of New England is a member of the
Green Press Initiative. The paper used in this book
meets their minimum requirement for recycled paper.

For permission to reproduce any of the material in this book,
contact Permissions, University Press of New England,
One Court Street, Lebanon NH 03766; or visit www.upne.com

Library of Congress Cataloging-in-Publication Data
Rasmussen, Karl Aage.
[Svjatoslav Richter. English]
Sviatoslav Richter: pianist / Karl Aage Rasmussen;
translated by Russell Dees.
    p. cm.
Includes bibliographical references and index.
ISBN 978-1-55553-710-4 (cloth: alk. paper)
1. Richter, Sviatoslav, 1959–1997. 2. Pianists—
Russia (Federation)—Biography. I. Title.
ML417.R38R3713   2010
786.2092—dc22   2009047996
[B]

5 4 3 2 1

CONTENTS

SVIATOSLAV RICHTER

Letting the Music Speak

Nobody who has seen the film by the French filmmaker Bruno Monsaingeon, *Richter, l'insoumis* (*Richter, the Enigma*), will forget the image of an ailing eighty-two-year-old musician who reluctantly allows himself to be interrogated about his life and art. Looking tired and resigned, and often with a melancholy or mischievous smile, Sviatoslav Richter recalls scenes from his long life. His was a full yet introverted life, punctuated by rounds of applause from an admiring public; his story is full of accolades and artistic triumphs. Richter had a restless career with nearly four thousand public concerts, which may well be a record. But in our protagonist's memory there is also loss, oppression, human frailty, and fear of being unable to meet the towering demands of his own art.

"I don't like myself," claims the celebrated pianist with head bowed (though his *"ya sebe nye nravlyus"* may be translated less harshly as "I am not satisfied with myself"). He may only be thinking about what he experiences when he listens—almost always with disappointment—to his own playing on one of the countless recordings that constitute his musical legacy. But when he lifts his head, looks directly into the camera, adds "That's the way it is!" (*"vsyo"*), and then hides his face behind his hand, turning away, the viewer hates the prying camera for a moment and senses that the remark may go deeper, touching on life itself. His comment is a reflection not just on a phenomenal artistic life that in hindsight did not realize the impossible dream—perfection, the ideal—but also on the personal struggle with fate and the meaning of life.

And yet, this fragile old man—a musician coming to terms with his life shortly before his death in 1997 and whose eyes shift from a world-weariness to a glowing intensity and an almost sardonic cheerfulness—still retains his status as an unshakable icon, a cult figure, alive and kicking, in the world of music. Not only was this status based on the fact that Richter was one of the greatest pianists of all time—one of those rare artists who are admired, honored, and beloved by their colleagues the world over—but it also hinged on a legend stemming from his personality, whose guardedness in private life was sometimes seen as shyness, sometimes as arrogance, a life filled with contradictions and riddles. A man of the world who hid behind his anonymity and isolation, an introvert who resigned himself to the rituals of the spotlight and officiousness of showbiz when his role as superstar of the piano required it. He was described as straightforward, full of *joie de vivre*, and at times almost bubbling over with humor, but also as distant and introverted, a man familiar with despair and depression. He was seen as a delicate flower, a mimosa, sometimes soft as velvet, sometimes hard as flint, especially when it came to art and its practitioners, a pianist with a repertoire so encompassing as to seem almost casual and yet a musician who throughout his life played only exactly what he wanted to, without considering the expectations of the audience or anyone else.

The tragic elements in a human life emerge more slowly and are acknowledged with more hesitation than success, glamour, and fame. Loneliness, wrecked love, unhappiness, illness, and death are the stuff of personality cults and myths, but the darker sides of great artists such as Maria Callas, Marilyn Monroe, Elvis Presley, Glenn Gould, Jimi Hendrix, or Janis Joplin came to the fore late, usually only after their deaths. The myth of Sviatoslav Richter is different. One ingredient is missing: the chasm between limelight and loneliness, the perilous balance between triumph and perdition, genius and fate, light and darkness. The Richter myth is in a way a pure myth about music, the story of a musician of enormous stature. In his final, difficult years, he did note that a musician's spiritual force becomes aimless without the participation of one's physical shell. But the tragic sides of his existence play out on the stage of life, not art. The perfect, the definitive in art, remains an unachievable dream. And this is not tragic. It is a condition of life.

Some of the components of the myth are self-evident. Richter possessed the ideal physical characteristics for playing the piano—unusually large, slender hands with a finger span that stretched easily across more than an octave between the index and the little finger. Very long thumbs with something resembling a third joint gave his hands unusual reach. A phenomenal musical memory allowed him to fix in his mind a piece of music he had played only once and then remember it half a century later. He could store entire operas in his head (a rare but not impossible feat, not unlike the photographic memory of chess masters who play blind chess with dozens of opponents at the same time). In addition, Richter possessed an exceptional ability to read music, which allowed him to play almost anything at first sight, "off the page," including orchestral music and operas. And with his colossal technical and mental reserves, he could memorize immense piano works in a few days. His repertoire stretched to almost all corners of the piano's domain—from Bach to our own times. He restored piano classics that had become rarities in the display windows of the concert world—Handel, Haydn, and Schubert—to their former glory. He played forgotten or overlooked music with the same commitment and empathy he invested in Beethoven or Brahms, Chopin or Debussy, Rachmaninov, Prokofiev, or Shostakovich.

He began late. He was approaching his twenties when he finally decided on a career as a pianist. And even though his father was a pianist and piano teacher by profession, Richter was, in most respects, self-taught. This made him into one of the piano world's great lone wolves, an outsider. His playing sometimes looked like a study of everything piano teachers warn against. And yet, he achieved the physical ability to create not only nuance—which turned him into one of the most sensitive creators of atmosphere of all time—but also an incredible range of dynamics and a palette of sound so rich that his interpretation of Mussorgsky's *Pictures at an Exhibition* makes Ravel's colorful orchestral version seem pale by comparison, and Richter does not need Vladimir Horowitz's pianistic "improvements" of the score. "The best Russian work *for piano*," Richter said with featherlight sarcasm.

Of course, colors in music and art are not equivalent, but they derive from the same sources in the imagination. Even in childhood, Richter was preoccupied with drawing and painting. On the walls of his Moscow apartment hung valuable works of art—Renoir, Fernand Léger, a drawing Picasso had given him, Kokoschka's sketch of him as a fifty-year-old, canvases by his close friend Robert Falk (whose experimental paintings were banned for a while), and sketches by Miró and by Alexander Calder. In the summer of 1950, a friend presented him with a set of pastels, and for many years thereafter, Richter indulged in this hobby as a form of relaxation from his nerve-racking concert life, with obvious talent. Later he often organized regular exhibitions for friends in his sitting room, including "forbidden" works by, for example, Robert Falk; in July 1979 he even showed his own gouaches and watercolors at an exhibition in Tbilisi, the Georgian capital. Throughout his life, Richter was passionately interested in all forms of creativity. He was a voracious art aficionado, to a degree that is rare among artists. He possessed a legendarily broad insight into not only the music of the concert hall and the opera house but also into theater, dance, art, architecture, film, and classical world literature.

As an interpreter of music, Richter was both simple and inscrutable. He did not doubt for a moment that music should be allowed to speak, and it should always be the composer's music—that is, the notes and directions in the score, for which he was both the guarantor and the sounding board. "I only play what is in the score," he stressed again and again. He quoted with satisfaction conductor Kurt Sanderling's characterization: *"er spielt nicht nur gut, er kann auch Noten lesen!"* ("he does not only play well, he can also read the notes"). "If you do not respect all the directions in the score, you begin to 'interpret,' and I'm against that," he said. "I try to play what the composer has written, nothing more, nothing less."

In a world influenced by technology, synthesizers, the MIDI, and computers, this point of view may seem simple-minded. A computer can be programmed to produce all the notes and other directions in a Beethoven sonata, for example, but a computer cannot play *the music*. Who would be satisfied with an actor who merely recited the playwright's words? What Richter means is that his performance of the notes is not about "putting something into" the work but about liberating the music from everything that can disrupt its trajectory from the sound board of the piano to the listener's mind. Richter wants to be the anonymous mirror that reflects the silent notes of the score and, thus, brings the dormant music to life. He wants to be not egotistical, but a sort of ethereal resonance, the conduit for a spiritualization of the meaning of the music.

But where *is* the music? Is it in the notes? In the piano? In the sound waves, in the ears, in the mind? Richter knew well that there is no definitive ideal, no "truth," and that the musical work exists only as an ever-new approximation. Can one speak of *the work* or *the music* in a definitive form?

And what role does the interpreter play for the musical work (particularly a heavyweight like Richter)? Can he hide behind the work as its faithful, anonymous mouthpiece? Should he? And even more important, can or should he forget his own time when he steps into the composer's? Do we not experience Beethoven differently after having heard Berlioz? Does not Schubert sound different after listening to Mahler? Can we hear Strauss or Debussy in the same way now that popular music, Hollywood, and Disneyland have used these sources for entirely different goals? Are we not all the result of an encounter with our own reality? Is Richter's Beethoven not read through Prokofiev? Did he not see Chopin through Scriabin or even Ravel in the light of Rachmaninov?

With his eminent ability to sense the dramaturgical flow of time, he could stretch out the first, dreamy movement of Schubert's final work, the Piano Sonata in B-flat Major, as an almost twenty-five-minute arc and yet keep the listener enchanted. This is overwhelming proof that the phenomenon of music contains elements that must be considered magical. But is this really just a mirror of the notes written by the genius Schubert, pure and simple? Or is it

Richter in the United States, 1970.

a depiction of Sviatoslav Richter's genius? What is an "interpreter"? Who can answer?

This problem preoccupied him all his life, which may explain his unbearable *Weltschmerz* virtually every time he listened to himself. His self-criticism was merciless, so total as to seem self-destructive. In his notes from the years 1970–95, parts of which Bruno Monsaingeon published in 1998, the year after his death, one sees him again and again rap himself on the knuckles ("most of my recordings are terrible. Listening to them puts me into a terrible mood. . . . I'm always disappointed"). It is shocking to learn that he is speaking of highly acclaimed recordings that are coveted as collector's items. It is hard to imagine what he is hearing!

Even when he failed by objective standards, it was on a scale that makes comparison with other pianists difficult. Half a century of music on records and CDs has accustomed listeners to expect music played flawlessly. Despite his background as a virtual autodidact, Richter possessed a piano technique and a dexterity second to none in the history of the piano. Nevertheless, there were evenings when he could be divinely inspired in one work and dryly introverted or exaggeratedly exalted in another. And there were evenings when he missed not just a single note here and there but a fistful. And apparently he did so without affecting the overall performance. Just as a newspaper photograph or the Milky Way seems to constitute a unified whole made of countless small parts, music arises as a spell-binding whole, not a sum of its parts. "Mistakes" are also music.

But everything looks different in hindsight. The slightest deviation from perfection made Richter feel like a fumbler. For example, after he heard a concert recording of seven of Liszt's *Transcendental Etudes* he made when he was seventy-three, he wrote: "This is yet another recording of a concert that, at the time, seemed to be fairly successful. How wrong you can be! True, it has a certain atmosphere, and everyone thinks this is the *prime* quality. But the blurred notes, the exaggerations, the absence of real concentration, and this quality that seems to be inherent in my playing—a sort of superfluous heaviness—it all makes me feel very sad (if not worse). I'd so much like to play better."

It can be difficult to come to terms with this feeling of inadequacy in Richter, his repeated disappointments with his performances, his dissatisfaction with the unique beauty he was able to create. But there is a psychological dimension to this, which shows up in an episode where acquaintances of his played for him two recordings of Prokofiev's Eighth Piano Sonata, one of Richter's favorite works. One of the recordings was his own; the other was by his friend and younger colleague Andrei Gavrilov (with whom he felt a close kinship as a pianist). His friends set a trap for him; they told him that Gavrilov's recording was his own. Richter suspected nothing and was highly dissatisfied with "his" performance. Then, upon hearing his own in the belief that it was Gavrilov's, he heard music "on a different, higher level." Understandably, his friends laughed long and hard. However, a deflated Richter called it "a dangerous game to play."

It can seem almost unreal that a musician of his Olympian stature could harbor so much insecurity, such a feeling of irredeemable inadequacy in the face of the challenges of his art, a consciousness that always renders perfect success an unreachable ideal. That Richter, with his virtually autodidactic background—as a young man, at any rate—needed to find security in the approval and applause of others seems evident from what students studying with Richter's beloved teacher Heinrich Neuhaus relate: even after he became famous and was lauded by musical audiences everywhere, he often returned to the Moscow Conservatory's piano class to try out a new program, with his young colleagues his loyal listeners.

The Richter myth crisscrosses the mysteries and questions of music. But as one delves into his background and personality, the myth broadens, deepens, darkens, and becomes a more complex story of the shadow sides, the costs and conditions associated with the gift we call talent or genius. And the long-term social, political, moral, and cultural consequences of the revolutionary movements of March and November 1917, together with Richter's unfortunate German-Russian background during two world wars in which Germany and Russia were on a war footing, are the stowaways that follow him most of his life.

In 1918, when the Russian czar, his wife, and children were executed and all privileges and most political rights were taken away from the upper class, Bolsheviks and rebellious peasants burned down several properties owned by Richter's mother's family. In 1938, during Stalin's purges, the secret police executed his uncle Rudolf as an "enemy of the people." And shortly before the German occupation reached western Ukraine and Odessa in the early autumn of 1941, the Soviet secret service forced his sixty-nine-year-old father to "confess" to collaborating in German counterespionage. This occurred under torture and, possibly, threats of reprisals against the unsuspecting twenty-six-year-old Sviatoslav, who at that point had begun his concert career in Moscow. The war made any communication with occupied Odessa impossible.

The NKVD, or the People's Commissariat for Internal Affairs (called the KGB, or Committee for State Security, after Stalin's death), made short work of it. Richter's father was summarily sentenced and shortly after shot. His mother remarried and emigrated to the southern German provincial town of Schwäbisch Gmünd following the withdrawal of the German-Romanian occupation forces. Not until a couple of years later did Richter learn that his father had been executed and that his much-loved and admired mother had left him for someone who had apparently been her lover.

Understandably, in his conversations with Monsaingeon, Richter describes his mother's new husband in very sinister, almost demonic phrases. In his hints that his father knew of his mother's infidelity and that the lover was an informant, a *stukach*, who was responsible for his father's death, one might see a Soviet counterpart of *Hamlet* unfolding. Richter saw his mother only a few times after that. Almost all of his other relatives emigrated or relocated to the West after occupation troops were finally driven out of the Ukraine in 1944.

Naturally, these losses left deep scars in his psyche. Many years later, he spoke reticently and aloofly about them. Sviatoslav Richter, the future icon of the socialist workers' state, the recipient of the Stalin Prize and the Order of Lenin, "artist of the Soviet people," a national cultural treasure of the Soviet republic, knew early on what a high price had been paid when revolt, revolution, and civil war swept over Russian society with a wave of violence that changed the lives and fates of millions of people. Along with his involuntary role as cultural figurehead of the Soviet propaganda machine and the artistic shackles imposed on him, this painful incident contains the seed of the repressions that characterized his self-understanding. Throughout his life, he was willfully ignorant of and uninterested in politics, which against this murky background resembles a tactic used by ostriches. Was this a flight from reality, self-protection, sticking his head in the sand? Or, looking at it from a more empathetic point of view, was it simply a routine acceptance of the social conventions of society? Yet this avoidance hardly constituted a naïveté or self-deception, words that seem inappropriate when applied to Sviatoslav Richter, a world-class artist who, when finally allowed to travel to the West, had to put up with surveillance by official traveling companions, the "secretaries" appointed by the Soviet Ministry of Culture.

The eighty-year-old Igor Stravinsky's reactions to his first and only visit to the USSR after fifty years of exile might illuminate Richter's complex of emotions. As a right-wing émigré, Stravinsky always gave vent to his violent, heart-felt disgust with the Soviet regime. But in connection with the visit, Stravinsky's assistant and famulus Robert Craft describes how half a century lived in the West can be forgotten in one night: the composer was more moved than Craft had ever seen him. Russian traditions, customs, conventions, and forgotten expressions overwhelmed him from the moment he stepped on his native soil. A cultural heritage expresses itself not primarily in terms of politics or art, but in terms of habits and conventions, signs, gestures, symbols, and rituals. It is an instinctual feeling that binds one to a place and a people, regardless of the form of government or power structure. Generally speaking, love of one's homeland is hardly ever a love of a country's political system. It is a love connected to one's spiritual life.

At one point in his conversations with Monsaingeon, Richter mentions that his mother's interest in social matters and politics may have contributed to his life-long aversion. He claims that she chastised him for not paying enough attention to what went on in politics and public life. But he does not go into any details. "I really wasn't interested in it in the slightest and have never paid the least attention to it before or since." One can believe *that*, but not the explanation. A totalitarian society permeated by lies and concealment leaves its mark. Criticizing policies in the Soviet Union (and how can an interest in politics not be critical?) carried the risk that a musician's music might be squelched. If a person retained the ability to think independently, this inevitably led to a sort of personality split. As the Russian saying goes, "An incautious word is not a bird; if it slips out, it cannot be caught again." After the collapse of the Soviet Union, the conductor Gennadi Roszhdesvensky said of the great violinist David Oistrakh, "If he had not kept his mouth shut, we would never have heard his violin!"

However, political freedom was a problem for only a few musicians; the issue mainly had to do with artistic freedom, the right to play what one wanted to play and how and where and with whom. Again and again, musical emigrants and defectors adduce this simple reason, adding: "I am a musician, not a politician."

But the problem is far more complicated. In the West, the generally accepted picture of life in the Soviet Union during the Cold War is one of empty shops, mile-long lines, alcoholism, the KGB, the Gulag, a gilded, mendacious bureaucracy, and a starved populace, making it all too easy to see the population as consisting of only three groups: a corrupt power elite, courageous dissidents, and a huge formless mass of silent fellow travelers. But the fact that most people preferred to comply with the state's norms and expectations and habitually practiced Soviet doublethink in no way made a rich spiritual climate impossible. After all, the Soviet era was an extension of the long Russian tradition of self-reflection and contemplation about existence, a tradition in which music, art, and literature are taken seriously in a way that is virtually unknown anywhere else and where kindergarteners flock to museums. Cultural life under Stalin, Khrushchev, and Brezhnev cannot be painted in dark colors only. Rather, it testifies to the ability of people to create spiritual values even under the most difficult circumstances. And a love of one's homeland, of one's national roots, can prevail in spite of despotism and oppression, making it difficult to distinguish that love from loyalty. Even today, political thought in Russia is decisively different from the way it is expressed in the West. The concept of democracy does not have the high status it does in the West. The role of the state is not to implement and ensure democracy but to show strength and exercise power. The state governs citizens, not the other way around. To have things "decided for you" apparently creates more security than annoyance among the Russian populace. Today's opinion polls indicate that almost a third of all Russians mourn the collapse of the Soviet Union. And the explanation might be rather straightforward: post-Communist Russia has developed into a country with possibly the greatest social inequality in the world between the well-to-do and the rest of the population.

And yet, memories of a childhood spent in Odessa in the mid-1930s, as recounted by the eighty-two-year-old Richter, are still permeated by fear, insecurity, and the brutal suppression of free expression and trade. People were arrested randomly in droves, often under the cover of darkness. Some were suddenly fired without reason, accusations of every sort were spread, including negligence of duty, corruption, embezzlement, dissolute lifestyle, and so on. Everyone feared others might be informants on the lookout for "enemies of the people."

For example, when Richter recounts how "somebody who toed the party line and was a Party member" suddenly took over a conductor's job he had been counting on or that the pianist Vsevolod Topilin—David Oistrakh's accompanist and partner until the war, a man whose playing had influenced the young Richter's decision to become a pianist—was arrested after the war "because he hadn't been killed in battle," this does not sound like an aversion to politics. It sounds like the experience of being helplessly subjected to a particular *form* of politics, a political vise that made resistance useless and pointless and led to a hatred of politics. And all Russians know the concept of *sudba takaya* ("that's fate"), an unshakable notion of a shared destiny that can, in many instances, lead to passivity and a shrug of the shoulders or possibly repression.

This side of Richter's personality reveals itself in many guises—so many that one may wonder whether *repression* is the right word. It is clear that, to a rare degree, he was able to deal with external pressure by going into a sort of internal exile. And this fatalism, which is a well-known aspect of the history of the Russian people, was evident in him. Disappointments can go so deep that they can be difficult to face. Whether the price for this inner harmony is too high, and whether forbearance, the shrug of the shoulders, a laissez-faire attitude over the long run gnaws at the soul in a man who, to an unusual degree, was willful and defiant is difficult to say. Not all demons can be tamed.

"Despite my temperament, I am something of a cold-blooded type," Richter remarked in one of his conversations with the Russian pianist and teacher Yakov Milstein, which after Milstein's death in 1981 were published in a slim book titled *O Svyatoslave Richtere* (About Sviatoslav Richter). "I look at what I do objectively." This detachment may have helped Richter's forbearance vis-à-vis the heavy-handed control of musicians, which was a fact of Soviet state culture and which, until Gorbachev's perestroika, turned many important Soviet soloists into defectors, for instance, Vladimir Ashkenazy, Kyril Kondrashin, Mstislav Rostropovich, Galina Vishnevskaya, Rudolf Barshai, Maxim Shostakovich, Oistrakh's student Gidon Kremer, Rostropovich's student David Geringas, and a number of others.

Officials in the concert bureau of the Soviet Ministry of Culture, the Goskoncert, determined everything of importance: where, when, with whom, and what music was to be played. Again and again, the bureau informed Western concert organizers that the musician they wanted to engage "did not fulfill travel or contractual prerequisites" at the moment, or that certain musicians "were not considered suitable." Goskoncert gave musicians the green or the red light, issued or canceled travel visas, set tours and concert dates, made decisions about the artist's "state of health," and so on. They negotiated all fees based on the performer's Western market value but normally paid the Soviet soloist only a small fraction of the fee. The reason the Ministry of Culture gave was simple: the Soviet state had ensured and paid for the soloist's high level of education. In her memoirs, soprano Galina Vishnevskaya wrote that soloists such as Richter, Oistrakh, Gilels, and her husband, Mstislav Rostropovich, were paid about $200 per concert in the 1960s, and singers a bit more. "When the Bolshoi was on tour, everyone, without exception—from the stagehands to the soloists—received the same payment: ten dollars a day. From that fee, they were to nourish themselves enough to avoid passing out from hunger during the performances." For the Soviet state, the business of touring musicians in the West was an attractive, almost cost-free source of income (that the Ministry of Finance tolerated the often restrictive exploitation of these opportunities is indeed surprising).

The fact that the deeply antiauthoritarian Richter put up with this system, which made musicians into a kind of serf, and that he lived with it almost his entire career must have made considerable demands on his "cold-bloodedness." But apart from his ironic bent, he never openly took exception to or criticized the Soviet practice of organizing concerts. He saw it as a condition of life, quite simply. It takes a dearth of imagination to fail to understand how and why it was (and is) possible for people at all levels of society to find a totalitarian regime repulsive and, at the same time, acknowledge it as a sine qua non; it is narrow-minded to overlook how and why citizens in an unfree society can be both its victims and its supporters.

Asked why Richter put up with these humiliations all his life, Rudolf Barshai, his friend of many years, the conductor and founder of the Moscow Chamber Orchestra, and former viola player for the Borodin Quartet, replies:

I don't know. You simply did not talk about it. The subject was taboo. It was a private matter. But let me assure you that emigration was an incomprehensibly difficult decision. You became a pariah. When I became a "defector," it amazed me how many close friends turned their back on me. I ran into friends on the street who walked over to the other side when they saw me.

But, for me, it was simply a necessity. My concert with the London Philharmonic and a concert in Lucerne were suddenly canceled. My English impresario flew to Moscow and interrupted me in the middle of a rehearsal: "Rudolf, pack your trunk. We have to go to London at once." I thought it was a joke. "I don't have a visa." He said, "We will lose a lot of money, it is already sold out." So he went to the ministry, where the deputy minister told him that Barshai was ill. "Ill? I was just with him!" "We know best about these things," answered the superior.

Later, these predators understood that it was stupid, that the state lost money when famous artists were not allowed to play abroad. You asked how much Goskoncert kept of a typical fee. Let me just say: I don't remember! I *won't* remember! It is a sad and dreary story. An uncivilized story.

But even though Richter describes it as "cold-blooded," his temperament sometimes took a violent, elementally physical form. Stories of this abound. In the mid-1950s, he played Liszt's Sonata in B Minor in a provincial town in Hungary. After the initial dark measures in pianissimo, he intoned the octaves of the fortissimo theme with a vigorous hop on the piano bench. It collapsed under him, and he fell to the floor. Shocked, he picked up the broken bench and disappeared behind the curtain. Then the frightened audience heard a tremendous noise from backstage: in a rage, Richter had smashed the piano bench against a wall!

The best-known episode is told by Hungarian pianist Zoltán Kocsis, with whom Richter rehearsed a Schubert program for four hands in a borrowed Parisian apartment (which belonged to his later film biographer Bruno Monsaingeon). It was a warm June day in 1977, and the musicians opened the windows. During the rehearsal, the doorbell rang. Kocsis opened the door, and a very agitated elderly woman began scolding him: the music was ruining her midday nap. When Kocsis returned and explained the problem, Richter exploded with a violent invective and threw his indispensable glasses on the floor, where they shattered. He then disappeared without a trace for more than a day.

Others tell of fits of rage that showed a Richter different from the introverted, slightly distant man most people saw if they were not close to him. At a concert in Italy, some technicians from RAI, the public service broadcaster, arrived with recording equipment and microphones shortly before Richter was to go onstage. Normally, he tolerated recordings of his concerts. This time, however, he was not informed in advance. He ripped the microphones from their stands and flung them on the floor in an uncontrollable rage!

The German pianist Andreas Lucewicz relates yet another story. Lucewicz played a special role in Richter's life after 1983, when he served as Richter's chauffeur, then page-turner, and finally duo partner. Together, they performed Max Reger's colossal Beethoven variations several times, including during Richter's very last concert in Lübeck on March 30, 1995.

In the 1960s Richter's close friend, the art collector Johannes Wasmuth, rented part of a beautiful old railway station in Bonn's southern outskirts and, among other things, created a museum for the sculptor (and Dadaist) Hans (Jean) Arp. One room in the building complex was converted to a concert hall, and Richter often returned there in the 1980s and 1990s. The audience sat close to the concert podium, and the sound of passing trains helped create a special, intimate atmosphere. In 1984, a few months after he turned sixty-nine, Richter walked onstage to play Brahms's Sonata in F-sharp Minor. But after a few measures, he suddenly stopped and left the stage with a darkened countenance, relates Lucewicz.

Wasmuth was waiting behind the stage with Lucewicz. *"Das Klavier ist kaput* [The piano is destroyed]," shouted Richter. *"Das Konzert ist kaput* [The concert is destroyed]." In his fury, he ripped off his bow tie and threw it into the air. Unfortunately, it landed in one of the crystal chandeliers of the high-ceilinged station. The technically proficient young colleague walked onto the stage to find out what was wrong. The pedal mechanism was askew, but he twisted it into place and garnered warm applause from the hall. However, Richter refused to go onstage without his bow tie. And it was twelve feet up. To the horror of his friends, he placed a table under the chandelier, put a chair on top of it, and crawled up to retrieve this article of clothing. But he still could not reach the last foot and a half. He balanced a stool precariously on the chair but still could not reach it (fortunately, there were no more chairs available). Wasmuth found a long pair of scissors and crawled up on the table. While he supported Richter's legs, the sixty-nine-year-old pianist knocked his bow tie down with the scissors. After a half hour's delay, the concert resumed.

At one point in the film, Richter tells Monsaingeon about a personal experience from his walks in Moscow's outer districts during the war: "I remember walking on my own through a forest and suddenly finding myself bellowing like a wild animal in a sort of atavistic reflex. All on my own and without warning: grrrr! Ow-ow-ow! Like a tiger, a lion or a wolf. It started up all at once, but I soon realized that I was doing something odd. It was as though I'd been turned into an animal wandering through a primeval forest. As an episode, it had no particular significance, except that it took place at all and that it occasionally resurfaces in my recollections."

Not all demons can be tamed.

Images and Chimeras

Antipodes often illuminate each other in a particularly telling way: Apollo and Dionysus, Holmes and Dr. Watson, Dr. Jekyll and Mr. Hyde, God and the Devil. Arthur Koestler spoke of "the differences that make a difference." The pointed difference provides clear markers and makes patterns visible. In his book titled *Philosophy of New Music*, the German philosopher Theodor Adorno used this method when he contrasted Schönberg and Stravinsky as exemplary antipodes in twentieth-century music in a large-scale attempt to say everything there is to say.

Richter's antipode might well be the Canadian pianist Glenn Gould. Gould's greatness is still controversial. He turned his back on the rituals of bourgeois musical culture and withdrew into the recording studio. Yet, he never became an isolated sectarian loner, but rather a media star with the status of omnipresent universal genius. And a galaxy of colorful details revolves around his myth: the far-too-low piano bench, the primal humming that accompanied his playing, the absence of the Romantic Golden Age of the piano from his repertoire, his absurd heavy clothes in the Canadian summer heat (wool sweater, mufflers, and gloves), the basin of warm water in which he dipped his fingers during his concerts, his phobia of any physical contact, the reverse circadian rhythm that turned night into day, and so on.

Richter was never controversial. He did not create his own media image, and his behavior was never strikingly eccentric. Whereas Gould recorded Mozart's sonatas so that even his most hard-core fans crossed themselves, or caricatured Beethoven's *Appassionata* with open malice, there is nothing similar in the Richter legend. Hardly any of Richter's interpretations through his long life were viewed as consciously provocative or fiercely controversial. Gould could direct a penetrating laser beam through the works he played that mercilessly revealed their weaknesses or flaws; Richter was always governed by love. "My favorite composer is always the one I am giving my attention to at the moment," he said. "You have to have complete trust in the composer and then . . . believe in yourself!"

Richter performs, illuminated only by his tiny personal lamp.

Richter always tried to avoid the spectacular, the showbiz sides of the traditional concert ritual. Later in life, he insisted on playing on a darkened stage. Only a single lamp illuminated the music rack (he had stopped playing from memory), and all attention was centered on the music. "You shouldn't care about the postman, only the post," as the Italian composer Giacinto Scelsi put it. Whereas Gould could be seen looming over the grand piano with his nose only a few inches from the keys, "conducting" his own performance as soon as a hand was free, Richter, as the years went by, would sit more and more quietly, often upright and almost motionless, before his piano. He harbored an intense hatred for TV transmissions of musical performances. "What is there to see other than the labor, the physical strain?" he asked irritably. "Only a voyeur could be interested in finger movements and facial expressions that do not reflect the music, only the labor." Or only the pianist, one might add. It is a classic problem. When we relate to art, when we listen, read, or watch, we often focus so automatically on the person *behind* the art that we can lose sight of the work itself.

Otherwise, Richter apparently accepted the traditional concert form as a fact of life. While Gould referred again and again to his lifelong "love affair with the microphone" and ultimately left the concert stage when he turned thirty-three, Richter usually despised working in a recording studio. A prominent member of the Soviet recording industry relates that Richter canceled more recording sessions than he showed up for—often at the last moment—and that he simply played through the music from start to finish, once or a few or, sometimes, many times. Fortunately for posterity, however, he tolerated the microphone without too much ado, when it came to radio transmissions, for example. He was even charitable toward the countless more or less dubious pirate recordings of concerts that appeared, without giving the lost income any thought. His discography is probably the largest of any classical pianist.

While Gould worked as an engineer behind the protective walls of the recording studio, tried countless possibilities, put them together in a clever, controlled jigsaw puzzle, wrote his own liner notes, and so on, Richter recorded reams of music without paying any attention to sound quality, microphone positions, remixing, or marketing. Several times, Gould expressed annoyance that Richter (whom he esteemed highly) had "betrayed his abilities" by representing them on some of the most awful-sounding and primitive recordings in the entire catalogue. At one point he even offered to be Richter's producer, "for anything in the repertoire, even Rachmaninov!" But it all went over Richter's head: "I have absolutely no understanding of this sort of thing; for me, it's completely indifferent. Many people today consider the quality of recording techniques to be quite significant. Probably, because this is something they understand, something they find more important than the music itself. They are simply incapable of appreciating the true worth of an interpretation." He later wrote: "I've always loathed technology and it repays me in kind. We're at cross purposes, and it's the music that suffers most." He often claimed that all his best recordings were pirated. Eventually, he began to avoid the recording studio with a consistency that almost mirrored Gould's reverse choice. At the end of his life, he played only when and where he felt the need for it, often in small, out-of-the-way concert halls, far from the traffic circles of classical music culture.

But there is no world fame without a personality cult. Of course, the Richter myth also has its hype—mostly spurious anecdotes, hearsay, rumors, and drivel, which the protagonist always contemptuously rejected. The media magician Gould more or less consciously invented most of the components in his mythology. Again and again, Richter found that his fanatical followers worshiped an invented Richter that had no basis in reality. One of the ineradicable fables has it that when he was ordered to play at Stalin's funeral, Richter chose a very long, dry fugue by Bach as a protest against the dictator. The audience began to hiss. The highlight of the anecdote is that the police finally had to drag Richter away from the piano, presumably under pain of death. "I could have been shot on the spot," he is supposed to have said.

The story is utterly absurd. A commission from the Ministry of Culture chose the music on its own; and the audience, of course, would never dream of hissing at Stalin's funeral. Richter relates: "I was in a confined space, completely surrounded by the orchestra and not even playing a proper piano, but a frightful upright. And it was the slow movement of Beethoven's *Pathétique*. We were so cramped that no one could have got to me!"

Even today, anyone interested in Richter can attest to how inaccurate or false rumors still spread like germinating seeds in authoritative lexica, in concert programs, CD booklets, and so on. For example, Richter studied at the conservatory in Odessa. No. He was assistant director of the Odessa Opera. No, never. Richter had a little sister. No, he was an only child. He was married in 1946. No, he never married. His mother married his father's younger brother. No, they weren't even related. He died in his dacha outside Moscow. No, he died in the city's most famous hospital. And so on and so forth endlessly.

The media's ritual worship of performing artists is an inevitable part of world fame in the information age. Today, more than ever, visibility is the number-one prerequisite for fame. You picture a pianist before you hear him. You have an *image* of a celebrity, not a sound, a tone, or a particular piece of music, not even when the celebrity is a musician. A musician without exposure on TV, video, the Internet, magazines, newspapers, and so on, simply does not exist in the twenty-first century. A musician who desires world fame must become his own brand, perhaps only by virtue of his manner, his choice of concert venues, his repertoire, his fee, or his private life, but preferably a brand that is *seen*, a brand suitable to TV. The *Three Tenors* is one of the most powerful examples in recent years. Alternatively, there is the image of Karajan with his trancelike expression and closed eyes, of Bernstein dancing like a tightrope walker on the podium, of Gould caressing his piano like an erotic object, of Nigel Kennedy with his punk hairdo, of sexy young women with violins.

In his film *Lisztomania*, Ken Russell made it likely that even the legendary Franz Liszt was fully conscious of the power of the image. In the overwhelming media hubbub surrounding Gould—the solitary TV star, the author, the composer, the journalist, the thinker, the self-promoter, the creator of radio montages, documentary films, and so on—the images are so omnipresent that one almost forgets the point: that the Gould legend is about a pianist.

This kind of hoopla would be inconceivable with Richter. Yet, it must seem surprising that the image of Richter as a person is still indistinct and enigmatic. Details of his geographic and family background are known by very few people. The story of his life and his personality remains shrouded. His attitudes and convictions, his thoughts about music and music interpretation are somewhat clearer, particularly since 1998, when Monsaingeon published his interview with the maestro in book form (and, as mentioned, expanded the book with a selection of Richter's notes on his music listening). But only a few of his admirers have a clear conception of the fundamental view of life and art that was the nutrient for his work.

The mercurially indeterminate creeps into his last encounter with the public, Monsaingeon's portrait on film. The touching ending ("I don't like myself") is, if you will, a fake. The sentence is a typical outburst expressing his dissatisfaction with his London recording of Beethoven's *Hammerklavier* Sonata ("there's something [what?] that doesn't entirely satisfy me"). Richter is actually reading from his notes. To create a deeper meaning, Monsaingeon has clearly edited the subsequent, unforgettable clip in which the pianist hides his bowed head behind his hand, for it shows a Richter in different clothes. Still, he does speak about the difficult life, the constant distractions, the superficial that so easily leads one away from what is really important. Monsaingeon has probably tipped the scales a bit but has done so in such a telling and sensitive way that one can only halfheartedly chide him for it.

While the legend, the symbol, the piano idol Richter may be examined in a clear light and in full form, Richter the man shows up only as confusing glimpses that shift between essence and appearance, surface and depth. It is a prerequisite for any postmortem biography that much of it must necessarily consist of recollections and experiences preserved in the memories of people who knew its subject to a greater or lesser extent, or of anecdotes, random thoughts, fragmentary flashbacks, or ephemeral opinions, often only passed from mouth to mouth. The risk of creating a cardboard figure without perspective goes hand in hand with the risk of accumulating a profusion of snapshots that never coalesce into a unified whole. And as we know from our own lives, we all sometimes wear masks suited for the occasion, or we disguise aspects of our personality, if only to simplify our relations with others. And, inevitably, we are influenced by the picture others have or form of us; we look at ourselves in a flickering cabinet of mirrors within mirrors. What "I" am and what my "role" is can be unclear to anyone, and especially to people constantly confronted with a public image of themselves. And in Richter's case, no confidential spokesperson or factotum exists—as, for example, with Goethe or Stravinsky. In themselves, concrete data and facts can never tell the story of a human being or a life. They are inevitably part of a tissue of ideas, feelings, and attitudes that consciously or unconsciously, for good or for ill, constitute the biographers' worldview. Any attempt is doomed in advance to be only partly successful. Any account of a life must recognize the risk that the essential core of a person remains a chimera.

Even the physical image of Richter the man can seem like a chimera: few people look so different in different situations and in different places as Sviatoslav Richter. Maybe that could blur his contours in the glittering spotlight of modern media. Yet, his personality as cult figure in a large part of the world is indelible as if protected by a Teflon coating. The explanation could be that he is strongly identified with his sound. But it is not that simple. Like a chameleon, Richter takes on the color of the music he plays. His piano sound is warm and singing when he plays Schumann; sparklingly brilliant or wildly effervescent when he plays Liszt; weighty and full-toned when he plays Brahms; aggressive and razor-sharp when he plays Prokofiev; glistening and pastel-colored when he plays Debussy. His trademark is not a particular "tone," sound, or playing style. The physical strength, the infinitely delicate pianissimo, the density of the sound, the architectonic clarity of the music, and the dizzying virtuosity are all part of his brand. But in Richter, caustic intensity alternates with measured inwardness.

What is unique is his ability to empathize with the whole pulsing microcosm that constitutes a musical work and to localize that particular area in which details and wholeness, expression and form, body and soul, find each other in that piece. This is a place where music does not appear in the form of a piano, but where the piano appears in the form of a particular piece of music. Music goes beyond the well-known expression of the Canadian philosopher Marshall McLuhan, "The medium is the message," because here, the medium is just the medium, and the *music* is the message!

After Stalin's death in March 1953 and especially after the 1956 Party Congress's critique of the Stalin era, a thaw in the relationship between the superpowers, the Soviet Union and the United States, began. Officially invited to the Soviet Union, the twenty-four-year-old Glenn Gould gave four concerts in Moscow and four in Leningrad in May 1957 as one of the first Western musicians to visit (only the violinist Yehudi Menuhin, who had Jewish-Ukrainian roots and close Soviet contacts, had been able to visit the country immediately after the war, before the Iron Curtain came down). Gould's Bach performance created a sensation and gave him immediate mythic status, although his choice of Alban Berg's atonal piano sonata created a certain unease in the hall; and when he closed a concert at the conservatory by introducing music by Schönberg, Webern, and Ernst Krenek, a few of the older professors left the hall. Richter heard Gould in the famous Grand Hall of the Moscow Music Conservatory, and he continued to applaud long after most people had grown tired. (Gould's interpretation of Bach's *Goldberg Variations* kept Richter from playing the work himself.) A couple of days before, on May 9, Gould had been present in the same hall for his colleague's piano recital including the music of Schubert and Liszt, composers with whom he had no affinity and of whom he never recorded a note. Gould despised Liszt, and he found Schubert "prone to repetitions," which made him restless and could even make him "writhe in the chair." But Richter's version of Schubert's final Piano Sonata in B-flat Major made such a strong impression on him that many years later he told a CBS journalist:

> It is a very long sonata—one of the longest ever written, in fact. And Richter played it in what I believe to be the slowest tempo I have ever heard, thereby making it a good deal longer, needless to say.
>
> But what happened in fact was that, for the next hour, I was in a state that I can only compare to a hypnotic trance. . . . It seemed to me I was witnessing a unity of two supposedly irreconcilable qualities: intense analytic calculation revealed through a spontaneity equivalent of improvisation. And I realized at that moment—as I have on many subsequent occasions while listening to Richter's recordings—that I was in the presence of one of the most powerful communicators the world of music has produced in our time.

"Gould doesn't understand; he's talking about me, not Schubert," Richter remarked dryly in an interview. Despite his deep respect for Gould's playing, it clearly annoyed him that Gould did not simply come to love Schubert from that moment on. "I only play what is in the notes!" The interviewer asks a little teasingly: "But if *I* play a Schubert sonata, people are not deeply captivated." Richter: "Then you're not playing what's in the notes!"

This mindset has the quality of a credo: "When I play the sonata, my colleagues often ask: 'Slava, why do you play it so slowly?' The truth is that I do not even play what Schubert wrote, *molto moderato*, but actually only *moderato*. Everyone else always plays it *allegro moderato*. Or simply *allegro*."

On August 1, 1997, plagued by illness, the eighty-two-year-old pianist died of heart failure at the Kremlin Hospital in Moscow, and on that day an appropriately shaken music world grieved over the loss accompanied by a tribute on several Russian and European television channels. A Russian newspaper called Richter "the messenger of the gods." But American television and the press greeted the news in almost total silence. Countless people all over the globe knew that Richter's existence had changed something crucial in their view of music, life, and the world, but the world hardly noticed that it had just become poorer. The American pianist David Dubal, author of several books on the piano and its most famous performers, relates that over the course of the day, his answering machine was filled with messages such as: "Richter is dead, he gave me so much." The special combination of openness, concentration, simplicity, and spiritual strength that characterized his playing had become, for many, a measure for their own lives.

After a short, unostentatious ceremony at the Ivan Voin Church, Richter was buried at the Novedevichy State Cemetery in Moscow, where members of the government, ministers, and the country's most important scientists and artists rest. This is where Prokofiev and Shostakovich are buried, as well as Richter's teacher Heinrich Neuhaus and colleagues such as David Oistrakh and Emil Gilels—great names that evoke images from one of the great chapters of music history. But the indispensable gifts musicians bear are by nature ephemeral; they are forgotten quickly, or they leave only indistinct traces in our memory. Like actors, singers, and dancers, musicians are time-bound, and the sad fact is that time dwindles away irretrievably. Even the remaining soundtracks fade and grow old in comparison with ever-newer soundtracks, new geniuses, new technologies, and new expectations and listening habits.

Nevertheless, the years since Richter's departure from the temporal world have not markedly diminished the spread and popularity of his recordings in record stores or on noncommercial radio stations. Many Richter recordings have been reissued in recent years. No one who once succumbed to the power of fascination his playing evokes forgets him easily (or will ever tolerate halfhearted attempts at the music they have heard him play).

Whether the world will remember and honor Sviatoslav Richter just as much in twenty years, no one can know. The pattern of history, however, suggests the answer is no. The magic, the presence, the empathy during a concert with Busoni, Schnabel, Cortot, Fischer, Gieseking, Horowitz, Arrau, and countless other great and influential pianists have long ago become feeble shadows or distant memories for most people. The performers' personal mythology or the reissue of old recordings keeps their names honored in music's Olympus, but they are rarely, if ever, players in the living musical culture.

If Richter can be said to have avoided this "fury of disappearance," it is surely because of the difficult-to-define universal aspect of his art: the interpreter as a sort of medium, a spokesperson who gives music permission to speak for itself. Perhaps this paradox—the interpreter as an unobtrusive and yet indispensable aura around the music—is what the pianist Arthur Rubinstein had in mind when he told an interviewer, "The whole world spoke of Richter. And I thought, oh well, let me hear this Richter. So I went. And it wasn't bad, good craftsmanship, professional, everything in order. At some point, I suddenly realized that my eyes had become moist, that tears were running down my cheeks, that my heart had contracted."

It is difficult to believe in music's ability to communicate without the presence of a great performer, difficult to accept that the score's directions and the necessary fingering techniques are the only things that a pianist brings to the mix. And it is difficult to see Richter's insistence that he did not contribute anything individual, anything "interpretive" to the music, as anything other than an oversimplification, an illusion. But it is possible to imagine that a person can dive in and become one with the music without wanting to re-create it in his own image. The American composer Morton Feldman once said, "When I try to push my music around, I know that in a moment I'm going to hear it crying *help!*" Perhaps Richter, too, had a sense and an ear for this quiet cry for help. He is always entirely on the side of the music. The music decides. Not the composer, not the pianist, not the audience, but the music itself!

PART **I**

"A Different Kind of Boy"

The world of classical music can seem like an ornamental garden surrounded by high walls. If you are not already inside the fence, any attempt to gain access to it may prove futile. But on this point the Fates mercifully smiled on Richter's talent. Geographically, he was an outsider from a provincial town in what at that time was called Little Russia (today it is called the Ukraine, an area northwest of the Black Sea whose capital is Kiev and which is an independent state since the collapse of the Soviet Union in 1991). But musicians were in his family going several generations back. His grandfather was German with roots in a part of Poland that is now the western part of Ukraine (the name means "at the border"). In the mid-1800s, many immigrants went to Russia from Austria, Prussia, and Poland to seek their fortune. His grandfather Daniel tuned pianos and organs and built pianos. Daniel settled in the picturesque provincial town of Zhitomir, eighty miles west of Kiev, where despite his modest social status, he achieved the rank of "personal honorary citizen" for his faithful service in maintaining the city's church instruments.

At that time, many Ukrainian cities had German sections with their own schools, churches, and so on. Richter's father, Teofil Danielovich Richter, was born in Zhitomir's German quarter in 1872, one among many siblings. Teofil's schoolteachers described him as a gifted, quiet, and modest boy, although one entry in his grade book from high school has a reprimand for "laziness in Greek and algebra." When he finished high school and was old enough for military service, however, he left his hometown to study piano and composition at the tradition-rich conservatory of music in Vienna.

A fellow student, the Austrian composer Franz Schreker, who later became one of the most successful opera composers of his time, was a close friend of Teofil. At the high point of his career, Schreker's operas competed with those of Richard Strauss for the largest audience, but unlike Strauss's, his name disappeared from the placards during the 1920s. For a long time, he remained a parenthesis in music history; but in recent years, there has been renewed interest in his music, lifting his name out of obscurity. In his time, however, his opera *Der ferne Klang* (The Distant Sound) caused quite a stir and was a topic of lively discussion among intellectuals—for example, in the highly regarded periodical of Klee and Kandinsky, *Der blaue Reiter* (The Blue Rider). In 1925, the same year the opera had its premiere in Berlin, it was put on at the Mariinski Theatre in Petrograd (St. Petersburg, later Leningrad). Teofil got hold of the score, and the music made a great impression on the young Richter. Three-quarters of a century later, he tells how, as a teenager, he played the entire work on the piano. And the eighty-two-year-old claims without blinking that he can still "remember every note"! When he saw a stage production of the work for the first time as late as 1990, however, he was rather disappointed.

Richter also tells that his father heard Johannes Brahms play in his hometown of Vienna and that he came to know the middle-aged Edvard Grieg. However, Grieg's concert tours with his wife, Nina, who was a singer, brought him to Vienna only for a short time in those years, and therefore this must have been more of a chance acquaintanceship. On the whole, Teofil thrived in the music metropolis and remained there long after the end of his studies. His abilities at the piano gave him enough income to support himself as a teacher and a musician, and he stayed in Vienna for more than twenty years. Later on, he returned there every summer to give concerts and to teach at Zhitomir's Artistic Society.

In 1912 the twenty-year-old Anna Pavlovna Moskalyova became Teofil's piano student. She came from Russian nobility, with Russian, Polish, Swedish, Hungarian, and Tartar blood in her veins. Among their more distant relatives, the Moskalew family possibly counted the legendary Swedish singer Jenny Lind ("the Swedish nightingale"), who was passionately admired by her contemporaries. Among her fans was the writer Hans Christian Andersen, who wrote one of his most famous fairy tales with her in mind ("The Nightingale," on which Stravinsky based his first opera).

Anna was highly gifted and had obvious musical talent. Her well-to-do family owned several manors and villas in the area surrounding Zhitomir and avidly pursued cultural interests. At the family manor in the village of Sudachevka, the staging of plays was a favorite pastime, and members of her large family were enthusiastic amateur actors. The family was also interested in art; Anna's father Paul Moskalew was an amateur painter and a capable violin player. But the noble family was content to invest their artistic abilities in cultural pastimes.

Forty-year-old Teofil and his student Anna Pavlovna fell in love. Despite the difference in their ages (she was half his age), they were bound together by a common interest in music. Both toyed with the idea of composing and were among the first to discover the qualities in modern composers such as Scriabin and Debussy. In fact, Teofil left behind several ambitious compositions, among them a Brahms-influenced string quartet and a number of lieder. But he had to court his Anna a long time before her noble father, Pavel Moskalew, a respected member of the local city government, consented to a marriage to a nonnoble, who in his opinion was also much too old for her. Religion may also have played a role; the Moskalew family was Russian Orthodox, whereas the Richter family was German Protestant—although Anna's deceased mother, Elisabeth, born von Reincke, belonged to the Evangelical Lutheran Church. Finally, the couple gained the Moskalews' acceptance, although without the dowry that was customary among nobles.

Many years later, a few years before she died in 1963, Anna Moskalew, now Richter, wrote her memoirs (*Aus meinem Leben* [From My Life]), which remain unpublished. She writes about her Russian childhood and youth, her mother's illness and death, and meeting Teofil (Theo) Richter. She admits that she had romantic reasons for choosing Richter as her piano teacher, and that for a long time her father was skeptical of the alliance. When, in the fall of 1913, Pavel Moskalew finally yielded to her wishes, the bishop of Zhitomir refused to marry a Russian Orthodox woman to a Protestant man. But they found a willing bishop in Kiev, and at the end of May 1914, families and friends went to the big city to witness their vows and celebrate the wedding at one of the city's hotels. The bridal couple had to commit themselves in writing to raise any children issuing from the marriage in the Russian Orthodox faith. The classic rituals and festivities were observed, and at seven o'clock on their wedding night, the newlyweds got on a train; their honeymoon destination was Theo's beloved Vienna.

According to Anna Richter, the five weeks "flew by with unforgettably blissful days." But on June 28, everything changed; in Sarajevo a young Serbian partisan murdered the successor to the throne of the dual monarchy Austria-Hungary. "On a very hot summer day," Anna writes, "we decided to go out to have a look at the aerodrome. Carefree Viennese sat outside eating their sausages and humming along to the melodies being played. Suddenly, the music stopped, quite abruptly, but in all the hustle and bustle we hardly paid attention. On the way home, however, I saw that some of the houses were flying flags with black mourning crape on them. No one could foresee that this was the start of a terrible time."

Not long after, they had to hastily make their way back to Zhitomir.

The shot in Sarajevo set off a chain reaction. The Balkans were a strategic area; freedom movements there threatened the Austro-Hungarian Empire and stood in the way of Germany's *Drang nach Osten* (Drive to the East), while Russia depended on the Bosphorus Strait for access to the Mediterranean. Two major power blocs—the Central Powers of Germany and Austria-Hungary against the communal interests of Russia, Serbia, and France—checkmated diplomacy. At the beginning of August, Germany declared war on Russia and France. Before the month was out, Great Britain and Japan had joined the Franco-Russian alliance, and Italy and Bulgaria soon followed. Gradually, even more nations became involved in the war, and the original conflicts led to numerous new ones. The First World War had broken out.

Earlier that year, composer Alexander Glazunov had offered Teofil a job as docent at the conservatory in St. Petersburg, where Glazunov was the director. But the outbreak of the war put an end to all these plans. The Richters remained in Zhitomir, and on March 20, 1915 (according to the Gregorian calendar), their first and only child, Sviatoslav Teofilovich Richter, came into the world in a beautifully appointed neobaroque home with four pilasters, granite stairs, elegant decorations above the entrance, and a façade decorated with plaster of paris vines. This was not a home for the petty bourgeois or for Theo and Anna. It was the local birthing clinic, donated to the city's social services by two brothers who ran the nearby ironworks. (Georgi Mokritsky, also born and raised in Zhitomir, has researched Richter's childhood and family connections in the city, and much of the information here derives from an essay he published in 2001.)

There is a simple explanation for why the newlyweds had their first child in a birthing clinic, and not in their own home or the home of Anna's well-to-do family. Those years were marked by great deprivation, social unrest, and poverty, and Teofil had lost many students. "We had to scrimp every cent," Anna Richter recalled. The couple's first domicile was in the big house of her father and later they found a nice flat close to her father. So as not to be an inconvenience, Anna went to the birthing clinic, which was on the same street. Normally, the clinic took in only indigent women. But they took Anna Richter, and thus the Darylin brothers' birthing clinic became the cradle of its first and probably only world citizen.

But regardless of this stately and idyllic setting, Sviatoslav Richter came into the world under dramatic circumstances. According to Mokritsky, Richter's ninety-two-year-old cousin Margarita remembered that this particular March was unusually warm, and the thaw brought great floods with it. The Teterov River (a tributary of the Dnieper) breached its banks and destroyed all the dams. In addition, the trenches of the First World War spread out in all directions. Shortly after Sviatoslav's birth, the report came that a cousin had fallen

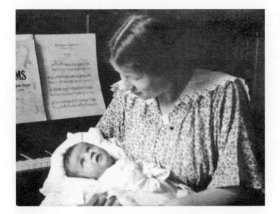

Little Sviatoslav (Svetik) in
the arms of his mother.

on the Rava Russkaya front, near the current Polish border. He was twenty-six years old.

Sviatoslav Teofilovich was not baptized in the city's Lutheran church, where his portly uncle Eduard was the organist and where his grandfather Daniel still maintained and tuned the organ. Not only had his parents agreed to raise their children in the Russian Orthodox faith, it was also simple common sense: professing allegiance to the Lutheran Church when Russia and Germany were at war could be viewed as a pro-German act.

The first few years of Sviatoslav's life were turbulent. The war brought with it increasing social unrest, unemployment, deprivation, and severe inflation; the country was debt-ridden; strikes and demonstrations were growing increasingly frequent. It became even more difficult for Teofil to care for his family, and economic dependence on the family of a much younger wife was inconceivable. It would stamp him as what Ukrainians called a *prijmak*, an "inferior" son-in-law. In the spring, however, they found a little house with three rooms near Anna's father. Despite these difficult conditions, Anna describes this period as a happy time.

But the war advanced ever closer. Anna recounts how one February night in 1916, the police suddenly appeared with orders to evacuate everyone with German ancestry. (The account here is based on Anna's detailed, handwritten memoirs.) She would not let her husband travel alone and, of course, she could not leave her son, who was less than a year old. Teofil's aging parents were also ordered to evacuate, even though the grandfather Daniel suffered from glaucoma and was almost blind. For several days the family traveled in an overfull, unheated train, before they finally reached the town of Sumi, about 150 miles east of Kiev. Here relatives were willing to take them in, as no one would lodge strangers of German descent.

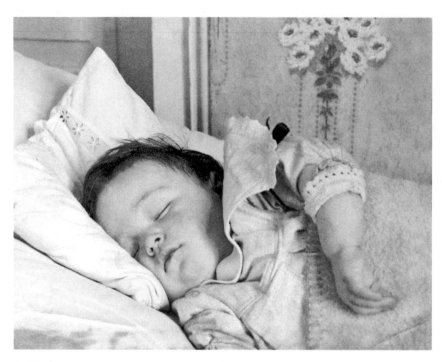

Svetik sleeps.

For several months, Teofil looked for work as a teacher. He made a long trek to the industrial town of Baku on the Caspian Sea but wrote to Anna that the city stank of oil (Baku was at the center of the largest and oldest oil fields in Russia) and that the bitingly cold climate was unsuitable for small children. He did not find a job. During the early summer, back in Sumi, he took on private students, and his teaching brought in just enough money to buy the necessities of life. Luckily, they saw a newspaper advertisement for an opening at the conservatory in Odessa. Teofil sought the position and got it. In the meantime, little Sviatoslav (called Svetik, "Little Light") had begun not only to walk and to talk, but also to show clear signs of musical ability. "When Theo rehearsed Liszt, he would stand up in his cot and wave his arms as if conducting. Whenever there was a *fortissimo* climax, he would cry out in ecstasy and shout out for joy."

The family once again packed their belongings and traveled to the dynamic and culturally active harbor town on the Black Sea. It turned out that Teofil found work as an organist at the German Lutheran church, which was just across the street from the conservatory. They established themselves in a small apartment ("full of bedbugs," Anna remembered), but money was still in short supply. After a while, mother and son visited the well-to-do Moskalew family in Zhitomir in order to put a little meat on their bones. But the growing political and social chaos in the years after the war broke out brought down the czar and led to the 1917 revolutions. The consequences of war, revolution, and class struggle became more noticeable day by day. Riots, starvation, and epidemics were now everyday occurrences. The takeover by the Bolshevik Party in November 1917 had removed the provisional government but brought a military breakdown in its wake. In March 1918 the socialist government entered into a peace accord with Germany. The war had laid waste to much of Russia, the losses had been enormous, and war weariness was overwhelming. And the fulfillment of Lenin's promise of peace, land, and bread was long in coming. The political and economic chaos led to an all-out civil war.

The year before, the United States had entered the war against Germany, and with the defense of democracy as its ideological basis (and out of concern that the proletarian revolution could spread to Central Europe), the American president Woodrow Wilson helped to mobilize White Russian rebels and Polish-German troops in the struggle against the newly formed Red Army. Shortly after, the French and the militia from the French colonies occupied Odessa. Thereafter, travel to the areas the Red Army controlled proved almost impossible.

The civil war dragged on for three years, subjecting the Russian people to even greater deprivation and plagues than the war. In the years after 1917, hegemony in Little Russia shifted back and forth between an independent local government, German or French occupation troops, Bolsheviks, and anti-Communist White Russians.

In the summer of 1918, while mother and son were on their way to Zhitomir, a typhus epidemic broke out. In her childhood home, Anna saw her younger sister Elena contract the infectious disease. In her memoirs she depicts her sister's delirium in frightening terms. However, when little Svetik was hit, the disease ran its course. In Odessa Teofil, also infected, was hastily admitted to the city's university clinic. Anna hurried back to her husband, leaving the ill Svetik with her family in Zhitomir. A few days later, her sister succumbed to the infection. Back in Odessa, Anna found the family's apartment partly destroyed by a violent street battle, but Teofil recovered.

While the civil war raged, the nascent Soviet Union was for all intents and purposes cut off from the surrounding world and, thus, from occupied Odessa. Svetik remained in Zhitomir with his grandfather Pavel and his aunt Tamara (Dagmar Reincke). His godfather, Uncle Nikolai, also took care of him.

The city's military command refused to allow Anna and Teofil to travel. But, of course, they missed their son. After "a couple of years of hunger, sorrow, and discomfort," it became too much for Anna. But the time frame is optimistically recalled; in fact, the separation lasted much longer. The account of how Anna struggled back to Zhitomir to get her son reads like a thriller. She got help slipping out of the city, fooling the Red Guards into thinking she was a Jewish doctor subject to German persecution. She boarded a northbound train carrying a medical kit to bolster her credibility; she then used a few drops of opium to ease the stomach pains some soldiers had incurred through an excessive ingestion of melons. But she had to change trains and ran far in the night with her baggage only to be turned away: the train turned out to be a field hospital, filled with wounded soldiers. When she got back to the original train, one of the few sober Red Guards offered to help her find another train to Zhitomir. They succeeded, and in the end she was allowed to sit in an open freight car. It was raining cats and dogs, and the temperature was approaching the freezing point.

Unfortunately, the train's conductor was dead drunk, incapable of driving the train. Anna sought shelter in the railway station. Some of the people there began to question her, but she faked a headache, a common portent of typhus, and they left her alone. The train finally departed, but it stopped again after a few stations. A couple of soldiers took pity on her; they eased her out of a window and into another train with Zhitomir as its destination.

> I crept into a dark luggage van. I had only just begun to distinguish the outlines of where I was when a Red Army officer entered. "Hey, Sister," said he with a sickly smile on seeing me, "where have you sprung from? You come along and sleep in my compartment." Then he went out again, and I crept behind the luggage and stayed as quiet and fearful as a mouse, hardly daring to breathe. Soldiers and officers came in and out, but as soon as the train started, all was still.

At dawn, when she reached Zhitomir, however, the train stopped far from the station. Once again, she had to drag her luggage a long way and could not find her way into town. A young woman came to her aid. "Oh, you must be the mother of Svetik, the little red-haired boy; he is the image of you."

One can imagine the reunion with the now much-grown Svetik. But life was also totally changed in the Moskalew family after the Revolution. Everyone had to work hard to produce something that could be traded for food. A money economy existed only in a truncated form. The journey back to Odessa and Teofil proved to be just as difficult. Again, she was refused a travel permit, and it took almost eight months to get one. Only through Teofil's contact with an NKVD official, who was married to one of his students, did she and Svetik finally obtain a permit to travel to Odessa. Three-quarters of a century later, Richter

Sviatoslav, aged three or four, with his aunt Dagmar Reincke.

still remembered the three-hundred-mile journey to Odessa: "My mother took me back by a freight train. The journey lasted a week. I found it exciting." When they arrived in Odessa, darkness had descended, and Anna did not dare set out into the lawless city. Mother and son waited until dawn at the railway station. Of course, Teofil was happy and relieved to see them again, but he had bad news: burglars had stolen practically everything in the apartment.

During the long separation, his aunt (*totya*) Dagmar (Tamara)—usually called Meri—raised him. And she became a pivotal point in his life. Early childhood surroundings and influences have a strong effect on the development of a child's psyche; Aunt Meri was a second mother for Svetik, and later in life they kept in close contact, often through an extensive correspondence. It is difficult to avoid feeling that in many respects, Dagmar stepped into his mother's place. As mentioned earlier, his mother disappeared from his life when he was in his mid-twenties, and she fled to Germany with her new husband. Almost twenty years would go by before they would see each other again.

During the war, in November 1943, Dagmar Reincke, her son Miroslav, brother Nikolai, and nephew Vitali Moskalew and his parents were evacuated from Zhitomir as *Volksdeutsche*. All six were interned in a refugee camp in the Black Forest, and shortly thereafter Vitali Moskalew's father died. The family were considered ethnic Germans—Dagmar's (and Anna Richter's) deceased mother, Elisabeth von Reincke, was German—and, after the war, they decided to settle in the southern German provincial town of Schwäbisch Gmünd, where Anna Richter and Sergei Kondratiev lived. The Germans changed their names, so Miroslav now was Friedrich (Fritz) Reincke and Vitali Moskalew became Walter Moskalew. Later, in the first half of the 1950s, they settled with their mothers in the United States (Dagmar Reincke now called herself Meri). After the death of their mothers, the two orphaned cousins and Moskalew's children remained Richter's only blood relatives.

Dagmar Reincke was an artistically gifted woman with a sharp eye for Svetik's peculiarities and personality. Throughout her life, she was active as an artist, illustrator, and painter, and during the years when she served as a second mother for Svetik, she worked as an illustrator for a publisher in Kiev. Richter's interest in drawing and painting undoubtedly has its roots there, and early on he began to draw fairy-tale creatures and characters. In 1964, the year after Anna Richter's death, Dagmar Reincke wrote a series of casual, slightly sentimental prose pieces, with recollections from Richter's childhood. She does not use dates, so it is not always clear whether the memories are from their time in Zhitomir, when she raised Svetik, or whether they are from her later visits to the Richter family in Odessa. The booklet takes its title from a telling episode in Odessa, when Svetik was presumably six or seven years old. She writes: "One day he was set upon by two boys from the Children's Home, who beat him up so badly that his nose bled and he got two black eyes. While the beating-up was going on, Svetik stood with his back to the wall without making a sound. He did not cry; nor did he try to run away or call for help."

Miss Stabusch (a Lithuanian, German-speaking teacher who had rented a room from the Richters and who taught Svetik German) must have seen the incident from her window; she rushed down to chase the young bullies away. Amazed at the boy's behavior, she asked him why he did not answer in the same coin. Aunt Dagmar continues: "Svetik looked amazed at Miss Stabusch and said: 'Surely you must understand, Fraulein Stabusch, that I can't fight, I'm a very different kind of boy!'"

This remark became the title of Dagmar Reincke's book. According to Dag-

A drawing by Dagmar Reincke from "Hanspeters Waldtraum" (Hanspeter's Forest Dream). Clearly, little Svetik served as the model.

mar, Svetik never played war; he hated games that entailed weapons, shooting, competition, or rough behavior. She describes him as a gentle, almost feminine boy with a lively imagination and great creativity; he particularly liked to make things from building blocks and homemade blocks of wood. He was an unusually patient child with a rare attention to detail. Economically, the postwar period was incredibly hard on almost everyone. Toys were not in the family's budget, and Svetik's imagination came in handy. Even as a four-year-old, he could sit for hours and carefully write out the alphabet on the empty backs of thick, used accounting books, each time with a new type of lettering.

But Dagmar Reincke stresses that his sense of being different was in no way a feeling of superiority. Rather, he seemed reticent, introverted, and somewhat shy.

Perhaps here one can sense traits that often characterize the closely observed, often spoiled only child. Such sheltered children have no competitors to threaten their time with and attention from adults, and they are often quite unprepared for clashes with other children. They know nothing of the herd mentality and are bullied more often than other children. It is not unusual for them to have difficulty connecting with others, and they sometimes develop

Svetik with his mother's family: in back, three uncles; in front, Svetik between his aunt and his grandfather, with his mother and father to the right.

a veritable hatred of school, ball playing, sports competitions, and anything else that smacks of competition or esprit de corps. Richter's lifelong dislike of any form of competition, in art, politics, love, and daily life, presumably has its roots here.

Aunt Meri also speaks of walks through the gardens and parks of Zhitomir, of Svetik's interest in theater, drawing, and painting, about music at home, play-acting, masquerades, and birthdays. She also organized theatricals in which they dressed up in imaginative costumes and even had their photographs taken with the cumbersome equipment of the time (in the Richter family, pho-tography was a bit of a hobby). In this light, his childhood seems happy, safe, and full of care and love. A beloved child has many names, they say, and Svetik was clearly a beloved child. Nicknames such as the one he invented, Tekota, Zibzik, and Tuksik, were often used. In fact, it is difficult in these downy, loving memoirs to find any hint of the precarious, unsafe, economically straitened, and politically tumultuous lives they led during the years ravaged by civil war after the Russian Revolution.

By the time the Richter family had finally gathered together again in their lit-tle apartment in Odessa in 1922, the *Sovietski soyus*, the Soviet Union, had been formed. This federation ultimately consisted of fifteen republics that were nationally, geographically, historically, and culturally very different from each other and were made up of hundreds of different peoples with different languages, divided into regions spanning a seventh of the total surface of the planet, more than seventy times larger than countries such as Germany and Italy (the USSR stretched over ten time zones).

Today, the post-Soviet region is divided into no fewer than eighty-nine territories, and some (for example, Yakutia in eastern Siberia) are ten times larger than the reunited Germany! Here Byzantine, western European, Persian, central Asian, and Mongolian cultural traditions continue either separately or tightly interwoven, and no single culture can claim to constitute the national heritage. But in Communist propaganda, the Soviet empire was portrayed as having established a magnificent, peaceful coexistence between people with colossal differences in lifestyles, cultural habits, climate, language, traditions, and so on. And everyone who has followed developments since the breakup of the Soviet Union knows that this was an impossible dream.

Obviously little Svetik had no idea of any of this. He lived a dreamy, carefree life, playing mostly alone, drawing, painting, and writing small theatrical pieces that were "performed" in the family kitchen or at modest gatherings held by his parents. Both Anna Richter and Dagmar Reincke tell of his passionate interest in acting and drama, an interest he retained all his life. As a nine-year-old, he wrote a play, "Dora," a short drama with thirteen characters in eight acts and fifteen scenes (Aunt Meri recalls that even as a six-year-old, Svetik designed a title page for "Dora," which at that time had only three acts). As a seven-year old, he saw an opera for the first time, a performance with piano accompaniment at the conservatory in Odessa. Such "family performances" were very popular in Odessa. He watched Verdi's *Rigoletto* for the first time in this form and was deeply engrossed in the final dramatic scenes. When he was nine, he saw Verdi's *Aida*, Rimsky-Korsakov's *The Tsar's Bride*, and, later, Tchaikovsky's *The Queen of Spades* at the city's famous opera house. His lifelong interest in film also began early. He was eight when he saw a movie for the first time, an American silent-film version of the story of Madame Butterfly; the desperate love and suicide of Butterfly made the sensitive boy sob out loud.

For a number of years from the beginning of the 1930s until around 1970, the Russian pianist and educator Yakov Milstein collected notes from conversations with Richter. After Milstein's death in 1981, these edited notes were published in a small volume entitled *O Sviatoslave Richtere* (On Sviatoslav Richter). Thus, the book in many respects is a companion to Bruno Monsaingeon's book of conversations—yet another "Richter in his own words." He spoke to

Teofil, Anna, Dagmar, and Svetik at a beach on the Black Sea.
It is evident that Svetik had very close ties to his aunt Dagmar.

Milstein of these years: "It was a period full of adventure and poetry. I lived in contact with nature, almost in symbiosis with it. My relatives were foresters, and in the family the virtues of the country life predominated. We loved nature, worshiped it: up until I was seven–eight years old, I believed in elves and mermaids. Nature was my contact to the supernatural, it was full of mysteries. Behind all its manifestations, there was something spiritual. I lived quite literally in a fairy-tale world." Throughout his life, Richter retained a pantheistic feeling of communion with nature and all its creations. His aunt and uncles were vegetarians. As a child, therefore, he had learned to have a deep respect for all living beings, though without acquiring meatless eating habits. But the child's experience of this dream world as a paradise never left him; even late in life, he insisted that he always had a burning desire never to grow up.

Yet another work of "Richter in his own words" exists in the literature. In her book *V puteshestvii so Sviatoslavom Rikhterom* (On Tour with Sviatoslav Richter), Valentina Chemberdzhy relates how, several times in 1986, she accompanied him on a colossal concert tour in a car back and forth across the enormous expanse of the eastern USSR. To her, too, he talks about his childhood: "As a child, I was a dreamer, I had no close friends, even though I got along well with everyone. During school hours, I played my favorite game (which I still love today): how would Aunt Meri, Mama, Papa, or someone else deal with this or that. So, I didn't listen to what was going on in the lesson. And when 'Richter' was suddenly shouted, I had no idea what they were talking about. . . . I didn't want to grow up!" However, he also says that he never read children's books.

He read *Pelléas and Mélisande*, the play by Maurice Maeterlinck about life's secret forces (and the basis for Debussy's opera), as well as Dickens and Gogol. He found literature such as Fenimore Cooper's popular books about the American frontier completely uninteresting.

Until Richter turned eleven, everything was apparently light and straightforward. But when he began attending a German school in Odessa, everything changed—"the most awful time in my life," he says (until then, he had been educated privately). Throughout his life, Richter hated any form of planning or compulsion from above. He felt disgust at the school's rote learning, considered most of his schoolmates "little scoundrels," and always had teachers breathing down his neck because he was unprepared and lazy. "By nature, I am passive," he admitted later unapologetically ("laziness and passivity personified," he said of himself many years later). He also had a reputation as a workaholic, which is just another one of those contradictions of which the Richter myth is made. At school, as in the Richter home, German was spoken; while in Zhitomir, he spoke Russian. During schooldays he often played truant—at one point, for more than a week—and he later believed he learned more as a part-time ragamuffin on the streets of Odessa than in the German school.

Their three-room apartment was located off a cramped square, and Svetik slept in a small room where the family's piano was kept. At his aunt Meri's (Dagmar's) in Zhitomir, there was no piano. Svetik was seven years old before he even had the opportunity to play the piano. As a teacher and pianist, Teofil often had to practice in the evening, and his son always listened. But when he himself began to sit at the piano, he just fooled around, and his father was almost appalled at the way the boy banged away. In the beginning, Teofil attempted a little teaching a few times; but even as a child, Svetik was willful and obstinate. So the gentle, soft-spoken, and forgiving father soon gave up. However, Svetik received a bit of tutoring from one of his father's students, but his real interest was not in playing the piano but *reading* music, playing reams of music "off the page."

Giving up on teaching him, Richter's father followed this development, and if, on rare occasions, he again tried to steer the boy in the direction of a piano lesson, his mother, Anna, intervened. As if by female intuition, she realized, probably correctly, that Svetik should not be subjected to any form of pressure to learn. As a result, young Richter grew up, for the most part, as a self-taught piano player and, practically speaking, avoided all the torments young piano students are subjected to: Hanon exercises, Czerny etudes, scales, chord progressions, finger exercises, "pentatonic pieces," and so on. Presumably, this is why, throughout his life, he resisted finger exercises and retained an overt skepticism toward all teaching. He never taught; "a waste of time," he called it and then asked rhetorically what there was to give to others. Inspiration? Personality? The special "mood" that characterizes an interpretation? Richter was the only prominent Soviet pianist who never taught, except sporadically as an instructor of chamber music. Later, the fact that he was able to avoid a heavy-handed mandate from the authorities was evidence of his high status in Soviet musical life.

The first piece he learned was Chopin's first nocturne, which he had often heard his father play. And then he went on without worries to Chopin's difficult E-Minor Etude from opus 25 (a feat that anyone who has some knowledge of the mysteries and obstacles of piano playing will find inconceivable). Soon, the boy was reading and playing most of Beethoven's sonatas.

Apparently, he was not primarily interested in playing the piano. He used the piano the way we use a CD or an MP3 player, as a means to listen to music we otherwise would not hear. Teofil's years in Vienna had made him into a passionate Wagnerian. Teofil had spent a great deal of time in Vienna's famous State Opera in the company of Wagner's music dramas, and he spoke with passion and commitment to his son about these works and about his operatic experiences. Young Richter immediately became a Wagnerian himself, a passion that never left him. With his fabulous sight-reading ability, he played the piano scores of *Tannhäuser*, *Lohengrin*, and *Die Walküre*, and then moved on to the operas of Verdi (*Aida* and *Rigoletto*), Mascagni, Puccini, Donizetti, Gounod, and, naturally, Tchaikovsky. Often he played these so energetically and persistently that he disturbed his parents' sleep at night. He played string quartets by Beethoven and Schumann and even tried Richard Strauss's symphonic poem *Aus Italien* from a pocket score. He heard and absorbed this music through the eyes, the fingers, and the piano keys! There is ample documentation that Richter, all his life, maintained his phenomenal ability to sight-read and his passion for bringing opera and orchestral music to life through the piano. His teacher Heinrich Neuhaus wrote in 1960: "I have had the good fortune, together with many others, to hear Richter at home. He played for us the operas of Wagner, Tchaikovsky, Richard Strauss, Debussy, and Schreker, and the symphonies of Mahler, Myaskovsky, and others. I'm not sure if this 'music-making' did not impress me even more than his recitals."

Theater and especially opera were the boy's true passion. When only eight years old, little by little he began to compose piano pieces, which his father helped him write down. And as a twelve-year old, he started to compose an opera about a character in the Russian poet Lermontov's famous novel *A Hero of Our Time*.

He showed Milstein piano pieces with titles such as "Evening on the Mountain," "Birds at Dawn," and "Indian Fort." And he mentions Puccini-like operatic fragments—based, for example, on the fable of Ariane and Bluebeard (by the poet Maeterlinck)—and several piano pieces composed after he turned twenty. The atmosphere in Odessa also inspired him to write foxtrot melodies, though with quirky harmonic changes and modulations. All this amounted to quite a bit of music. At one point, he was taught composition by his future stepfather, Sergei Kondratiev. But even back then, the relationship between the two was explosive. "Endless discussions," he remembers. "All that chitchat took away my desire; had it not been for Kondratiev, I would probably never have stopped composing."

Perhaps. But his compatriot the pianist Vladimir Viardo, who was much younger than Richter (and yet the two were friends for more than thirty years), relates that every so often Richter would begin to play one of his own works for him and then break off after a few measures with a scowl or a disgusted grimace. "I think he was very skeptical of his abilities as a composer, much more skeptical than of his talent as a pictorial artist. But his early experiences as a composer were a part of his lifelong and deep respect for composers; he considered the composer's score as sacred, nothing less. When Russians say about someone that he 'plays like a composer,' it is not kindly meant. It means that he has not practiced enough. But in Richter's case, it had a completely different meaning. The poet Osip Mandelstam wrote in a poem: 'I am at the same time the gardener and the flower!'"

Later, however, Richter gave yet another reason for losing his desire to compose: he had begun to imitate other composers' music—for example, Puccini and Franz Schreker's *Der ferne Klang*, to which his father had introduced him. Also Richter played another, often overlooked German music drama from the period, Hans Pfitzner's great choral opera *Palestrina*, whose bulky piano score Teofil Richter had acquired. The choice shows how unusually broad-minded Teofil's approach to music was, and Richter admired, memorized, and publicized this work vociferously again and again for the rest of his life.

His enthusiasm for opera, rather than the piano, was the life nerve of his musical interest. He was only nine when he tried to play the notes in an elegantly bound volume his father had gotten from Vienna with the piano score for Wagner's entire *Ring*. As a twelve-year-old, he spent a whole summer familiarizing himself with *Die Walküre*. "Opera gave me all the most important things in my education," he later claimed. Beginning with Wagner and Verdi, the young opera lover collected scores, and soon he had accumulated over a hundred volumes. "I played unceasingly."

Odessa: The Light and the Dark

Once, Odessa was the gateway to the vast Russian hinterlands in the same way Hong Kong was the gateway to China. In the early 1800s, the harbor city on the Black Sea was among the wealthiest in Europe. But its prosperity (which depended on the export of Russian grain to Western Europe) came to an abrupt halt when American wheat flooded the market at the end of the American Civil War in 1865. With its somewhat faded charm and narrow streets, however, the city still has remnants of its golden age. From Primorski (Lake Shore) Boulevard's acacia trees and neoclassical architecture, a broad stone stairway with 192 steps and ten landings leads down to the water. As a tribute to the famous scene in Eisenstein's film classic in which an abandoned baby carriage bumps its way down the many steps, it is now called the Potemkin steps. The architect was Italian, and probably only Bernini's "Spanish steps" in Rome compete with these stairs as Europe's most famous stairway.

In the city's heyday, opera was so popular that an opera bulletin was published several times a year, even before the city's first Russian-language newspaper was established. In the first decades of the century, Odessa was a center of literature, science, art, theater, and especially music (sometimes ranking next to Moscow and St. Petersburg). The city's vigorous cultural life continued unabated during the economic downturn, and musical activities prevailed even during times of war, revolution, and starvation. An astounding number of the twentieth century's most significant musicians grew up in Odessa in the first decades of the twentieth century. In addition to Richter, there were world-class names such as Emil Gilels, Shura Cherkassky, David Oistrakh, Mischa Elman, and Nathan Milstein. The city was a cradle of the Russian-Jewish violin tradition, and Yehudi Menuhin, himself of Russian-Jewish extraction, relates that when he played in the town, people came behind the stage after the concert not to thank him but to ask what fingering he had used for certain passages!

For the teenage Sviatoslav, a career as a concert pianist was hardly within the realm of possibility. However, in the summer of 1930, he began to work as an accompanist, and the Seamen's Club in Odessa became a frequent employer. He was motivated not only by the musical challenge but also for financial reasons. A lack of money was a fact of life for almost everyone. In the 1930s Odessa experienced frequent bouts of starvation. At the Seamen's Club, Richter accompanied amateur singers who aspired to a singing career ("incredibly dreadful voices!"), most often in music by Tchaikovsky, excerpts from operas such as *The Queen of Spades* and *Cherevitchki* (*The Slippers*, an almost overlooked opera in the West, which Tchaikovsky himself and Sergei Prokofiev believed to be his best). The numerous societies and associations in the Odessa region became a natural playground for Sviatoslav (now called Slava) and his musical abilities; factories, nursing homes, and collective farming associations in the city and the surrounding villages served as his concert podium. In the following years, he accompanied virtually everything performed in Odessa on the piano, whether outdoors or indoors, for circus performers, comedic actors, variety entertainers, jugglers, singers, and instrumentalists, always without rehearsals, always here and now, as a sight-reader.

For three months he improvised music for silent films in a movie theater ("I don't think I did it very well, because I always wanted to see the film myself"). Throughout his life, film was yet another one of his passions. As a soloist, he performed a motley opera repertoire in piano versions: the "Ride of the Valkyries" from Wagner's *Die Walküre*, the final scene of his *Tristan und Isolde*, the Polovetsian Dances from Borodin's *Prince Igor*, the coronation scene from Mussorgsky's *Boris Godunov*, excerpts from Tchaikovsky's *Sleeping Beauty*, and so on. The meager supplementary income he earned in the form of cash contributions or goods, such as a sack of potatoes, was welcome but hardly a motivation.

Every summer the Richter family spent two months in his childhood home of Zhitomir, and it was there that the teenage Slava appeared as a piano soloist for the first time. He tells Bruno Monsaingeon about the place and the audience. Among his father's friends and admirers was a family of no fewer than eight sisters (the Semyonovs), who all lived together—"delightful women, but slightly comical, because they behaved like girls although they were in fact around seventy and always wore very old-fashioned clothes. Everyone made fun of them." The Semyonov sisters organized a family concert in their home and, at sixteen, Richter played both the solo and the orchestral parts of Schumann's piano concerto on the sisters' piano. In his view, the concert was a success: "Suddenly, I discovered I had admirers. Imagine! Eight at once!" Richter later believed that this event led to his decision to become a pianist. But there are indications that the final decision was made considerably later.

Slava plays the Schumann concerto in the home of the Semyonov sisters.

Since his arrival in Odessa, Teofil Richter had earned extra money by playing the organ at the local Lutheran church; but in the mid-1920s, he left this job to assist as organist at the city's opera house whenever the repertoire required it. He must have felt nostalgically at home here because the external architecture of the building was a faithful copy of the opera house in Vienna. His opera-loving son was often present at performances in the orchestra pit. And from the time he was sixteen, Slava began to perform as an accompanist at concerts organized by the Odessa Philharmonic. This led to an offer to work as an accompanist, a *répétiteur* for the ballet. He was all of eighteen. He worked at the ballet for about a year and then continued as a *répétiteur* at the city's opera houses. This gave him experience in following a conductor, which had obvious advantages later. Odessa's opera was a respected and farsighted organization with several excellent conductors and a large repertoire of Russian and classical operas. The first Russian performances of new Western operas such as Puccini's *Turandot*, his trilogy (*Gianni Schicchi*, *Il Tabarro*, and *Suor Angelica*), and even Ernst Krenek's much-discussed jazz opera *Jonny spielt auf* took place here. The latter was a short-lived world success—even the stately Vienna Opera staged it. In Odessa it remained in the repertoire for several years before it was banned by the authorities—presumably because it depicts a love relationship between a black man and a white woman. When more than fifty years later he heard it again, Richter remembered it "to the last detail."

The young Slava gradually began to spend all his days and nights at the theater. In the daytime he participated in rehearsals, and in the evening he

A wild witch and Pan, the god of the woods: Aunt Dagmar and Slava having great theatrical fun.

attended the performances. He made himself so noteworthy that at one point he received an offer to conduct some of the rehearsals for Alexander Glazunov's popular ballet *Raymonda* (it remained in the repertoire for several years). But at the last minute, the job was given to an *apparatchik*, a Party-faithful functionary, and the young, up-and-coming musician had to settle for playing a long piano solo in the ballet's third act. As usual, when the eighty-two-year-old Richter is reminded of the political machinations of the totalitarian system, he shrugs them off, saying: *"Ladno"* ("It doesn't matter!"). But early in life, he admitted, it made him rather bitter and made him feel that there was nothing for him in Odessa. So the truth is that it contributed to his decision to leave the city.

The musical and cultural life of the city was lively and varied, and not just at the opera. For example, Richter watched Nikolai Malko conduct Scriabin's colossal *Poème de l'extase* (Poem of Ecstasy), and he attended rehearsals and concerts where Glazunov conducted his own music. Soon after, both Malko and Glazunov emigrated to the West. Richter also heard noteworthy pianists such as Egon Petri, Robert Casadesus, Arthur Rubinstein, and Ignaz Friedman in

Domestic theater performance in the Moskalew family, with the teenaged Slava between his uncle Nicolay and his aunt Dagmar.

Odessa's concert halls, and both Petri and Friedman made a huge impression on him. He even mentions Petri's interpretation of César Franck's *Prelude, Chorale and Fugue* as having played a role in his decision to become a pianist, and he claims that he would always be able to recall Friedman's tone in Chopin's nocturnes in his inner ear. However, he was unable to hear his later idol, the renowned Russian Vladimir Sofronitsky. Sofronitsky's piano recital was completely sold out.

At the beginning of the 1930s, Teofil received an official request from the German consulate to teach Consul Roth's children, a job he kept for several years. The period was still marked by unrest and economic depression; many people in the country and in the cities were starving. Any opportunity to earn a little extra money had to be exploited. The consul was a competent amateur musician and a frequent guest at the opera. He had heard Slava play the piano solo in Glazunov's *Raymonda* and invited him to perform at one of the consulate's soirées (Teofil Richter suffered from an irksome nerve inflammation in one arm and had developed intense stage fright; he no longer performed publicly).

Thereafter, the young Richter performed at cultural evenings at the consulate on a number of occasions. When Paul von Hindenburg died in August 1934

Coffee table in the Odessa home of Anna and Teofil.

(a year and a half after having stepped down as the German chancellor in favor of Adolf Hitler), Richter even participated in a memorial service at the consulate by playing two classical German dirges, "The Death of Siegfried" from Wagner's *Götterdämmerung* and Beethoven's "Marcia funebre" from the Piano Sonata in A-flat Major, opus 26. As the commander of the Eastern Front in 1914, Hindenburg had won decisive victories over the Russian army. And Wagner's dirge was usually performed at Nazi statesmen's funerals.

Thus actively honoring a great German army commander and chancellor could be interpreted as a pro-German act. But the Richters were on a familiar footing with the consul and his family, and the two families celebrated New Year's Eve together on several occasions, until shortly after Hindenburg's death the consul was called home. This open *liaison dangéreuse* with official Germany would later have fateful repercussions for Teofil Richter.

Richter still had no experience as a solo concert pianist. He worked primarily as an accompanist and *répétiteur* and was apparently still not especially attracted by piano music as such. Concerts tended to bore him. He missed action and flourish; a love of theater was deep in his blood. But he loved playing symphonies and other orchestral music arranged for four hands. At the age of fifteen, he often played four hands with Yakov Zak, yet another of the supertalents from Odessa who later became one of the country's premier pianists. A local music historian helped them, lending them scores from his library, and together they played, among other things, Stravinsky's *Sacre du Printemps*.

Against this background, it may be surprising to find out that as a nineteen-year-old, Richter suddenly got it into his head to arrange a piano recital. In the summer of 1933, the violinist David Oistrakh (to whom his father had introduced him several years earlier) and his accompanist, the pianist Vsevolod Topilin, gave a concert in Zhitomir. Topilin's performance of Chopin's F-Minor Ballade had such a powerful effect on Richter that he immediately decided to prepare a whole Chopin program. He began to rehearse seriously. But whenever he asked his father for advice, he always got the same answer: you know best. "My father and I understood each other without words; we didn't speak much, but I always had a sense that he understood me tacitly."

The concert took place on March 19, 1934, the day before his nineteenth birthday. He put on the concert in a small hall that the Engineers' Association of Odessa made available, playing for a large audience composed in part of family, friends, and acquaintances. He recalls his preparations and performance as "amateurish." To attempt Chopin's huge *Polonaise-Fantaisie*, his ingenious, virtuoso Ballade in F Minor, the Scherzo in E Major, and several of the neck-breaking etudes from opus 10 must, at any rate, be called ambitious, if not reckless. But in a wondrous way, the program was a foreshadowing of his whole later career—Chopin's fantasy was the major piano work he played most often throughout his life. With the wisdom of hindsight, he spoke very negatively about his performance but nevertheless recalled that he was rather satisfied with Chopin's Ballade and that his encore, the Fourth Etude from opus 10, was very successful. "I had practiced quite a bit and could play it at a neck-breaking tempo." The Etude in C-sharp Minor is a dizzying piece of finger acrobatics, which Richter later mastered with inconceivable precision in a breathless and stormy *prestissimo*. And his lifelong respect for the composer's specifications is also apparent here. Many years later, he said, "I have been criticized for playing this etude too fast. But the tempo designation is *presto*. It is Chopin's etude that is fast, not me! I have no idea why so many play it in the same tempo as the first etude, which is *allegro*." The simple answer is probably that only a very few are able to play it at Richter's tempo. However, almost twenty years went by before he played this virtuoso etude again in public.

If critics from the Odessa newspapers were present, they did not mention the concert. The great Richter began his career as a concert pianist almost unnoticed by the public. And a number of years would go by before he tested his abilities again with a piano recital.

The story is a bright point in a time otherwise marked by yet another wave of violence in the form of brutal Communist purges. As soon as he acquired dictatorial power at the end of 1927, Stalin implemented a heretofore-unknown regime of political and economic terror: mass arrests, show trials, indoctrination. The violence was directed particularly at intellectuals, who were predominantly considered counterrevolutionaries. The first "five-year plan" in 1928 introduced extremely restrictive reforms in connection with the forced collectivization of agriculture, and Stalin fine-combed the army, the state administration, and society's leadership structure for "state enemies." With a steady stream of images, slogans, signs, and icons, the power apparatus gilded daily reality or masked it to the point of unrecognizability. And in most essentials, the people went along with this sham world in their public and private lives.

On December 1, 1934, Sergei Kirov, the party chairman in Leningrad, was murdered (it is still unclear whether Stalin saw him as a dangerous competitor and was responsible for the murder). A political insurrection was brewing, and the result was a yearlong bloodbath. By staging political trials everywhere, with mass arrests, deportations, executions, and liquidations, Stalin resolutely strangled any opposition in the party apparatus, whether real or imagined. His motives were cynically pragmatic and often inscrutable; executions and deportations were like a lottery of death. The Red Army's supreme commander was sentenced and executed in June 1937. Even highly placed Party members were shot for "treasonous activity" of all sorts, among them Lenin's close friend, the highly regarded Marxist theoretician and for many years chief editor of *Pravda*, Nikolai Bukharin (who had criticized Stalin's cultural policy).

In 1937–38, article 58 of the Soviet Penal Code on "anti-Soviet activities" (espionage, sabotage, and propaganda against the regime) was methodically and painstakingly used at the slightest hint of skepticism or criticism; the result was countless accusations and arrests of people from every social class. Thousands of intellectuals, authors, journalists, scientists, cultural workers, and so on disappeared or were executed. The public reacted with anger and mutinous feelings; everyone realized that they or their family members risked random arrest. But anyone who asked questions or expressed disagreement was automatically branded a counterrevolutionary. In this environment, the young Richter had good reason to have no interest in politics.

A standing joke in Odessa was the story of a man who asks his barber why he is always talking about politics. The answer was: "Because it's much easier

Slava Richter.

to cut your hair when it's standing on end." Countless people were interned in Stalin's Siberian "work and reeducation camps" along with murderers, thieves, and criminals, a man-made hell called the Gulag (the name of the state institution that had overall responsibility for the camps). At one point the number of interned people reached several million, and starvation, exhaustion, and disease increased the number of deaths dramatically. But many years would go by before the world would learn of these concentration camps, and even today they are hardly part of the general historical consciousness in the same way as Hitler's camps are, even though they lasted for a longer period and cost many more lives. Scholars estimate that the number of victims of political crimes in the Soviet Union approaches a mind-boggling seventy-eight million.

In vivid and frightening language, Richter evokes the fear that permeated everything and plagued everyone when sixty years later he relates a strange dream that recurred during that period: "There's a ring at the door. I go to answer it. 'Who is it?' And from the other side of the door comes a terrifying voice: 'Don't open up. I'm a burglar!' And I would wake up, bathed in sweat. My dream was clearly bound up with this fear of the doorbell ringing, as, needless to say, there were arrests." The memory of this dream lasted all his life; but with characteristic deprecation, the eighty-two-year-old Richter calls the dream "amazingly silly."

The young pianist.

His debut concert was Richter's first but also his last in Odessa. As things developed, both privately and politically, the city later became a symbol of the darkest chapters in his life. Not only was it the place where his father was later executed, but already in 1933 the regime had begun systematically to destroy Odessa's churches. In 1934 the cathedral was blown up. In Zhitomir the Lutheran church was converted into an indoor football field.

Denunciations, anonymous or not, were part of the day's agenda, and, understandably, this led to cynicism, a situation in which benefits were routinely obtained at the expense of others. Often an anonymous letter to the NKVD was enough to get rid of a competitor, a difficult neighbor, or a hated family member. The purges also reached Odessa's opera house. The man who had staged Ernst Krenek's *Jonny spielt auf* was now accused of treason. The entire staff was encouraged to report anything that could be used against him. His photograph was posted on the theater's walls with the inscription "enemy of the people."

For the young apolitical despiser of violence, weapons, and compulsion, the situation became more and more intolerable. The fact that he was passed over as conductor and thereby robbed of his dream of a conducting career at the Odessa opera house further aggravated his negative feelings. But the situation reached its apex when a close friend, the talented young Ukrainian composer

Sergei Orlov, was arrested. At the same time, there was a possibility that Richter would be drafted. The military symbolized everything he despised, and he acted swiftly. The year was 1937. He was ready to burn his bridges, to leave his parents, friends, obligations, and hopes. He was twenty-two years old. A number of music celebrities who had heard him play the piano and sight-read, among them the influential composer and critic Boris Asafyev, had recommended that he go to Moscow to obtain a musical education of the highest level. Richter wanted to find out whether he could become a conductor or a pianist there, or perhaps even a composer. He dreamed of someday conducting an opera.

Suddenly the opportunity to study piano arrived in the form of Heinrich Neuhaus, the famous teacher at the Moscow Conservatory and one of the country's greatest musical personalities. Richter had met him at one of his concerts in Odessa. His performance of Beethoven's *Hammerklavier* Sonata had made a colossal impression on the young Slava, and he had an intuitive sense that Neuhaus was the right teacher for him.

The goal was now Moscow, but this was easier said than done. No one could just move to the incredibly overpopulated capital city; permission from the authorities was needed. It was also enormously difficult to find a place to live, and it required money. Acquaintances—among them the well-to-do parents of Teofil's students—provided financial help. And some friends, a young couple, offered him a place to live in their diminutive Moscow apartment in a large, cooperative complex. The woman of the couple also studied with Neuhaus. The fact that Richter could find a roof over his head without having to wait in line with others may have paved his way. It is also probable that the highly respected Heinrich Neuhaus acted as a fulcrum.

"I Have Had Three Teachers: My Father, Wagner, and Heinrich Neuhaus"

Among admirers of the piano's more or less forgotten greats, pianist Heinrich Neuhaus is something straight from the horse's mouth. As an interpreter of Beethoven, Chopin, Schumann, and especially Scriabin on the recordings that have survived from the Soviet radio archives, he still elicits interest among connoisseurs and collectors. As a piano teacher, as one of the fathers of the "Russian school," and as a teacher and mentor for a host of significant pianists for more than forty years, he is still honored in his homeland (in addition to Richter, for example, he taught Emil Gilels, Yakov Zak, and many years later the Romanian-born Radu Lupu). But in the West, he remained relatively unknown; whether due to personal choice or a politically motivated ban on travel abroad, he apparently never performed outside the Eastern Bloc.

Like Richter, Neuhaus was born in Little Russia, now the Ukraine (Russians know him as Genrikh Gustavovitch Neigaus). His musically gifted family was of German-Polish origin; he was a half-cousin of the Polish composer Karol Szymanovsky, and the great pianist and teacher Felix Blumenfeld was his mother's brother. Like Teofil Richter, he was educated in Vienna, at the Wiener Hochschule, although it is not clear that the two piano-playing German Russians ever met in the musical metropolis. He was a student of the fabled Lithuanian-born Leopold Godowsky (who was educated by Blumenfeld, his uncle), and even as a young man, he counted future stars such as Vladimir Horowitz and Arthur Rubinstein among his friends; Horowitz, too, was a student of Blumenfeld. In 1922, at the age of thirty-four, Neuhaus became a professor at the great, tradition-rich Tchaikovsky Conservatory in Moscow, and from there his immense influence on the Russian piano tradition spread until his death in October 1964.

In November 1941 he was arrested, presumably for anti-Soviet behavior (Richter tells Monsaingeon that the reason was Neuhaus's German derivation, but that is incorrect). Because of an aging and sickly aunt, he had refused to be evacuated; he was now sentenced to five years in a labor camp near the

Vsevolod Topilin and Heinrich Neuhaus.

remote industrial town of Sverdlovsk in the Urals. After a year, however, influential friends and students (particularly the young Emil Gilels) were able to obtain his release. Only in 1944, after a few more sad war years as a poorly paid teacher at the conservatory in Sverdlovsk, did he obtain permission to return to his position in Moscow. During the war, in his absence, Richter took shelter in his apartment for extended periods.

Neuhaus was a colorful and wide-ranging cultural personality who spoke most of the primary European languages and was well read in literature, philosophy, and art history. He was a small, intense man with the stature of a typical German intellectual at the beginning of the century, an Albert Schweitzer or an Einstein. His views on education and the literary quality of his 1958 book *The Art of Piano Playing* still attract readers today.

For the young Richter, Neuhaus was the right man in the right place. In many respects, he reminded Slava of his father, Teofil, although Neuhaus was more cheerful and carefree. Neuhaus's book attracted some attention in its day. In it he argued that the heart of a pianist's education must be the content of the music, not virtuosity, accuracy, and technique. Neuhaus commented ironically on the pianists "whose fingers are lightning fast and smooth, while their brains are slow and listless," emphasizing again and again that "the more musical self-confidence, the less technical uncertainty."

According to Neuhaus, talent is not about fingering skill; it is "passion combined with intellect." "Is someone a pianist because he has a good technique? Of course not; he has a good technique because he is a pianist, because he finds meaning in sounds, in the poetic content of music."

The young, self-taught Richter felt he was on the same wavelength as Neuhaus. And he made an immediate impression on Neuhaus, as is apparent in Neuhaus's description in his book of the way his teacher Leopold Godowsky played, an account that bears striking similarities to descriptions of Richter's playing: "Turn your gaze from his hands to his face, and you will see the incredible concentration: the drooping eyelids, the position of the eyebrows, the forehead, everything mirrors thinking, enormous concentration—and nothing else! You immediately discover the cost of this apparent lightness, this effortlessness; what colossal spiritual energy it requires to create it. This is where true technique comes from!"

Richter admired Neuhaus's piano playing from the start, and later in life he consistently refused to play several of the standard works that Neuhaus, in Richter's opinion, had played in such an exemplary fashion that there was nothing to add: Chopin's first piano concerto, Schumann's *Kreisleriana*, and Beethoven's fifth and final concerto, the *Emperor*.

When Richter arrived for his audition at the conservatory in the hope of being admitted to Neuhaus's class, the teacher was amazed to learn that he lacked any kind of preparatory education. "It is a bold fellow who wants to enter a conservatory entirely without any musical schooling," he later wrote. "I was curious to get to know him." The young genius who traveled from the provinces to the capital, with a talent not beaten into submission by schooling, is a favorite theme in European Romantic literature, and it was exploited by writers such as Stendhal, Jean Paul, Balzac, Flaubert, and Hans Christian Andersen. But it is not a typical Russian theme. When Richter arrived in Moscow, from the beginning he was apparently quite unique.

Neuhaus writes:

A young man arrived, tall, thin, fair-haired, and blue-eyed. His face was alert and incredibly intense. He sat down at the piano, placed his long, supple, and powerful hands over the keys, and began to play. His style of playing was reserved, simple, and austere. The extraordinary musical perception that he showed won me over from the outset. I whispered to a female student sitting beside me: "I think he is a musician of genius." Following Beethoven's

Sonata in A Major, opus 101, he threw himself into Chopin's F-Minor Ballade, then played some works of his own and sight-read. Everyone present wanted him to go on and for it to last forever. That day, Sviatoslav Richter became my student.

Slava was not satisfied with his audition. His work as *répétiteur* had taken up so much of his time that his preparation was inadequate. But he remembered that after his audition he chatted with Neuhaus about this and that, especially about Wagner. "I must have made a good impression on him, as I was admitted without any examination or competition, on the one condition that I would attend the mandatory courses. These courses, however, had nothing to do with music but were a half-baked political and philosophical shambles that I could not bring myself to attend. I was twice expelled from the conservatory during my first year."

Undoubtedly, among the subjects Richter hated—and he was definitely not the only student to do so—was what went under the label of *diamat*—dialectical materialism! But conservatory students were also taught political economy, "scientific communism," Party history, and even military science. Despite many rebukes by Neuhaus, Richter, who hated any form of compulsion, could not bring himself to attend these lessons and was expelled.

The rebellious student traveled back to Odessa, having resolved never to set foot in an educational institution again. But Neuhaus, who at that point was also the principal of the conservatory, wrote a heartfelt letter to Anna and Teofil, in which he called Richter "my best student" and encouraged him to return. The generous and diplomatic Neuhaus was able to resolve the bureaucratic problems that Richter's willfulness had created. Richter continued in Neuhaus's piano class, now with no other requirements except the piano. Even the obligatory exam was waived. When Neuhaus was banished to Sverdlovsk, Richter repeatedly put off his graduation until his teacher returned to Moscow. Technically, therefore, he was a student for almost nine years. And Neuhaus succeeded in replacing his final exam with a number of concerts under the aegis of the conservatory.

Richter admits that he was not a model student. He often forgot to attend his lessons or arrived late. But Neuhaus's admiration for his talent apparently always brought out the teacher's indulgent side. Later, Richter consistently spoke of Neuhaus in the most endearing terms: "I've never met anyone with so much charm; such a delightful man, so utterly lacking in gravitas. He was like a second father to me."

But Neuhaus was more than a father to Richter. As a teacher, he had an influence on Richter's playing that cannot be overestimated. Until then, the voracious young accompanist and *répétiteur* had hardly given attack, tone, and physiology much thought. As a phenomenal sight-reader, his attention was undoubtedly directed toward reproducing the notes in the score as precisely and correctly as possible. And he must have played on quite a few run-down, pathetically maintained third-rate instruments. For him, tone was just a byproduct.

This is precisely where Neuhaus came in, even though he repeatedly claimed that there was nothing he could teach Richter (in a laudatory essay he wrote when he was seventy-two, he repeated that "when it comes to talents like Richter, it really does not matter with whom they study"). Neuhaus's incredibly stubborn and willful young student, who later in life never played a note he did not want to play, resigned himself to the fact that he had to study Beethoven's great, penultimate sonata, opus 110, in A-flat major, even though he did not care for it. He tells Monsaingeon that as a hotheaded young man, he even criticized Beethoven for his "bad taste" in this sonata. However, he later admitted that with Neuhaus at his side, he discovered "a singing tone, the tone I'd always dreamed of." And one can believe it when listening to the poetic, singing, vibrant tone in Neuhaus's own recording of the sonata. And as to "bad taste," Richter had to eat his words later. The Sonata in A-flat Major became one of the most frequently recurring works by Beethoven in his programs. (Moreover, there may be a memory lapse; at one point, Richter remembers it as Beethoven's much earlier sonata in the same key, no. 12, opus 26. But it hardly seems likely that this warm, melodically flowing piece would annoy him. And of the twenty-two Beethoven sonatas he played, opus 26 is the one he performed most frequently during his long life!)

Neuhaus recommended that he loosen his muscles, relax his hands and shoulders (on the existing film clips with Neuhaus, one sees him play with an incredibly relaxed, softly caressing body language), and sit upright in front of the piano. (Later Richter said: "He was right, everything depends on that!") The relationship between the two artists was clearly marked by mutual love and respect, but not by intellectual, verbal communication. At one point, Richter claims (incorrectly, as it turns out): "I have never been good with words." As a young man, however, he was sometimes described as taciturn or completely silent in the presence of others. And the almost wordless atmosphere surrounding teacher and student (this, too, must have reminded Richter of his father) placed the focus even more on the music. Playing, listening, and playing again was part of the educational communication, creating a situation that realized in the simplest way Neuhaus's concept of a proper musical education: about music, in music.

Richter's admiration for his teacher was boundless. He tells Chemberdzhy enthusiastically: "Actually, no others had the *élan* Neuhaus possessed. . . . At that time, I would simply hide behind the piano and cry. As a seventy-year-old, he achieved perfection. He decided to take on Reger's Bach variations. Such a difficult work, simply awful, and with an incredibly complex counterpoint. He played like he was twenty. . . . He was unique. But he spent too much time on teaching. Neuhaus was a musician. At the highest level, and with a wide horizon."

"In the course of six months, he liberated my fingers. He helped me get rid of the harsh sound ('one must fly, fly,' he said)." Richter had found a teacher with an amazing ability to teach by example and who allowed him to find new sides of himself without molding or repressing the self-conscious student. As Richter explains, "Neuhaus put the finishing touches on what I was looking for." Neuhaus himself described his role as that of an adviser in an atmosphere of "friendly, diplomatic neutrality."

The remark indicates a well-developed sense of humor in the teacher, which his book on the art of playing the piano and the many anecdotes about him demonstrate again and again. A number of his students were the pretty young daughters of well-to-do, artistically hopeful parents, but these girls were without much talent. After listening to one of them along with the young Richter, Neuhaus exclaimed: "My God, since the girl looks like the Venus de Milo, why did she get hands?" Another young lady, the student of a colleague, performed on the piano like a washerwoman, according to Neuhaus. When Richter and Neuhaus heard a new recording by Horowitz, this very conservative colleague exclaimed: "Good grief, he plays like a whore!" "Better a whore than a washerwoman," Neuhaus remarked.

In his 1960 essay on Richter ("Portrait of an Artist"), Neuhaus writes:

> Only a pianist whose genius is a match for the composer's, a pianist who is the composer's brother, comrade and friend, can play like this. . . . One talks so much about "style" as if style were a thing apart from a given work, a given composer. Style is merely a word. When Richter began to play Schumann after playing Haydn, everything changed—it was a different piano, a different tone, a different rhythm, a different character of expression, and the change was so easy to understand: that was Haydn, and this was Schumann. . . . His singular ability to grasp the whole and at the same time miss none of the smallest details of a composition suggests a comparison with an eagle who from his great height can see as far as the horizon and yet single out the tiniest detail of the landscape.

However, in a letter to Richter, Neuhaus admitted that he would have to "write for 50 years to be able to write about you in a proper way."

Richter did not want any "style" other than that of the music. Neuhaus was right, of course, even though Richter was ever changeable and unpredictable, a restless, searching wanderer, a Janus who could play Chopin so monumentally that it almost acquired a German accent or Schumann so nervously and passionately that it took on Slavic features or, sometimes, Bach with a Romantic coloring. But he insisted on the right of the artist to put trust in inspiration, even when inspiration did not arrive. He also insisted on the right to allow curiosity and intellect to govern, the right to experiment with tempo, tone, pedal use, and so on, as long as it was the music itself, its unique mysteries and questions, he was relating to and trying to penetrate.

Sometimes one can see Richter's playing described as measured and even cool. But there is a big difference between the younger Richter and Richter in the final twenty-five years of his life, which anyone with access to just a few of the numerous Russian recordings from the 1950s can ascertain. In a short essay from July 1985, the Russian composer Alfred Schnittke relates that even as a teenager Richter was his musical idol. "I was astonished at his temperament and willpower. I marveled at his conquest of technical difficulties. But I did not appreciate his easy posture at the instrument; I thought he was trying to impress the public." When Schnittke heard Richter again a dozen years later, he was amazed at the change. "The easy posture had gone, there was a sage, an ascetic at the piano, one who knew something of which music was merely a part. . . . The temperament was as vigorous as before and yet somewhat different, not subjectively romantic but objectively elemental. The objectivity, however, was not retrospectively classicistic, but perfectly new in kind. . . . It was the grandeur and might of one who had renounced ambition and power."

If a certain coolness may sometimes be felt in the late Richter, it is a coolness naturally connected to seeing and experiencing the world from on high, perhaps the kind of coolness that the composer Anton Webern described after a hike in the mountains: "Quite literally to reach the greatest heights, to find the connections in that mountain nature which expresses itself literally 'in the highest of places,' and which for me represent ideals I would like to feel within myself. It is as if the reality of heights contains all wonders at once."

Moscow

Moscow was to become the focal point of the rest of Richter's life. "Moscow is a city of contrasts, a place where everything puts down its own roots. Everything that can seem foreign, it makes its own. The beautiful and the monstrous stand side by side; buildings in one style stand door to door with buildings in a completely different style. And yet everything is harmonious. That is what is attractive about Moscow," he told Milstein.

After the strains of life in Odessa, student life in Moscow opened up new horizons for Richter. There he heard music by the most significant Soviet composers of the day—for example, the first Moscow performance of Shostakovich's Fifth Symphony in January 1938. In Neuhaus's class, he had not only friends and admirers but also classmates whom he might have seen as competitors. Richter's temperament, however, was never inclined to competition or jealousy. "Jealousy is a feeling that is alien to me, in all areas," he claimed. And one believes him.

He began to perform at student concerts Neuhaus arranged in the conservatory's Small Hall, and he played not only the flagships of piano music—works such as Schumann's C-Major Fantasy and Schubert's *Wanderer* Fantasy, but also new classics, such as Debussy's preludes, Ravel's *Valses nobles et sentimentales*, and the modern works of that time, for instance, music by Neuhaus's half-cousin Karol Szymanovsky. He found rehearsal space when and where he could; he might turn up at friends' homes at any time, night or day, to borrow a piano. He rarely had a fixed residence and then only for a short time. "I slept where people let me," he said. Neuhaus took care of him more than anyone else; for many years Richter lived with his teacher for varying periods. "He [Neuhaus] was so generous that his students could call on him without warning, even at four in the morning. If you turned up in the middle of the night, his wife would say: 'You've nowhere to sleep? Well, you can spend the night here.'" It may sound almost too good to be true, but that sort of hospitality was quite common in the USSR at that time.

The Neuhaus family lived at the Specialists' House, an imposing, ungainly

Anatoly Vedernikov.

building near the Kursk metro station in eastern Moscow, where apartments were made available to people who had contributed something special to the Soviet state (later Gilels and Oistrakh also lived there for a time, as well as the author Boris Pasternak). The apartment was small, but the budding pianist had no need for creature comforts: he slept on the bare floor, under the grand piano. Almost every day he met a composer who lived in the same building—a tall, elegant middle-aged gentleman clad in light yellow shoes, a Parisian jacket, and an orange tie: Sergei Prokofiev.

The student closest to Richter in Neuhaus's class was Anatoly (Tolya) Vedernikov, a great talent who apparently never gained the recognition he deserved in the USSR and has remained virtually unknown in the West. Vedernikov was five years younger than Richter. The son of a Russian couple who had emigrated to Japan and later to Manchuria, Anatoly came into the world in the Chinese city of Harbin, where a significant portion of the population spoke Russian. His concert career took off in China and Japan, while he was still a teenager. But when his parents were forced to return to the USSR in 1936, in the middle of Stalin's purges, they were immediately arrested. And then the story becomes depressingly familiar: Vedernikov's father and brothers were accused of espionage and executed; his mother spent eight years in a labor camp.

The two young great talents became friends immediately. They played music together, and for long periods they were roommates or stayed with Neuhaus. Before the war, a fellow student, the composer Grigori Fried, shared a dorm with them for a time. Since they had only one sofa, all three of them decided to sleep on the floor. The eighty-nine-year-old Fried recalled in his Moscow apartment: "We lived in many different places. We were close friends; I had close contact with Vedernikov up until he died in Hamburg during his first and only concert tour to the West in 1993. Richter, on the other hand, I saw only rarely after he became an international celebrity. At that time Richter was a tall, thin man with hair that was almost orange. We read books aloud all night long— Maeterlinck, for example—and Richter especially was unstoppable." To the question of why Vedernikov's parents were arrested, Fried answered simply, "Nobody asked why. My own father was arrested. At that time you just did not ask such questions."

In 1939 Richter and Vedernikov performed together publicly for the first time. The concert was Bach's Double Concerto in C Major (many years later they recorded the work with Rudolf Barshai and the Moscow Chamber Orchestra). And with two other Neuhaus students, they later performed Bach's version for four pianos of a Vivaldi concerto on Soviet radio. The young German Kurt Sanderling conducted, and Sanderling became one of Richter's favorite conductors. Before Stalin's purges accelerated in 1936, the Soviets offered asylum to political refugees. Many German conductors escaped from Hitler's Germany to the USSR and were appointed as heads of a number of the best Soviet orchestras. Sanderling, who was Jewish, emigrated with his family in 1936. He worked with the Moscow Radio Symphony Orchestra and headed the orchestra in Kharkov, Ukraine's former capital, until the German invasion in 1941. Although many exiled Germans were arrested during the war, Sanderling was appointed as the alternating principal conductor of the Leningrad Philharmonic and was to hold this post for almost twenty years (his partner was Evgeny Mravinsky, "undoubtedly our best conductor," according to Richter). In 1960 Sanderling was appointed head of the symphony orchestra in East Berlin (which later became the Berlin Symphony Orchestra); the East Germans wanted to have the counterpart to the famous Philharmonic Orchestra of West Berlin.

Asked to tell about his times and his relationship to Richter, the ninety-three-year-old Sanderling explains:

Even in the spring of 1937, they demanded that foreigners either accept Soviet citizenship or risk expulsion. What saved me was that my passport

Kurt Sanderling.

said not "German" but "Jew." My uncle had told me that would be the best. The situation created new job possibilities. Otherwise, for example, Mravinsky would never have gotten the post; until then, he was an almost unknown ballet director at the opera. They had no one else, he looked good, he had successfully conducted Tchaikovsky's fifth symphony, but he would have preferred to decline [the post]. It was a long time before he received his due. He was a close friend of Shostakovich, which is why he premiered so many of his symphonies.

When Maestro Sanderling hears about Richter's admiration for Mravinsky, he arches an eyebrow. "In my day," he continues,

he was not particularly enthusiastic about Mravinsky. Or, rather, he liked him because Mravinsky was always a fanatical worker. Most soloists were not so happy with Mravinsky because he could only do it the way he himself understood the music. He did not have the ability to accommodate the soloist's uniqueness or peculiarities. He was always frightfully nervous when he was to accompany. In fact, I can only remember a single time when he performed with Richter. It was the Tchaikovsky concerto. Mravinsky was decidedly not

Richter's comrade from his student years, the composer Grigori Fried in his Moscow flat, 2006.

someone who wanted to discover new works, whereas Richter selected his repertoire like an *enfant terrible*. You could never know what he would play.

As early as 1941, before the war reached the Soviet Union in June, Vedernikov and Richter arranged a recital for two pianos with music by Chopin, Liszt, Debussy, and Rachmaninov. They must have felt an extraordinary musical concord, and later they collaborated repeatedly. In 1938 the composer Grigori Fried had already formed a study group at the conservatory (named "the creative circle"). In his Moscow flat, Fried related, "The circle was organized by a five-man group: Richter, Vedernikov, pianist Vadim Gusakov, music scholar Kira Masova, and myself. The intent was to listen to unknown or 'forbidden' music that, in theory, was banned—for example, Stravinsky before the war. We each had our own special area: Vedernikov took care of Debussy and Ravel, Gusakov was responsible for Scriabin, and I took care of Stravinsky and the newest music. But Richter played everything. Especially opera, Krenek's *Jonny spielt auf*, Hindemith's *Mathis der Maler*, Debussy's *Pelléas et Mélisande*, but also, for example, the music of Berlioz."

The circle met every Thursday to play pieces for two and four hands for and with each other. Gradually, other students, teachers, and friends turned up in increasing numbers as listeners. Richter played large-scale operas such as Wagner's *Tristan und Isolde* and *Die Meistersinger von Nürnberg*; he played Richard Strauss's *Salome* and *Elektra*; and with colleagues he played versions for four hands of symphonies by Bruckner and Myaskovsky or Mahler's gigantic Third Symphony, which otherwise was impossible to hear in the USSR. Completely new music, the avant-garde of that day, also gained a footing in the program, as with the music of Szymanovsky. Neuhaus believed that his students learned more from these get-togethers than from anything else at the conservatory.

But the circle's piano soirées gradually began to engender serious competition for the conservatory's official concerts. The two famous conservatory halls were half-empty on Thursdays. In 1941 Vedernikov, Richter, and their colleagues decided to play Wagner's entire *Ring Cycle* on the piano. On the evening of June 21, just as Richter and Vadim Guzakov were ready to go onstage to perform the last act of *Götterdämmerung*, the conservatory's principal showed up demanding that the concert be canceled, Richter recounts. Not a single listener had shown up at the official concert in the Great Hall!

The Wagner evening would have been the circle's hundredth Thursday-evening concert. But the next day, according to Richter, the German army's invasion of the Soviet Union put a stop to the circle's activities. However, this must be a memory lapse or a slight dramatization on Richter's part. June 21, 1941, was not a Thursday but a Saturday.

Two years earlier, Grigori Fried had been drafted. In 1940 he was stationed in Odessa and, at Richter's encouragement, visited Teofil Richter at the city's opera house with greetings from Slava. He described Teofil as a very lively, warm, and receptive man in his late sixties. "I heard afterwards that he had been executed," he said; "that was terrible." Later, Fried energetically continued the work of the student circle. In fact, to this day he is still active (now in the Musicians' Club), and with him as president for all these years, the group has, at the time of this writing, reached concert number 1,145!

In the following years, Tolya Vedernikov was a sparring partner and a peer for Richter. A certain rivalry seems, especially in the beginning, only to have increased their friendship. A fellow student, Richter's long-time friend Vladimir Tchaikovsky, said that they loved to improvise together. "Once they agreed on a key and a character, they nodded to each other and took off. It was very funny when the music drove them each in their own direction, and, in unexpected ways, they found their way back to the key." They often performed together in the company of friends. For example, in 1942, two years before their first concert performance, they played the entire piano score of the first version of Prokofiev's new Tolstoy opera *War and Peace* for a group of musicians, among them Dmitri Shostakovich.

Vedernikov's musical interests were comprehensive, and Fried especially admired his advocacy of the new Soviet music. Richter, on the other hand, never played lesser-known, younger Soviet composers. Vedernikov was also enthusiastic about the latest Western music; works such as Stravinsky's piano sonata, Hindemith's *Ludus Tonalis* (twelve preludes and fugues), and Debussy's etudes for piano were pieces no other Soviet pianist would dream of including in his repertoire shortly after the war. The list of new Western works he premiered in the Soviet Union is long and impressive. Later, for example, he recorded Arnold Schönberg's Piano Concerto (which uses Schönberg's heretical twelve-tone method).

Vedernikov can still be heard on various recordings (in 1999 the Japanese company BVCX even published a Vedernikov Edition). For extended periods, his concert activities were limited, but in contrast to Richter, he loved working in the recording studio. As a pianist, he was similar to Richter in some aspects. His interpretations of Beethoven and Schumann were often innovative, and his technical abilities dizzying. Due to the phenomenal clarity and stringency in his performance of works such as Brahms's Paganini variations and Stravinsky's sparkling piano version of three movements from *Petrouchka* (a commission from Arthur Rubinstein), his recordings deserve greater dissemination. But on one point he is Richter's opposite: his playing is devoid of Romantic depth of feeling and of poetry; his tone is sober, almost hard, as far from Neuhaus's introverted singing sound as can be imagined. And the aging Richter is unwilling to accept this tone as a conscious, well-considered choice. He calls Vedernikov "pig-headed" because in his student days Vedernikov ignored Neuhaus's advice and insisted on playing only with his fingers, not his whole body. "Stubborn as a mule," Richter says as he looks back on it.

Or stubborn as Sviatoslav Richter? The eighty-two-year-old Richter did not have much patience for Vedernikov's notion that a musician's individuality and idiosyncrasies can stand in the way of the music, which inevitably leads one to think of his own intellectual problem with the role of "interpreter." Could his lifelong insistence on the inviolability of the notes and the composer not be expressed in a similar way? Nevertheless, Richter calls the idea of the musician's anonymity monstrous and remarks—with a logic that can also apply to himself—that Vedernikov's playing often contradicted this.

Richter's admiration for Vedernikov's musicianship, however, is evident. He praises his friend's sense of form, virtuosity, concentration, and taste. He puts Vedernikov's playing of Bach on the level of Glenn Gould and praises his Debussy to the skies, for example, the twelve etudes; Richter was seventy-five before he played seven of these etudes.

In his conversations with Monsaingeon, however, he also recalls his colleague as a pure "contrarian," somebody who opposed everything and everyone and who easily made enemies. "He was terribly pig-headed, out of a spirit of contradiction; he rubbed people up the wrong way." This statement may sound like misanthropy but might also describe a man with the courage of his convictions, a disposition that, for obvious reasons, is problematic in an authoritarian society characterized by power and control from above. The explanation for why Vedernikov was able to perform only in the West after the fall of the Soviet Union could well be this undiplomatic obstinacy. In the Soviet cultural environment, "individualism" was a dirty word, a rebuke for having independent opinions; obliqueness was a necessity, and it was an accepted habit to say one thing and believe another.

A second area of disagreement between the two stubborn individualists was the instrumental physiognomy of the piano. Vedernikov believed that the piano was, in reality, a percussion instrument, since the tone dies away quickly after the string is struck. The fact that the instrument can "sing" is mere theory, a pretty illusion. Richter, of course, disagreed. Their debate reached its peak when they listened to a Richter recording of Mussorgsky's *Pictures at an Exhibition*. The final, powerful bass note in the "Catacombs" movement is meant to resonate for a long time. "You see, you can't hear a thing," claimed Vedernikov to Richter's understandable chagrin. A number of years later, they studied the score of Dvořák's rarely performed piano concerto together, and they agreed that the work contains many interesting passages. Richter decided to take on this overlooked, technically difficult concerto and played it for the first time with Eugene Ormandy, during his first trip to the United States in 1960. But after a Moscow performance, Vedernikov turned up in the artist's dressing room and asked, "Slava, why do you play such worthless music?"

Together, they listened to a recording of Benjamin Britten's opera *Peter Grimes*, and they were both deeply moved. But when Richter later became acquainted with Britten personally and developed a warm friendship with the world-famous Englishman, Vedernikov suddenly announced that Britten had never written anything but indifferent music. Richter presented Vedernikov with the score to Pfitzner's opera *Palestrina*, the work his father had introduced to his opera-loving teenage son and which Richter considered in every respect an important work with a splendid libretto. According to Richter, Vedernikov responded: "Impossible to imagine a stupider subject!"

All this is the reminiscence and point of view of an eighty-two-year-old. But the fact that in his conversations with Monsaingeon Richter devotes so much attention to the friend of his youth testifies to the significance of the friendship in his life and development. His description of his friend in rather negative terms—for unfathomable reasons—in no way signifies that the friendship was broken off. In the evening of his life, Richter apparently felt the need to distance himself from Vedernikov's turn of mind and from aesthetic attitudes that might resemble the Western intellectual avant-garde. But it is evident that he admired his friend's independence and personal courage. The two colleagues gradually stopped performing together because of Richter's all-consuming international concert calendar and the ban on Vedernikov's foreign travel. Much later, however, Richter kept in close contact with Vedernikov and his wife, Olga, and when the opportunity presented itself, he spent Vedernikov's birthday with his colleague.

In his conversations with Monsaingeon, however, Richter plays a trump card in his account of Vedernikov's stubbornness by claiming that his friend refused to get medical help for his young son, even though the boy was seriously ill with meningitis. "I have no faith in doctors," he reports Vedernikov saying. And Richter claims that the son ended up a deaf-mute. But here, as elsewhere, Richter is revealed as the child of a society where rumors and more or less invented anecdotes were part of the social conventions of the time. Others describe the Vedernikovs as splendid parents. And their son became known as an illustrator and painter, with both hearing and speech intact.

In fairness, it must be said that a number of people who were close to Richter were amazed at the often cynical and, at times, almost bitter tone in his characterizations of some friends and colleagues over the course of a long life, both in his biographical monologues and in his diary. They find this uncharacteristic of him.

The person in Neuhaus's class from whom everyone expected the most was Emil Gilels — at least before Richter began to vie for this rank. When admitted to Neuhaus's class, Gilels, a year and a half younger than Richter, was already known as a supertalent. In 1933, at the age of seventeen, he had won the state piano competition and, two years later, was awarded second prize at the international competition in Vienna. He and Richter had Odessa in common as the city of their youth, and they met for the first time when Richter was seventeen. A music critic took Gilels along to a recital when Richter, as usual, was playing a piece for four hands with a friend: Liszt's *Les Préludes* and movements from Myaskovsky's symphonies. Richter relates to Chemberdzhy: "Gilels was already a celebrity. He listened for a while and said about me, 'He's good, but the other won't do.'" So obviously, the other was hardly Yakov Zak.

The young Gilels never had the same father-son relationship with Neuhaus that Richter did. He apparently did not enjoy his colleague's almost telepathic connection with his teacher. In an early interview with the music scholar and pianist Alexander Vishinsky, Gilels mentioned that he definitely wanted more verbal communication with his teacher. "I understood when something was wrong, but I never understood what I was supposed to do. Neuhaus never explained anything. He just sat at the piano and played. We had no conversations, no discussions. . . . But later, during the war, I visited Neuhaus in Sverdlovsk. We played some quartets by Beethoven, Brahms, Schubert, Schumann, in versions for four hands, and we found a sort of common language. It was a most interesting period."

For many years the two Odessa boys pursued their careers side by side, with mutual respect and increasing status in the musical world as the Soviet Union's brightest piano stars. In a radio transmission in 1942, they played together for the first and only time; the work was a bit of a rarity, Saint-Saëns's variations for two pianos on a theme by Beethoven (a work that Gilels later recorded with their mutual friend Yakov Zak).

In 1955, after the Stalin era, when Gilels was the first Soviet soloist to tour the United States, the eyes of the Western media were seriously opened to future sensations in the concert hall. Gilels's status as the "second great Russian," alongside Richter, was cemented right up to his death in 1985. But in contrast to Richter, he appreciated "the American way of life," taking advantage of the variety of goods in shops, which were suddenly within the reach of a Soviet artist with dollars in his pocket. For example, rumor has it that he unexpectedly showed up at the Steinway sales offices in New York to buy a concert grand piano (including transportation to Moscow), paying cash for it. Goskoncert must have given the international star special treatment. Normally, only a fraction of the foreign fees ended up in the artist's pocket.

For almost two dozen years, Gilels organized major concert tours to the United States. He was the very image of the piano virtuoso, a born stage artist who enchanted the audience with his commanding body language, unruly red hair, vitality, full piano tone, and a primal pianistic force that at times could seem almost frightening.

With his powerful playing, he earned a reputation as a pianist who excelled in big halls with a large-scale, full-toned repertoire: Brahms, Liszt, Tchaikovsky, Rachmaninov. His unpredictable, sometimes awkward, impulsive, and even sloppy playing earned him the nickname "the Butcher" among Russians at one time. Critics objected to what they believed was an exaggerated use of the pedal and tempos that were sometimes too slow. But everyone praised his masterly technique, his drive, his fluid, plastic delivery, and the expanse of his huge repertoire. And his powerful playing did not preclude an incisive and expressive simplicity in Mozart, a reticent calm in Beethoven, or an elementally infectious charm—something that is rare in Richter, as in, for example, many of Grieg's *Lyric Pieces* or Scarlatti's sonatas. The highly respected German critic Joachim Kaiser wrote in 1965 that Gilels "again and again plays in a more compelling way than even a Rubinstein or a Horowitz. . . . Many professionals believe that Gilels is one of the world's greatest pianists, if not the most significant at the moment."

The relationship between the two pianists, however, gradually cooled. Richter describes Gilels as a "complex personality," a man with a belligerent temperament and a nervous, rather joyless, spirit. And unlike Richter, he suffered from violent jealousy, which plagued him to such a degree that in Richter's memory he always seemed unhappy or dissatisfied. Richter tells of an episode he heard secondhand in which a woman greeted the great Gilels and asked the little girl who was with her, "Do you know who this is? The greatest pianist in our country." The girl exclaimed, "Sviatoslav Richter!" Instead of being amused, Gilels turned on his heel and slammed the door behind him.

Gilels's sensitive, touchy temperament led to other awkward episodes. By all accounts, at the high point of his career at the end of the 1950s, when he was famous in the East and the West, he wrote to Neuhaus claiming that he had learned nothing from him (according to Richter, he also wrote to newspapers, but that is not true). As mentioned, he never had the same deep personal relationship with his teacher as Richter, although Neuhaus always worshiped him. Richter believes that the explanation has to do with a lack of self-esteem. Gilels did not tolerate criticism, and he was known for an almost pathological sense of pride. His annoyance might conceivably have derived from Neuhaus's 1958 book on the art of piano playing, a book in which Neuhaus often refers to both Richter and Gilels. Neuhaus notes that spiritual qualities cannot be measured in a simple way, like "Elbrus is the highest peak in the Caucasus and Mont Blanc is the highest in the Alps." But in his choice of words, he could not hide the fact that he placed Richter at a higher level. Of the young Gilels's musical background and development, he writes: "When Emil Gilels came to study with me at the Moscow Conservatory, I was forced to say to him at one point: 'You are already a grown man, you can eat steak and drink beer, but until now you have been bottle-fed.'"

Nina Dorliak, Richter's lifelong companion, reportedly claimed that the infamous letter arrived at a point when Neuhaus and his wife were staying with her and Richter, and that Neuhaus never showed the letter to anyone but his wife, his son, and her. Gilels himself apparently never referred to the letter that ended his contact with Neuhaus. But Richter must have heard about the letter, and it upset him so much that from then on he refused to greet Gilels when they happened to meet.

The ninety-three-year-old Kurt Sanderling sheds light on the tense relationship between the two Soviet piano giants.

Richter was immensely favored by Neuhaus. And it harmed him really more than it benefited him, because it led to many of his colleagues not caring for him. Neuhaus spoiled him to an almost ridiculous degree. If one spoke about pianists in the presence of Neuhaus, you could be sure he would immediately say: "Yes, yes. But *Richter . . .* !" So, his most famous colleagues were not his friends. Gilels was just as great an artist, although entirely different. If you spoke to Neuhaus about Gilels, once again he would immediately say, "But *Richter . . .* !" I knew Gilels better than Richter, and I know that Gilels did not always behave properly towards Richter. But he had a reason for it. Neuhaus spoke of Richter as if, yes, almost as if he was in love.

Sanderling can also confirm the remark Richter often cited him for (*"Er spielt nicht nur gut, er kann auch noten lesen"* [He not only plays well, but he can also read music]). "In 1961, after I had moved to the DDR [East Germany], I came to Moscow and, along with Neuhaus, heard Gilels play the last three piano sonatas of Beethoven. Neuhaus threw himself once again into one of his paeans to Richter, and I said, 'What is special about Richter, however, is not merely that he plays well but that he reads the notes!' " Neuhaus must have passed Sanderling's remark along, and, understandably, it pleased Richter.

However, musically and as a pianist, Richter admired Gilels unreservedly. He asked in amazement why Gilels's colossal talent had not made him happy as an artist (and, again, one is tempted quietly to redirect that question to him). Richter is normally stingy with superlatives, but he calls Gilels's premiere of Prokofiev's Eighth Piano Sonata—the piano work by Prokofiev that Richter came to appreciate most—"phenomenal." And Gilels's interpretation of the composer's short Third Sonata, another of Richter's favorite works, was so exemplary that Richter never played it. "There was nothing I could add," he said.

Richter speaks to Monsaingeon about Gilels's death in 1985, but again, by all accounts, his story is based on groundless rumors. Numerous Western musicians and other visitors recount that the Soviet musical world was always a wasps' nest of half-truths and whole rumors, an environment that made it almost impossible to distinguish between fact and fiction. In countries where truth is routinely perverted by the state, more or less paranoid rumors enjoy an ideal breeding ground. And Gilels was not reticent; he passed on, for example, the story that a young Chinese pianist who had been highly placed at the first International Tchaikovsky Competition in 1958 (where Gilels was chairman of the jury) had both his hands cut off upon his return to Mao's China. However, according to the American journalist Paul Moor, someone visiting Beijing a few years later met the Chinese pianist, now a highly respected artist in his homeland. And in possession of both hands!

Here is the story of Gilels's death as told by Richter: Shortly before a concert tour, Gilels had a check-up at the world-renowned Kremlin Hospital in Moscow, a hospital reserved for the elite. He was injected with a sedative, but a few minutes later he died. "Everyone knows that, at that hospital, the doctors are chosen because of their political background," says the apolitical colleague. "Through sheer incompetence, they gave him the wrong injection and killed him."

Emil Gilels's family, upon being asked, insists that the story has no basis in reality. According to them, the pianist suffered from severe diabetes and heart problems. He died of a heart malfunction on October 14, 1985. No one can say where Richter got his story. Perhaps it is a bizarre manifestation of his perpetually ambiguous and often irritable relationship with the Soviet social order (and social systems in general). Richter was never in doubt about his national loyalties; he accepted the political realities as a fact of life, usually with a shrug of the shoulders. But his hatred of authority of any sort is clear.

The cellist Mstislav Rostropovich, who was twelve years his junior, came to play an important role in Richter's life, both as a friend and as a musical colleague. Despite the significant age difference, they became friends even in their conservatory days. Unlike Richter, Rostropovich began his studies very early. Richter describes a man who loved silliness and parties and who shared his sense of life's odd, theatrical sides. He tells Monsaingeon of masked balls in Moscow, once in the small apartment of the widow of the writer Bulgakov, where they decided to dress up as crocodiles. A costume designer helped them, but the costume was so complicated that they were delayed for several hours. When they were finally attired, their simultaneous entry on all fours, each through his own door, elicited shouts of joy and horror.

Later, at the end of the 1960s, they lost contact to some extent. Whereas Richter consistently maintained his dismissive attitude toward social-political issues, Rostropovich, particularly when he became a close friend of the dissident author Alexander Solzhenitsyn, was fiercely political. He left the Soviet Union with his family in 1974, shortly after Solzhenitsyn was expelled. Thereafter, he repeatedly criticized the Soviets' suppression of human rights and artistic freedom.

As a student at the conservatory, Richter performed at a large number of private concerts for the institution's teachers and students. His first true public solo recital was scheduled to take place at the conservatory's Small Hall in October 1941. But the Germans were less than seventy miles west of Moscow, and his "debut" was canceled, probably to Richter's surprise because true to form he had hardly noticed what was going on in the world around him. And at this time he had no idea that his father had just been executed by Beria's henchmen. A few weeks later his teacher was arrested.

However, his reputation was already solidified. A year earlier he had been praised for his Prokofiev at a public piano recital with Neuhaus, a program they repeated soon after. And at the end of December 1940, at the age of twenty-five, he had his real breakthrough when in the conservatory's famous Great Hall he played, for the first time, the crown jewel of Russian piano music, one of the best-loved musical works of all time, Tchaikovsky's First Piano Concerto (even today it is the best-represented piece in the world's CD catalogues, rivaled only by Vivaldi's *Four Seasons*). A few weeks later he again played the concerto with success. And in March 1941 he elicited enthusiastic applause for his interpretation of Prokofiev's Fifth Piano Concerto, which was a bit of a stepchild in the composer's oeuvre.

At the beginning of July 1942, he finally had the opportunity to make his delayed solo debut. However, he was not allowed to have his own way. He suggested a program of Beethoven's *Pathétique* Sonata, Schubert's *Wanderer* Fantasy, and music by Chopin, but was told to replace the Chopin with Prokofiev. He played Prokofiev's D-Minor Sonata (number two) and preludes by Rachmaninov in the last part of the concert. But he found the program to be something of a muddle. Later he always put together his programs with great care, so that the individual works "spoke" to each other. In December of the same year, therefore, he arranged yet another solo recital, now with a purely Russian program that he himself had put together.

World War II from the Sidelines

In the spring of 1941, German troops occupied most of Europe and the Baltic countries. But Stalin put his faith in the nonaggression pact that the foreign ministers Ribbentrop and Molotov had signed. So, the USSR was completely unprepared for the German attack on June 22. In a shockingly brief time, the Germans moved through the Ukraine and advanced toward Moscow. In October ministries and institutions such as the Bolshoi Theater were evacuated, and Stalin kept a plane ready for his own use. The city and its hinterland made their stand, but a month earlier Leningrad had been besieged; for the next three years, the blockade cut Leningrad off from the rest of the world, and hundreds of thousands of people starved or froze to death. A harsh winter and the mounting Soviet mobilization, however, slowly gummed up the German war machine. For varying periods, most musicians were evacuated and sent to central Asian republics or the Urals. From 1943, the government gave several significant composers the opportunity to work in peace at a former poultry farm, north of Moscow. Kurt Sanderling recalls, "It was one of the few virtues of the regime at that time that they endeavored to get the great cultural institutions away from the frontline. Moscow's operas and theaters, the State Orchestra, Leningrad's opera, the Dramatic Theater, etc., were all evacuated for a period; the entire Leningrad Philharmonic was evacuated to Novosibirsk. Huge trains came from Siberia with ammunition and soldiers and returned with cultural institutions. It was magnificent!"

But many of Moscow's most famous musicians refused to be evacuated— among them pianists such as Maria Yudina, Vladimir Sofronitsky, and Yakov Zak. They helped make sure that the musical world prevailed, and Soviet radio transmitted concerts and recordings throughout the war. At that point, the young Richter was hardly in a position to oppose evacuation. In fact, most students in the country's conservatories had to work at the end of their studies as musicians or teachers wherever the state found it expedient, most often in the provinces. However, the apolitical but often quite astute pianist did not want to leave Moscow, and he managed to stay. Sometimes he worked as a guard dur-

Vera Prokhorova with her cat, 2006.

ing air raids or as a guide to the expansive Russian capital. Later, he was sent to the front to cheer up soldiers and the wounded with his piano playing.

All his life he was an indefatigable walker, and he claimed that he often walked more than thirty-five miles in a single day. He came to know Moscow and its suburbs like the back of his hand. His cousin Fritz Reincke tells that many years later, during his visits to Boston, he went on similar extended walks and that he had an incredibly well-developed sense of place. A Japanese piano tuner remembers how, after a concert in the 1970s, Richter insisted on walking the five or six miles back to his Tokyo hotel. None of the Japanese present were sure they could find the hotel, but Richter reached his destination without difficulty.

Schubert's piano fantasy based on his lied "Der Wanderer" played an important role in Richter's repertoire through most of his career. And his own self-imposed life as a "wanderer" characterized his entire adulthood to a degree that is unusual even for a world-famous musician.

During the war years, Vera Prokhorova and her family came to play an important role in Richter's life. In her declining years, the charming and linguistically gifted teacher is one of the few sources of insight into Richter's life during these years. In her Moscow apartment, she recalls that distant time with warmth and engagement. Her aunt was Neuhaus's wife, Sylvia, and she was close to several of Neuhaus's young students; she came to know Richter shortly after he arrived in Moscow. She met both Anna Richter and *totya* Meri when they came to visit Slava before the war. She describes Anna Richter as a very charming, wise, witty, receptive, and generous woman. Prokhorova's uncle, an aunt, and a nephew had been arrested. So the family had an extra room, and when Neuhaus was interned, her mother decided that Richter, too, risked internment if he stayed in Neuhaus's apartment. (She tells a grotesque story that the KGB had already made an unannounced visit, searching for a certain "Lichter," but they left empty-handed. This idiotic mistake may explain the fact that the pianist avoided evacuation or worse. He spent long periods during the rest of the war as a member of the Prokhorova family.)

In all essentials, musical life in Moscow and eastern Russia went on relatively unhindered during the war, even though the concert halls were warmed to only five or six degrees above freezing during the winter, and audiences often listened dressed in furs and felt boots. In the summer of 1943, Richter was sent to the Caucasus, and for months he gave concerts in Georgia—at that time, a wealthy region between the Black Sea and the Caspian Sea. He performed in urban areas such as the Georgian capital Tbilisi, in Baku (in today's Azerbaijan), and in cities such as Yerevan, Grozny (capital of the Chechen Republic), and Sukhumi, at the western shore of the Black Sea. He was able to eke out a living, and he experienced Georgia as a quiet, slightly sleepy enclosure behind blue mountains, a world away from the horrors of the war. Tbilisi, a cosmopolitan city of a million people, with Russian, Turkish, and European traditions and always one of Richter's favorite cities, has a subtropical climate with sun and palm trees, and the city was known for its opera, its conservatory, and its theaters. Young men and women promenaded peacefully on the boulevard in the evening. No one was rushed into the military, and there was food enough for everyone; the city is still famous for its gastronomy. At that point, Georgia was something of a cozy corner in the Soviet Union.

In Tbilisi Richter played Mozart's Piano Concerto in D Minor for the first time. The performance took place in a radio studio, where he collaborated with a conductor who was clearly connected to a unit under the NKVD (later, the KGB), and he found the man incompetent. But in his conversations with Monsaingeon, with characteristic self-irony, he recalls other obstacles:

> I'd been given a room on the sixth floor of the hotel that I had to share with an accompanist. . . . I had friends in the town and I sometimes spent the

night at their place, and each time I returned to the hotel, I had to account for my absence. One day, I told my room-mate that I'd return to the hotel in two days time and collect the music for the Mozart concerto I was to record the next morning. When I returned, fairly late at night, the door to the room was locked. I knocked . . . knock, knock . . . "I have to collect the score!" knock, knock, knock! There was no answer, and I could hear a stifled laughter coming from inside the room. What should I do? A few doors away lived a circus artist, extremely likeable, and I'd noticed from the outside that his room gave on to a ledge that ran all round the building. He agreed to help. It was raining. It was also about one o'clock in the morning, and here I was, scrambling from one ledge to another, six storeys in the air, in an attempt to get back to my room. As it was war time, it suddenly struck me that if anyone saw me, they'd shoot me like a rabbit but nothing of the sort happened. A few minutes later I entered my room through the window, greeted by shrieks of terror. I realized that my room-mate wasn't alone. "Don't be afraid," I said, "I shan't even put the light on." I stretched out on my bed. I didn't sleep a wink all night, but the next morning I was at the radio station at nine, playing the Mozart Concerto with my NKVD official.

When he later told his friend Vera ("Vipa") Prokhorova about the event, she asked him, shocked, if he was not terrified doing that tightrope act sixty feet up in the air. He answered, "Why? If you walk down a sidewalk, you only use a small part of it. The ledge was wide enough." Prokhorova generally describes the young Richter as a man who, in a wonderfully simple, almost Siegfried-like way, knew no fear, and she remembers other examples. When they spent Christmas Eve with her family, their spartanly decorated Christmas tree suddenly caught fire. Slava calmly put out the fire with his bare hands; if you do it quickly enough, you suffer no harm, he claimed. One night Slava heard a noise—a burglar was opening a window and trying to crawl inside. Soundlessly, the pianist crawled toward the window and, with his huge fists, grabbed the thief's hands. The man emitted a terrified scream and woke the whole house. Richter let him run away.

The time Richter spent in Tbilisi was a welcome interlude. It was here, in the beginning of 1944, that Richter decided to perform the second volume of Bach's *Well-Tempered Clavier*, and in the course of a month, he was able to play all twenty-four preludes and fugues by heart. However, he made do with playing smaller portions of the work for an invited circle of students, and not until a year later did he perform twelve of the twenty-four at a concert in Moscow.

This slightly hesitant, reticent approach to Bach had its reasons. Piano recitals were (and still are) dominated by Romantic music, and this was particularly so in the "old-fashioned" USSR. Bach was considered erudite and difficult, and *Das wohltemperierte Klavier* was a bit of a dust collector—a mandatory part of every piano exam, but not a work for the concert hall. If Bach's fugues ever showed up on concert programs, they were in the form of Liszt's or Busoni's monumental piano adaptations of his organ works. Only the incredibly self-willed Maria Yudina had played Bach's fugues at her concerts as early as the end of the 1920s. Once, while on tour, Richter had to practice on a worn-out upright piano in a banquet hall, and people constantly came by asking whether he would entertain them with a bit of music. He quickly discovered that he could drive them away by playing the Bach fugues!

It was definitely not typical of Richter to play an entire cycle from A to Z. He liked to describe himself as "omnivorous" but stressed that the prerequisite was always love. "I care for so much music, and I can't seem to get rid of the desire to pass this love on to a listener." But without love for a piece, there is no desire to play it. For example, he never played all of Chopin's etudes, all of Debussy's preludes, or all of Beethoven's sonatas, not even the ever-popular *Moonlight* Sonata, "for the simple reason that I do not care for all of them!" he explains with a poker face. And he admits that in the case of *The Well-Tempered Clavier*, from the outset it was mostly a matter of the challenge itself, of testing his mental ability to learn it by heart. In addition, he had a lifelong awe for music he had become acquainted with through his father. Perhaps it was a sort of defiance; at first he nourished no warm feelings for Bach's erudite polyphony. A few years later, he remarked in an interview with Alexander Vishinsky: "You are not seduced by Bach as such; it is not possible. You have to really get into his shoes to understand him. You have to develop a trusting relationship with him. To become passionate in your relationship with him, that would seem to me almost frivolous."

But as his work progressed, he did in fact come to love Bach's universal, self-contained music passionately, and he realized why the work almost had the status of a Bible for many musicians. Robert Schumann had recommended playing these preludes and fugues every single day; a number of music's legendary figures—Pablo Casals, Carl Nielsen, and Igor Stravinsky among them—often began their day by playing a fugue. For the great pianist and conductor Hans von Bülow (who, in 1875, premiered Tchaikovsky's First Piano Concerto), the work was simply "the Old Testament of the piano."

It was also in Tbilisi that Richter learned and performed for the first time one of Beethoven's most magnificent piano works, the Sonata in F Minor, the *Appas-*

sionata, a sonata that is generally considered very technically demanding. But Richter remembers that "beside *The Well-Tempered Clavier*, it seemed almost easy to me." (Later, however, he changed his mind, calling the sonata "a monster" and playing it only a few times in the last thirty years of his life.)

A couple of years later, he also memorized the twenty-four preludes and fugues that constitute the first volume of Bach's major work. Thereafter, he played "the 48" everywhere he went, with a stubbornness that elicited snappish letters from female admirers ("When are you going to stop tormenting us with Bach?"). But normally he prescribed Bach in moderate doses, eight preludes and fugues in the concert's first part and, after a break, well-known music by, for example, Mozart, Beethoven, or Brahms.

The eternal controversy on whether Bach should be played on the modern piano or on the harpsichord did not interest Richter. But he made no secret of what he preferred: "You can also play Bach on the harpsichord. But an entire concert on the harpsichord seems so impoverished!" Was it not likely that Bach himself realized the limitations of the harpsichord in relation to the dynamic possibilities and phrasing he knew from strings and wind instruments, and was it not possible that Bach heard such nuances and refinements in his inner ear?

In Baku Richter discovered that he was being shadowed. During Stalin's vendetta as well as during the war, the iron fist apparently did not come down on musicians with the same zeal and brutality as it did on poets, writers, and theater folk. But even the most remote family ties to Germany were looked upon with deep suspicion. One late night, as he was heading toward his hotel, in order not to be locked out he began to run. When, by chance, he looked behind him, he discovered a man running after him. To find out what was going on, he ran past the hotel's entrance and around the next street corner, where he waited. When the pursuer approached at full speed, Richter stepped out in front of him. They were both knocked down. The man pretended it was just an accident, but Richter was in no doubt; when he later looked down from his balcony, the man was still there, now in the company of another.

The surveillance continued for several months, and it is easy to imagine his apprehension. Richter was shadowed everywhere, but he invented his own little stratagems. Once, in a cable car, he asked his "shadow" whether he was going to get off at the next stop. "Yes," the man answered. "I'm not!" Richter said, remembering that the man looked very hurt.

He knew that the NKVD had questioned several of his friends for information about him. And his friends did not hide the fact that Richter knew what was going on. But the surveillance continued anyway throughout the winter. Not until the following spring did it suddenly cease.

After several months in Moscow, in March 1943 Richter was sent out to the northwestern front and the trenches to play on a dilapidated piano for soldiers and the wounded in military hospitals; he traveled in unlighted, unheated trains to Vologda, Molotovsk, Archangel, and Murmansk by the Barents Sea, close to the Finnish border. On March 28, in Murmansk, the country's northernmost city, he played one of his standards, Rachmaninov's 1901 marchlike Prelude in G Minor (opus 23, number 5). He learned later that his great countryman and colleague had died in New York on that very day (according to legend, with the words "Farewell my beloved, my poor hands").

But Richter's stay on the front was short. When the authorities learned that he was of German descent, they immediately whisked him back to Moscow. For Richter it was one of fate's happy ironies: just when he arrived in Murmansk, the air raids stopped, and just as he left it, the bombs began to fall again. The city, an important harbor, lay in ruins.

A particularly ambivalent war memory is his visit to Leningrad, one of the war's hardest-hit cities, which was besieged for nine hundred days. Richter arrived on December 31, 1943, in the middle of an air raid, and he spent a lonely New Year's Eve accompanied by hollow explosions from detonating shells, staring out his hotel window across the city at the Neva River with its many bridges and the gilded dome of St. Isaac's Cathedral. For most people, the experience would probably have been frightening and depressing. But Richter was more depressed when he returned a year later, in January 1945. Now the curfew was over, the siege was at an end, and the streets were full of people. The busy rush hour almost nauseated him. To Monsaingeon, he says: "The first time everything was dark, beautiful, mysterious, there were shells . . . now it was utterly banal!"

What Richter means exactly is unclear. Perhaps this is yet another particularly ambiguous expression of his compulsion to see the world only from an aesthetic point of view, never from a political one, of his lifelong idiosyncratic discomfort with everything that seemed mundane, boring, and trite. On New Year's Day in 1944, he had practiced at the Philharmonic, and in the evening, as he was walking back to his hotel, bombs began to rain down on the city. Bricks and wounded and dead people were lying everywhere. But Richter continued walking back, unconcerned, to the nearby Astoria Hotel and described the experience as "exciting." Vera Prokhorova's characterization of Richter as a young Siegfried, unfamiliar with fear, was hardly an exaggeration.

The next day, when he returned to the Philharmonic, all the windows had been blasted out. A bomb had destroyed the museum across the street, but the concert was performed in front of an attentive and rapt audience dressed in heavy winter coats. Richter was satisfied with his playing. "As soon as you begin to play, you stop being cold," he said (by his own account, during the long siege of Leningrad, his famous colleague Vladimir Sofronitsky played numerous concerts in the same hall wearing fingerless gloves, with temperatures hovering three degrees below the freezing point!).

But once again, a security check of Richter's identity papers revealed that he was "German." He had to leave Leningrad immediately because the risk that he might be harboring pro-German feelings or intentions was too great for the authorities. "Russians tell me I am German, Germans tell me I am Russian," the eighty-two-year old mutters with a dark irony.

Nina Lvovna

When Richter began Neuhaus's class, he had yet another defining event: a respected clarinetist had died, and at the funeral, in accordance with Russian custom, there was a memorial concert that attracted musical colleagues. Among the performers was a singer who performed songs from Grieg's *Peer Gynt*. "It took my breath away," Richter says; "she was extraordinarily pretty and a true princess, to boot!" The singer, eight years older than Richter, proved to be a certain Nina Lvovna Dorliak, a gifted lyric soprano and an experienced lied singer who often performed on this sort of occasion (she herself described her role as a "paid mourner"). She was born in St. Petersburg in 1908 to parents with noble French and German ancestry. She spoke fluent French and went to the city's French school. Her mother, Xenia Dorliak, was a well-known opera singer and an excellent voice teacher who taught at the conservatory and performed in the West. Later she accepted a teaching position at the Moscow Conservatory, and Nina Dorliak took her degree from there with her mother as her teacher. From 1947 on, Nina Dorliak taught at the same institution, later with the title of professor. Among her many students was Galina Pisarenko, who became an acclaimed international opera star; Pisarenko joined the inner circle around Richter, and in the 1980s they performed together several times.

A relationship between Nina Dorliak and Slava Richter, however, did not arise at that early point. Vera Prokhorova relates that Richter knew Nina's mother, but that the relationship between the two artists, which lasted more than fifty years, developed slowly at the end of the war years. Before the war was over, Richter introduced Dorliak to the Prokhorova family. Vera Prokhorova says that "she really looked like a pre-Revolutionary fairy-tale princess; she was in a long dress. But Nina's warm and friendly manner made everyone like her." She continues:

It never occurred to us that the beautiful, distant princess could have anything in common with the spirited nature-child Slava Richter—beyond music, of course. She seemed to be above the everyday—gentle, elegant,

Richter and Nina Dorliak at a concert commemorating the
125th anniversary of Franz Schubert's death, USSR, 1953.

and good-hearted. And at that time, the significant age difference between
the two was unusual. She lived in the Arbat Quarter of Moscow, and I visited her now and again. We talked a lot together, and when my mother died
in 1945 of cancer, she comforted me; her own dearly beloved brother had
recently died of typhus. Materially, they were very harsh times. I was deeply
depressed after my mother's death; Slava began to come more rarely, and
Nina gradually stopped coming. Little by little, we understood that there was
a love relationship.

One musician acquaintance—possibly Nina Lvovna's mother—suggested
that Richter give some concerts with Dorliak, and he found the idea attractive.
She had already made a name for herself. In a conversation many years later
with the then world-famous Richter's Japanese interpreter, Midori Kawashima
(Richter: "I won't walk one step in Japan without her"), Nina told that she and
Richter had a common acquaintance, a female painter. At one point during the
war, Nina Lvovna was evacuated to Tbilisi, and Richter came to town to perform. "He came to see me to deliver a present from my friend, the painter. It was
the first time we met. But the important meeting was in 1943, after the funeral
of the great theater director Nemirovitch Dantchenko. As I was walking home,
I suddenly heard someone speak from behind: 'Let's do a concert together.'

It was Slava. 'But what sort of concert? Will you play one half and I'll sing the other?' 'No, I will accompany you.' Then we began to rehearse together. But our first concert did not take place until two years later, in Leningrad in 1945, the year my mother died."

Their first performance included music by Prokofiev. The work was a typically courageous choice: the composer's five songs from 1916 to texts by Anna Akhmatova. From 1940 on, the poetess was persona non grata, condemned as "an enemy of the people" and pardoned only in 1958, under Khrushchev.

After that, Richter and Dorliak cohabited most of the time, almost always traveled together, and pretty much lived as husband and wife. But this was not a traditional relationship. There is no doubt that for most of his life, Richter was attracted to men. But it is uncertain how early his sexual inclination became clear to him. Prokhorova relates that, before the war, Slava was deeply in love with a beautiful young dancer who rejected him in an unusually cruel fashion. Dorliak shared Richter's homosexuality. She was—or became—a lesbian. It was an unusual relationship, indeed. But in the more than fifty years they spent together, they seem to have considered this a fact of life, a sine qua non.

Countless lexicons, CD liner notes, and so on, reiterate the fact that they were married, but Richter never married Nina Dorliak. "I see no reason for it," he told his friend Prokhorova. He and Nina always addressed each other formally (in the second-person plural). In a society in which homosexuality was illegal and, according to the letter of the law, criminal, it is clear that their relationship—in addition to being an extremely close friendship—had great practical value as camouflage. It was an ideal façade to a world and a society that would not recognize or even allow their natural urges. When they attended social gatherings and society dinners on their trips in the Soviet Union—and later in the West—everybody took them to be husband and wife. Again and again, one encounters the erroneous statement that they were married in 1946. As well-known artists, they were eventually able to acquire a reasonably spacious residence in a country where the state firmly controlled the living quarters of all inhabitants. This meant that unlike gay and lesbian Soviet citizens who had to live in crowded apartments, they did not have to resort to boulevards, parks, and public toilets to explore life's erotic side unmolested. In an overpopulated Moscow, privacy was a luxury.

People who knew of the nature of their relationship tell that it was quite common for Richter to be accompanied by his erotic liaisons on his concert tours and that Dorliak apparently accepted this and even showed these men genuine affection. The smokescreen around the real nature of their relationship was a prophylactic strategy. Russia had no tradition of open-mindedness with respect to homosexuality, although before the turn of century it was wide-spread in the upper class. Tchaikovsky presumably committed suicide in order to avoid a political scandal in case his "subversive passion" became known to the czar and his cabinet. Sergei Diaghilev, the creator of the Ballets Russes, was the first famous Russian to openly acknowledge his homosexuality, and it was the main reason that his company never visited the USSR and that he remained persona non grata in his homeland for most of the century. In the 1950s, regular purges of homosexuals took place at the university, in the State Film Society, and at the Moscow Conservatory. A young homosexual pianist who was praised at the Tchaikovsky competition of 1958 was jailed and deprived of what might otherwise have been a promising career. A year later, a teacher at the conservatory was sentenced to five years in prison for allegedly having sexual relations with his male students. It should be remembered, though, that in the strait-laced United States of the McCarthy era during the Cold War, there were similar—if not so actively oppressive—attitudes toward homosexuality. In most American states, so-called unnatural relations were a crime (in some states this is still the case, at least in theory, and it is still legal to fire people for their homosexuality).

Nina Dorliak's significance for Richter cannot be overestimated. Clearly, they lived as a couple in practice, and in practice and to all appearances, she acted as his life companion. She was far better suited to handling life's more down-to-earth matters than he was. To a large extent, she took care of the long-term planning necessary for a concert pianist but which Richter despised. And since Richter was completely uninterested in money, she apparently took full control of that side of his life as well. With tremendous reserves, she combined the roles of partner, private secretary, assistant, organizer, administrator, and much else. In many respects, she was the indispensable intermediary in Richter's unique career. Genius alone would not suffice. She spared him most of the headaches of everyday life, secured contacts, arranged meetings, remembered appointments, answered letters, and planned tours. Everyone who was close to them testifies that Richter—hardly easygoing as a life partner—had deeply affectionate feelings for her. Richter hated talking on the telephone. He reserved this technology for special situations. During the relatively infrequent trips on which Nina did not escort him, however, it was his habit to call her immediately after a concert.

Between 1945 and 1961, the pair gave countless concerts together in the Soviet Union and in the Eastern Bloc, but never in the West. Richter's first performance in the West coincided with the end of Nina's concert career. In addition to a great deal of Russian music, they performed songs by Debussy and Ravel. For a long time after the war, however, the classics of the proud German lieder tradition could hardly be sung in their original language in the USSR, and a German lied composer such as Hugo Wolf was totally unknown. Even Schubert's or Schumann's lieder were rarely performed at that time.

In late 1945, Slava moved in with Nina Dorliak. She had a couple of small rooms at a cooperative, which was also inhabited by two other families. Until then, the closest he had come to a permanent residence was with Neuhaus, the Prokhorova family, and the student dormitory at the conservatory. The story of Richter's residences is a lesson in Soviet bureaucracy, and only his complete indifference to anything that had to do with bourgeois comfort enabled him to fulfill his comprehensive concert obligations without a fixed roof over his head. Again and again, people tried to help him with local or state authorities, but to no avail. Ironically, he earned too *much* to apply for an apartment in a cooperative. But without official permission, he could not obtain an apartment. And, of course, he needed a place where he could practice for long periods and regularly, sometimes in the evening, without bothering his neighbors.

In 1952, almost forty years old, he was finally granted—after endless negotiations, cries of distress, and pleas—a spacious apartment near the conservatory. And Nina Lvovna succeeded in obtaining an apartment adjoining his; thus, by removing a separating wall, they could in part live together. Also later, their flats were always divided into two completely separate domains, each with its own interior decoration and lifestyle: ornaments and comfort for her, spartan simplicity for him.

It goes without saying that this unusual relationship—characterized in equal parts by love, friendship, partnership, and dependence—became one of the magnetic poles in Sviatoslav Richter's time on earth. Their relationship was something other, and more than, that of a harmonious, uncomplicated couple. But it has proved to be incredibly difficult to gain insight into these aspects of Richter's life. Even today the topic of homosexuality is still taboo in Russia. Richter himself never spoke about it. His close friends not only accepted this as self-evident but also apparently still view it as a breach of confidence to speak about it, not because they think it would besmirch his memory, but in order not to break what they view as an implicit promise to a beloved and admired master who never touched on the subject. This topic inevitably makes a biographer feel like a gossip columnist and a snoop. "We have the music, why should anything else be important?" is the typical reaction. But however compelling this thought may be, it is also clear that the topic is a big one and an essential chapter in the story of the pianist's life and work. In the West many people saw Richter in the company of his lovers. One who did, the American-born,

German-naturalized journalist Paul Moor (the man who tracked down Richter's mother in Germany) points out that Heinrich Neuhaus was fully aware of Richter's homosexuality. So, whether taboo or not, this topic obviously has not yet been exhausted.

Vera Prokhorova always saw the two artists as totally different in their attitudes toward life. Despite his mother's well-to-do family (as landed nobility), Richter had grown up in straitened circumstances. He was a child of nature who treated everyone equally and who had neither a sense of nor an interest in class differences. Nina Lvovna, however, was very conscious of her noble origins; Prokhorova does not hesitate to call her a snob. She believes that Nina allocated to herself the role of a protective governess and controlled all of Slava's contacts with the outside world. She wanted to secure a high position in society and a respectable, *haute bourgeoisie* status; Richter loved scandals. This deep difference in their nature and temperament made Richter feel confined, and many people say that he often felt a compulsion to indulge in provocative behavior when he was with Nina. In 1998 Monsaingeon related (to a London newspaper) a telling episode. He was finally able to persuade the reluctant eighty-two-year-old maestro to accept the presence of a film camera. At that very moment, Nina came into the living room and expressed her delight at his decision. "It ended there. He became violent and began to smash things. He felt caught in a trap."

Grigori Fried also views Nina Lvovna as a protective wall around Richter. He relates:

> When he became famous, you could only reach him through Nina. She kept him in a golden cage. For example, when you were invited to their apartment to see an art exhibition by him or others, you received an official invitation: "We, Dorliak, Nina, and Richter, Sviatoslav, hereby invite . . ." And it was a very limited circle of people who came. It was like a ritual theater. If I tried to get him to play at our "club," like in the old days, Nina always reported that he had a cold or felt ill. You couldn't call him; he never picked up the telephone. When one of my operas was performed for the first time in the USSR, it took place in the Moscow Composers' Union, and Nina and Slava lived in the same building. I approached her a number of times to ask Slava to attend the performance. I also asked her to give him the score. But nothing happened. Anti-Semitism was quite common in Russia. Perhaps it played a role for her that I was Jewish.

To be fair, this is hardly likely. Throughout her life, Nina Lvovna had close friends in the circle around Shostakovich, and the composer had many Jewish friends. At one point (1948), he had personally selected Dorliak to try out his song cycle *From Jewish Folk Poetry*, at a time when the systematic persecution of Jews led to arrests, torture, and executions.

Admission into the circle around Richter was not granted to everyone; people other than Fried describe his social circle as a sort of royal court. Pianist Vladimir Viardo relates that his teacher, one of Neuhaus's assistants, introduced him. "You had to earn acceptance, and my knees were shaking the first time I came. I didn't care for this 'courtly' game, but suddenly I saw a glint in Richter's eyes. He did not take it seriously at all. It was all theater!"

Thanks to Nina Lvovna, Richter was protected from life's practical, mundane aspects. And, of course, it became not only a habit but, gradually, a prerequisite for focusing his spiritual energy entirely on music. "Nina was gentleness itself," Prokhorova remarks. "But she was also hard as nails. And she was by nature suspicious, jealous. She created a protective wall around him." Vladimir Viardo (who lived close to the couple in the 1980s) remembers that Richter sometimes felt the need to escape. He might suddenly turn up unannounced at Viardo's, and despite self-recriminations, his friend had to lie and deny that Richter was with him when Nina Lvovna called!

However, she was apparently not jealous of Richter's erotic acquaintances. She must have felt safe in the knowledge that the foundation on which their relationship rested was not a sexual attraction. And when a childless relationship between two such strong personalities lasts more than fifty years, its indissoluble necessity for both parties must be obvious.

It may have been his collaboration with the lied singer Nina Lvovna that led Richter to move Franz Schubert to the top of his list of favorite composers. A few of Schubert's piano works, of course, belonged to the standard repertoire in concert halls throughout the world: the popular *Impromptus* and, naturally, the *Wanderer* Fantasy. But apart from the final Piano Sonata (in B-flat major), no one played Schubert's sonatas in the Soviet Union at that time, and except for Wilhelm Kempff and the recently deceased Arthur Schnabel, only a few did so in the West. When Richter began to include these piano works in his programs in the 1950s, people considered him mad. But they were wrong; Richter laid the foundation for a veritable Schubert renaissance.

His love of Schubert began in his student days. He told Jürgen Meyer-Josten, head of music at Bavarian Radio, that he listened to one of his fellow students play the Sonata in D Major (Deutsch 850) and that it seemed "frightfully long and boring, almost unendurable. But I said to myself: it is impossible that Schubert can be so boring, and I decided to play the sonata myself." (Like his conversations with Monsaingeon and Milstein, his conversation with Meyer-Josten, titled *Musiker im Gespräch: Sviatoslav Richter 1982*, is the interviewer's own condensed version of a number of conversations that took place over a longer period.) This reason for playing a work was typical of Richter. But it also worked the other way around: as a reason for *not* playing. For example, on Rachmaninov's enormously popular Third Piano Concerto, he said, "Why? Because I enjoy it a lot when other people play it. If I did not enjoy the way others play it, then it would certainly be in my repertoire!" So much for the interpreter's anonymity, one is tempted to say.

PART **II**

Prokofiev

Two composers exemplify Russian music in the twentieth century with the same clarity as Tchaikovsky and Mussorgsky did in the nineteenth: Sergei Prokofiev and Dmitri Shostakovich. Of course, Igor Stravinsky and Sergei Rachmaninov were also Russian by birth and descent, but they were not a part of Soviet musical life. Stravinsky left Russia before World War I and returned for only a few weeks in 1962 at the personal invitation of Khrushchev. Rachmaninov settled in New York after the Russian Revolution and spent his summers in Switzerland and Paris. He never saw the land of his birth again. For extended periods, the authorities in the USSR denounced and criticized the music of the two exiled Russians. Not until the 1960s and 1970s was their music once again viewed with unconditional respect and admiration.

Other significant musicians emigrated because of the Revolution and civil war, among them conductors Serge Koussevitzky and Nikolai Malko, violinist Jascha Heifetz, and, a few years later, the great singer Feodor Chaliapin; and thereafter, pianist Vladimir Horowitz, violinist Nathan Milstein, and cellist Gregor Piatigorsky. But it is an oversimplification or a distortion to see this exodus as purely politically motivated. In an impoverished and shattered country ravaged by hunger and misery, many musicians felt they had no future there.

The twenty-six-year-old Prokofiev was in Petrograd (St. Petersburg) during the February Revolution and left the country in 1918—first for the United States, then, in 1922, the German Alps at Oberammergau (Garmisch), and, in 1923, Paris. But he never put down roots in the West and always traveled on a Soviet passport. In the early 1930s, he spent several extended periods in the USSR, and throughout his life he considered himself a Russian-Soviet composer. After 1933 he lived primarily in Moscow but still commuted between the East and West. In 1936, just as Stalin's purges gained momentum, he became a permanent Muscovite.

Prokofiev's entrance into the world of music resembles Richter's. He also came from a provincial town in the Ukraine, and his family background bears striking

Prokofiev in front of his dacha in Nikolina Gora, 1952.
Seated on the stairs, Anatoly Vedernikov.

similarities to the pianist's. His mother was an eminent pianist, and as a nine-year-old, he wrote theatrical music—including an opera in three acts ("The Giant," with his own libretto), which was "performed" at his uncle's summer residence with family members playing various roles. He eminently deserves the label child prodigy, as confirmed by the fact that he presented four operas, two piano sonatas, and a symphony upon his acceptance to the conservatory in St. Petersburg. He was thirteen years old!

His special turn of mind, the aggressive, roughly hewn, and emotionally tempered tone, is already present in the works he wrote during his student years in St. Petersburg's lively environment, which fostered compositional experimentation. Whereas Stravinsky, nine years his elder, began his career with an entirely conventional E-flat major symphony in four movements, the young Prokofiev was by nature an *enfant terrible*. His early works annoyed and offended his teacher Rimsky-Korsakov, whereas Stravinsky, Rimsky's private student, was an obedient apprentice. Prokofiev claimed—perhaps correctly—that as a very young concert pianist, he was the first to play the atonal music of Arnold Schönberg in Russia.

The motoric drive and dissonant harmony in Prokofiev is an innovative counterpart to Stravinsky's rapidly maturing style in the ballets from before the war that made him world famous. But then Prokofiev's style developed in a much less directed way than Stravinsky's, in violent leaps between biting, mocking sarcasm (one piano work is even called *Sarcasmes*), playful irony (for example, the opera *The Love for Three Oranges*), melodic lyricism as in his First Violin Concerto, and highly charged expressionism. In a splendidly written autobiography on which Prokofiev worked in 1937–45 but that he only took up to 1936, he describes five stylistic features as typical of his music: the classical, the innovative, the "toccata-like" (the motoric drive), the lyrical, and the scherzo-like humoristic (often bitingly grotesque in his youth but, later, with a much more kindly disposed humor). The description is found in the chapter called "Youth," but it is apparent that Prokofiev has his entire oeuvre in mind.

He conducted the perennially popular *Symphonie Classique* from 1916 at its premiere only a month before he left the Soviet Union in May 1918. Many people consider it the very prototype of neoclassicism, but in fact it was only a phase he was passing through on his intuitive search for forms of expression. The classical symphonic form (the Haydn model) is put into a sort of mirrored cabinet: tonal cadences and classical figurations of melody and accompaniment are shifted, turned, twisted, and combined like building blocks, pulled out of the tradition, and reused in consciously "oblique" patterns.

Even though music publishers, conservatories, and theaters were nationalized after the Revolution, musical life in the early Soviet state remained in many ways relatively unchanged despite the economic and political difficulties. The cultural climate within music was still dominated by the ideas of a "new music for a new time." The prerevolutionary desire to experiment blazed up again, but now with a clearly antiromantic and antimystical turn, directed against, for example, Scriabin's egocentric individualism. St. Petersburg (rebaptized first as Petrograd, then as Leningrad) was still the hotbed of experimentation. A nephew of Rimsky-Korsakov, for example, worked with quarter tones, and in 1920 the physicist Leon Theremin (Lev Termen) constructed the first purely electronic musical instrument; in the early 1930s this aroused much attention in the West.

Contacts with the West were renewed. In the 1920s conductors such as Bruno Walter, Pierre Monteux, and Otto Klemperer visited the USSR. Bruckner's and Mahler's symphonies were played to full houses. Mahler's music was a revelation to the young Dmitri Shostakovich; and only a year after Nicolai Malko's world premiere of the work in Leningrad, Bruno Walter, in February 1928, conducted Shostakovich's First Symphony in Berlin and laid the foundation for the composer's world fame. Composers such as Hindemith, Darius Milhaud, and Franz Schreker were invited to the USSR; Ravel's *Bolero* was performed in Moscow a few weeks after its Parisian premiere. And even though the term

"expressionism" was a curse word, viewed as the equivalent of bourgeois deca-
dence, Alban Berg's atonal, decidedly expressionistic opera *Wozzeck* was performed in 1927 with success in Leningrad. Stravinsky's ballets also enjoyed
great attention in these years.

Before his death in 1924, Lenin had repeatedly stressed that schools were
more important than art, that "while, perhaps, ten thousand people go to the
theatre, millions are trying to learn to write their own name . . . or to count."
And in accordance with classic Marxist ideology, the new state viewed art as a
superstructure for a social and economic foundation; changes there necessarily led to corresponding changes in art. However, there was an immediate con-
sensus that the "revolutionary" should characterize both art and society.

The ideological overseer in those years was author-politician Anatoli Lunacharsky, commissar for education in the first Bolshevik government from 1917 to
1929. For a long time, Lunacharsky was able to convince politicians that the
education of the masses and the gradual acknowledgment of artists' new social
obligations were connected vessels. He introduced the idea of *proletkult* as a
question of prioritization. Highly regarded artists such as Marc Chagall, Was-
sily Kandinsky, Alexander Blok, Ilya Ehrenburg, and Vsevolod Meyerhold were
placed in important administrative positions. And even though agitational art
and "utilitarian music" had the highest priority, Lunacharsky also made room
for experimental composers such as Nikolai Roslavetz and Alexander Mosolov.
Lunacharsky personally authorized the Soviet passport that made it possible
for Prokofiev to travel wherever he wanted.

Even though in his day Lenin had warned against Stalin, Stalin fought his way
into the post as the undisputed leader of the Communist Party after 1929, and,
almost immediately, the cultural situation changed decisively. Lunacharsky,
the guarantor of enlightened cultural policy in the 1920s, was removed from the
Ministry of Education. Author Maxim Gorky's doctrine of disciplined "socialist realism" in art began seriously to influence cultural life (the slogan does not
entail what we today understand by the term "social realism" but promotes a
socially and politically constructive art). And the curse word "formalism," used
about politically incorrect art, began to make a career for itself, which may
have made Prokofiev somewhat hesitant to return. As early as 1929, the stage
director Vsevolod Meyerhold was forbidden to go ahead with planned performances of Prokofiev, Hindemith, and Shostakovich at the Bolshoi. So, when
Prokofiev finally decided to return, he knew the price: unmusical bureaucrats
would subject his music to censorship. But he felt increasingly like an outsider
in the cultural life of Paris, with its cliques, disputes, and feuds about who was

more "modern." And he lacked his colleague Stravinsky's talent for attracting well-to-do patrons or obtaining lucrative commissions.

The movement toward simplification had already been long under way in his development. In his ambitious, edgy, and experimental Second Symphony (of "iron and steel," he claimed), he had tried, without luck, to strike a chord with the Parisians' taste for modern "noise music," *bruitisme*, in the 1920s. For a number of years, he also worked on an intensely expressionistic opera, *The Flaming Angel*. But he did not succeed in having the work performed. Not until a few years after his death did it have its premiere in Venice, and it was more than half a century before it could be seen in the Soviet Union; he used part of the opera's thematic material in his Third Symphony.

In the latter half of the 1920s, therefore, he gradually turned away from this jarring, dissonant style. By simplifying and systematizing his tonal language even further during the 1930s, he attempted to create a balance between politically correct music for a broad audience and artistically more ambitious projects. His ballet *Romeo and Juliet* was written in 1935, when he spent most of the year in Moscow. In the fall of 1936, again in Moscow, he wrote what was to become his most popular work, the musical tale *Peter and the Wolf*. Later he produced three very different symphonies, innovative film music for the film director Sergei Eisenstein, chamber music and ballets, and the grand-scale opera *War and Peace*, based on Tolstoy's novel. Today many people believe that the music he composed between 1935 and 1948 contains the high points of his life's work. His four last piano sonatas are milestones in the century's music for the instrument and may be the last solo works for the piano to achieve an entrenched place in the international standard repertoire.

But as a "political" composer, he was disappointed again and again. His first attempt, a huge cantata for orchestra, two choruses, four ensembles, and sound effects for the twentieth anniversary of the October Revolution was immediately archived by the government and not performed until more than ten years after his death. His attempt to create "Soviet" operas fared no better. Richter describes a man who "had the easy, arrogant charisma of fame, a man you turned around to look at when you saw him on the street." But on those occasions when he consciously angled for approval from the authorities, he easily lost his artistic self-assurance. It says something about his artistic integrity that political cautiousness, halfhearted socialist realism, and brutal pressure from bureaucrats and ideologues usually extinguished his creative spark.

Richter's first encounter with Prokofiev and his music goes back to a concert his father took him to in Odessa, when he was twelve years old. He does not mention the date, but the exiled Prokofiev performed only once in Odessa during those years: two piano recitals of his own music in March 1927. Also present were ten-year-old Emil Gilels and eighteen-year-old David Oistrakh; and, probably, it was on this occasion that Teofil Richter introduced his son to the violinist who, forty years later, would be a highly treasured musical collaborator. But Oistrakh already knew about Svetik. His future wife, Tamara, was a student in Teofil Richter's piano class at the Odessa Conservatory, and later she told her son Igor that she often saw little Svetik hopping around on one leg outside her windows.

Oistrakh remembers that Prokofiev played "without any superficial movement, not a single external demonstration of emotion, nothing that could be interpreted as a desire to impress. . . . It was unforgettable." For the teenage Richter, the impression was just as durable. "He wore a fashionable suit that was clearly of a foreign cut, short in the arm and leg—it looked almost as if he had outgrown it. It amused me when he bowed. He sort of bent in two—crack! . . . part conjurer, part character out of the tales of Hoffmann." The young Richter noticed that the composer's face was entirely expressionless, that he played almost without any pedal work, and that the music was "different from anything I had heard before." And he adds: "As a result of my childish stupidity, I also had the impression that everything he played sounded exactly the same. (Bach's works had the same effect on me at this time)." When he later encountered Prokofiev's music, he found it interesting but not appealing. He was brought up on the Romantics. Prokofiev's music must have seemed cool, mechanical, and severe.

But fate played its hand. In the Paris of 1934, Prokofiev had written a cello concerto with which he was not satisfied. So, in 1938, on a commission from a Soviet cellist, he rewrote it. The highly regarded musician Lev Berezovsky (first cellist at the Bolshoi) was proud of being the first musician to perform a cello concerto by the great Prokofiev, but modern music was alien to him. He engaged Richter as a rehearsal pianist, and, for a few months, Richter accompanied him often. Richter slowly grew to like the music, and when they performed the work at a private concert at the Composers' Union, everyone agreed that a thundering success was imminent.

Among the few texts Richter published is an essay entitled "On Prokofiev": "very impressionistic," he thought. To his great annoyance, the text was censored and altered. But it has retained a colorful, oddly ironic narrative style that must make everyone bemoan Richter's literary reticence. He wrote his essay a few years after the composer's death in 1953 and says about the cello concerto:

We went to play the concerto for Prokofiev. He opened the door himself and let us into a little canary-yellow room. . . . Berezovsky looked terribly confused, and it was no doubt because of this that Prokofiev, clearly in no mood for compromise, immediately sat down at the piano himself and began to say things like: "Here it should be like this, there it should be like that." I stood in a corner, out of harm's way. Prokofiev was businesslike, but not pleasant. Berezovsky's questions clearly annoyed him. . . .

I attended the first performance. My heart was beating wildly, and I was suffering from stage fright, simply on account of the work, but also for Berezovsky, of course. The ground seemed literally to be pulled from under his chair while he was playing, as the conductor's tempi were as impossible as they were wrong. It seemed to me that he utterly failed to grasp the work's inner essence. It was a total fiasco.

And it was not only the audience who reacted negatively. The critics denounced the work as "lacking" and "anti-artistic," and not until February 1952, after several rewritings, did the work find its final form in a close collaboration with the young Mstislav Rostropovich, now with the title Symphony-Concerto (often, misleadingly, translated as "Sinfonia Concertante").

Richter's feelings about Prokofiev's music gradually grew warmer. He was won over after hearing the First Violin Concerto shortly before Prokofiev left the Soviet Union, indeed, even before he heard the violin part, just after hearing his friend Vedernikov rehearse the piano version of the orchestral score. And his relationship with the composer gradually grew into an acquaintanceship. By the end of 1938, he had performed with Vedernikov a piano version of Stravinsky's oratorio *Oedipus Rex*; Vedernikov played the part of the orchestra, Richter the chorus. It took place at the Composers' Union, and Prokofiev was present. The composer had no great expectations for this "economy version," but he was persuaded to listen to the performance. And to Richter's relief, he was pleased, amazed that the music actually sounded interesting for two pianos.

Prokofiev's hyperintense, colorfully orchestrated Third Symphony overwhelmed Richter when he heard it in 1939. In the scherzo, he felt "as though the air itself were on fire," and in the finale, he heard "a veritable apocalypse. . . . I sat there as though turned to stone. I wanted to hide. I glanced at my neighbor, who was crimson and sweating profusely. Even during the interval, shivers still ran up and down my spine." Prokofiev had taken some of the material for this symphony (from 1928) from his opera *The Flaming Angel* (it was never performed in his lifetime)—Richter's experience of "the air on fire" would probably have gratified him.

In 1940 Prokofiev's opera *Semyon Kotko*, a conscious attempt to write a Soviet musical drama, had its premiere. This work was a parable about a virtuous young peasant and freedom fighter who defends the young Soviet Union against German occupation troops during the civil war in 1918. However, the composer emphasized that he wanted to avoid anything dogmatic and moralizing. He wanted to describe the Soviet state's new social conditions through "living people with living passions." Several times during the rehearsals, however, the opera was "corrected" pursuant to demands from the authorities. Nevertheless, immediately after the first performance in June 1940, it was criticized for its "formalism" and for being "incomprehensible to the masses," and it disappeared from the repertoire for a quarter of a century (even today it is almost totally unknown in the West, as is yet another "Soviet" opera by the late Prokofiev, an entirely uninspired attempt at political correctness). But Richter remembers the enthusiasm of his youth: "Without a doubt, the finest Soviet opera," a national music drama that "followed the path traced out by Mussorgsky" and which he saw three or four times, before the opera had to wait for a revival long after the composer's death. Prokofiev's music for Eisenstein's film *Alexander Nevsky* also filled him with admiration ("Never before had film music impressed me to such an extent. I have still not forgotten it to this day").

In May 1940, a month before *Semyon Kotko* finally had its premiere, Prokofiev first performed his grand Sixth Piano Sonata, finished the year before. The concert took place at the Composers' Union and was not public, but was transmitted by radio. Richter turned pages for the composer (who played from his own manuscript), and Prokofiev's self-confidence and authority made a strong impression on him. He decided to look more closely at the sonata, and when he returned to Odessa on vacation, he had a copy packed in his suitcase. His father, Teofil, had some appreciation for Prokofiev's music, but, in his view, this work was too grim. "It's like being slapped in the face again and again," Richter remembers him saying.

Prokofiev had admitted to Neuhaus that as a matter of fact the Sixth Sonata was beyond his own abilities as a pianist, and Neuhaus suggested letting the young Richter try his hand at it. Prokofiev must have consented, because Neuhaus suggested that Richter take part in one of his piano recitals with Russian music (Neuhaus claimed to have practiced too little, but Richter understood that this was a very unusual gesture, since he was still a student). Before a responsive audience, Richter played some minor pieces by Prokofiev in the second half of the concert and then the Sixth Sonata. True to habit, he was practicing up to the last minute ("I know it is a disaster, but that's the way it is with me, always!"). Not until the day before the concert did he have the music down pat after practicing around the clock for several days. His performance on November 26, 1940, at the conservatory's Small Hall was open to the public and, therefore, considered the work's true premiere.

The sonata, the first of three piano sonatas Prokofiev worked on more or less concurrently before and during the war years (often referred to as the "war sonatas"), was a bit of a tour de force, an aggressive, dark, virtuoso piece of music whose four movements demand great technical and physical reserves; lasting more than half an hour, the sonata is the longest of Prokofiev's nine piano sonatas. But after the concert, Prokofiev congratulated Richter heartily and flattered him by suggesting that he play the solo in his Fifth Piano Concerto with himself conducting. His Third Piano Concerto had long been a worldwide success, but this concerto had never gained public favor. Prokofiev had premiered it himself in October 1932 with no less than Wilhelm Furtwängler and the Berlin Philharmonic, but nobody else had played it. His first two piano concertos were youthful works; the fourth was commissioned by the one-armed pianist Paul Wittgenstein (brother of the famous philosopher), for whom Ravel wrote his often played concerto for the left hand. Unfortunately, Wittgenstein did not care for Prokofiev's concerto, and it had to wait for a performance until after his death. Regarded as a whole, today only Prokofiev's five piano concertos compete with Rachmaninov's five works for piano and orchestra as the genre's most often played and recorded works of the twentieth century. (Bartók's 1945 Third Piano Concerto is the last work for piano and orchestra to have achieved a fixed place in the standard repertoire.)

The challenge from a musical colleague with a worldwide reputation seemed attractive to the twenty-five-year-old pianist, although Neuhaus was worried. He believed that the most popular of Prokofiev's concertos at that time and now, the Third, would be a safer choice. But Richter stuck to his guns. When he studied the score in depth, however, he was not enthusiastic. The music seemed to him even more challenging and caustic than the Sixth Sonata, light years away from the Romanticism with which he was raised. The concerto was typical of Prokofiev's "toccata" style from the period before he once again became a Soviet citizen: energetically chiseled, marching in measured steps, but not "Romantic" in the least. In February 1941, however, Richter traveled back to his family in Odessa, firmly resolved to learn the concerto. And a month later he played it for Prokofiev in the apartment of his neighbor Neuhaus with Tolya Vedernikov as his accompanist. Richter narrates:

Prokofiev had brought his wife with him, and the room was filled with the powerful smell of French perfume. He suddenly started to tell us some tall stories about gangsters in America, everything told in his inimitable way, extraordinarily businesslike and yet not without humor. We sat at a small table with barely enough room for our legs, drinking tea and munching the slices of ham that Neuhaus invariably provided.

Then we played.

Prokofiev was clearly pleased. He had been standing in front of us, facing the two pianos and conducting, and at the end he produced two bars of chocolate simultaneously from both his pockets and presented them to us with a grand gesture.

On March 9 Prokofiev himself conducted the concert, which also included the *Lieutenant Kijé Suite* (another work originally created for film), a highly aggressive work of his youth; the *Scythian Suite* from 1914; and the ever-popular *Symphonie Classique*. Richter remembers that the piano concerto went rather well, but that he was incredibly nervous and derived no pleasure from it. Not long before, a packed hall had heard him play the most popular of all piano concertos, Tchaikovsky's first. Now the hall was half empty and virtually unheated.

But the work, until then generally disliked, was an outstanding success. Both the composer and the pianist had endless encores, and Prokofiev was amazed. Richter remembers that he suddenly exclaimed: "Ah, I know why they're clapping like that—it's so you will play them a Chopin nocturne!"

Richter was happy. "At the same time, though, I had a feeling of dissatisfaction caused, in part, by my nervousness (try playing the Fifth Concerto, and you will understand) and, in part, by a vague premonition that I would not play it again for a long time." And he was right. Seventeen years would go by. At the beginning of May 1958, when the "thaw" under Khrushchev created new possibilities for cultural exchanges between the superpowers, Eugene Ormandy visited Moscow with his Philadelphia Orchestra and conducted Prokofiev's Fifth, with Richter as soloist.

A few months after war broke out, the concert was Prokofiev's last in Moscow. For the next three years he was evacuated to the Caucasus, to Tbilisi, and later to Alma-Ata, the capital of Kazakhstan, several thousand miles from Moscow. Several years would go by before Richter saw him again. "I had more contact with Prokofiev's music than with the composer himself," he admits. Only rarely in the dozen years before the composer's death was he alone with Prokofiev, and he notes dryly that "if there was a third person present, it was always he who had the floor." But even though he believed, reasonably enough, that the most important thing he could say about Prokofiev was through his music, he clearly had a need to recount the strong impression the person behind the music made upon him.

Prokofiev's piano sonatas became one of the cornerstones in Richter's repertoire. But true to his nature, there were several of the sonatas he never played: in addition to the First (written when the composer was only sixteen), there were the Third and the Fifth of the nine—Emil Gilels played the short, one-movement Third, and according to Richter there was nothing to add. The Fifth (about which the composer himself had doubts, revising it shortly before his death) became a sort of trademark for his friend Anatoli Vedernikov, who was also close to Prokofiev. Of the others, he felt a special connection to the Second, Fourth, Eighth, and Ninth, and throughout his long career, he had a Prokofiev sonata on the program again and again.

Prokofiev asked him to premiere the best-known sonata, the Seventh, in January 1943, with only a few days to prepare for the concert. As usual, Neuhaus's little apartment was the only place he could rehearse, and he worked at it day and night. Neuhaus's wife was ill with a high fever in the room where the grand piano was, and, as Richter remembers it, he made life pretty impossible for her. But the work was a triumph for both composer and pianist. The audience included several famous musicians, among them, David Oistrakh, and even after the lights in the hall were dimmed and most people had left the hall, the applause continued until the lights were finally turned on again, and Richter played the work *da capo*.

The Seventh Sonata was (and is) always a hit, and it brought Prokofiev his first Stalin Prize (although the authorities were still so guarded about the "international" composer that he had to make do with second place). But Richter had the strongest feelings for the Eighth Sonata, although it was his colleague Gilels who premiered it in December 1944. It is "the richest. It has a complex inner life, profound and full of contrasts." Prokofiev worked on it throughout the war, and the sonata became the most inward-looking, most transparent, most "classical" of the three "war sonatas." In 1946 it brought him the Stalin Prize, first place. In the same year, he was awarded a prize for his ballet *Sleeping Beauty* and for his film music to Eisenstein's *Ivan the Terrible*. The total sum of these monetary prizes corresponded roughly to the lifetime wages of two workers.

Richter chose the Eighth Sonata when he, quite reluctantly and irritably, was persuaded to participate in the State Piano Competition in 1945; "complete waste of time," he thought. His participation also immediately led to diplomatic complications. With his German ancestry, he could not win first prize so soon after the war. But Foreign Minister Molotov called Shostakovich, the chairman of the jury, and gave the green light to allow Richter to share first place with someone else. "So, they could put it on my concert posters," the pianist comments acidly. Two days later, he was again to perform Tchaikovsky's perennial First Piano Concerto, a solo part he played more than fifty times in his lifetime and, in his opinion, one of the most technically demanding in the entire canon. The preparations for the competition exhausted him completely, which took its toll on Tchaikovsky. "I only had the strength to practice on the day of the concert itself, and I played terribly."

In 1947 Prokofiev dedicated to Richter his Ninth, and final, Piano Sonata, an unusually simple, melodic, and sometimes almost cheerful piece of music even for the late Prokofiev, which aimed at what the composer called "new simplicity." Richter later described it as a "cozy," idyllic sonata, a *Sonata domestica*, referring to Richard Strauss's symphonic poem *Sinfonia domestica* (which he esteemed highly). Prokofiev gave him the manuscript when Richter visited the composer's *dacha* (summer house) for the first time in the woods around Nikolina Gora, west of Moscow (a recreational area on the banks of the Moscow River, today a part of Moscow's "whiskey belt"). "It's hardly the sort of work to raise the roof of the conservatory's Great Hall," the composer admitted. At first, Richter was a bit disappointed, but he does not remember much, other than the fact that it was spring (it was Prokofiev's birthday, April 23, 1947). The thirty-three-year-old pianist, already quite famous, was still shy, reticent, and taciturn in the company of the composer.

But the planned premiere of the sonata was canceled. In 1948 the Central Committee and Andrei Zhdanov (the Party's chief ideologue since 1939) began a cultural-political vendetta aimed at all "formalists." He demanded a straightforward, conformist, nationally based socialist realism, and he turned his critique directly against composers like Prokofiev and Shostakovich. Richter was furious, and his friend Rostropovich remembered that he threatened to go on "strike," which must have required courage. But the opposition to Prokofiev's music persisted. Not until late April 1951 was Richter allowed to present the work in public, and at that point the singing, inward-looking tonal language could well have been perceived as a concession to Zhdanov's criticism of any form of "formalistic deviations and antidemocratic musical tendencies that are foreign to the Soviet people." The cultural atmosphere in the Soviet Union at the end of the 1940s was dominated by the public flagellation of famous composers and may be best characterized by a cartoon in the satirical periodical *Crocodile*. A young couple are lying on a bench listening to a bird singing. She says: "Don't you love the song of the nightingale?" He replies: "I dare not say before I know who wrote the song."

Music, Power, and Musical Politics

Prokofiev was a tall, solidly built man who exuded health and self-confidence until health problems began to plague him at the age of fifty. In every area of his life, he was governed by discipline and precision and organized his career according to strict rules. He was a cool and rational intellectual, well versed in international politics, well read in areas such as mathematics, physics, and engineering, and a highly gifted chess player (even Mikhail Botvinnik, world master in 1948–56, considered him a difficult opponent). However, his fiery temperament and sharp, often sarcastic, and at times tactless behavior only rarely put a hitch in his travels through the labyrinth of Soviet musical life. He was a pragmatist with no firm principles, and he was indifferent to ideology in a country permeated by ideology. But the laissez-faire attitude that is sometimes ascribed to him is misleading. As an individual, he was brave, ready for a scrap, and proud of always saying what he meant (which most people avoided in public places). The later years of his life, however, became difficult.

In 1948 the Ministry of Culture reorganized the State Composers' Union, and Stalin installed the politically adept thirty-five-year-old composer Tikhon Khrennikov, a member of the Supreme Soviet, as its first secretary (and, in practice, chairman). Khrennikov developed a meticulous system of total control, and he remained at the top of this power pyramid until 1992. In practice, the Composers' Union controlled every composer's career, just as the Goskoncert, the State Concert Bureau, did with musicians. Everything was controlled from above: commissions, performances, recordings, publications, awards, appointments, and so on. For more than forty years, Khrennikov was the uncrowned king of the Soviet music world. Clever, opportunistic, and without scruples, he was able to adapt to the constant pendulum swings in Soviet cultural politics.

Already in the fall of 1946, film, theater, and literature were subjected to the intense state criticism of Andrei Zhdanov, Stalin's powerful commissar for cultural control and, in practice, minister of culture. In February 1948 Zhdanov introduced the notorious decree in which the Central Committee accused the country's most significant composers of "antidemocratic tendencies," of composing "bourgeois decadent" or "formalistic" music (Zhdanov made up the concept "antipopular," which did not exist in any dictionary). Zhdanov was also the instigator of the vicious political attack on Shostakovich in 1936 (which almost crushed him and prohibited the performance, among other things, of his Second and Third Symphonies and his successful opera *Lady Macbeth of the Mtsensk District*) while Prokofiev was out of the country. The attacks in the government newspaper *Pravda* were directed at Shostakovich, but many of his colleagues saw the writing on the wall, and Prokofiev cannot have been in doubt that he, too, was in the line of fire. In principle, artistic and aesthetic "crimes" now had the status of political crimes. And it is ironic that this development began just as he had decided to return to his homeland. In 1941, the war had made a return to the West impossible.

Wreaking brutal vengeance upon the German people, Soviet forces moved into Berlin in May 1945 and raised the hammer and sickle over the German Reichstag. Nazism had been conquered, and because of the "grand alliance" against Hitler, intellectuals in the USSR hoped for a more enlightened, more "Western" era. But the war and its massacres had destroyed and impoverished great portions of the country, and at least twenty-seven million Soviet citizens had lost their lives. At the Yalta Conference in February 1945, Roosevelt, Stalin, and Churchill agreed to divide Germany into four occupation zones: American, Soviet, French, and English. As the victorious power that had struggled and lost the most, the USSR was to receive billions of German marks in war reparations. But the situation changed completely when the agreement was later ratified at Potsdam, now with President Truman as part of the game. After a successful atom-bomb test in New Mexico's desert, Truman decided to demonstrate his superiority in the power play with Stalin; the A-bombs were dropped on the civilian populations of Hiroshima and Nagasaki even though Truman knew that Japan was prepared to surrender. Then he did everything he could to isolate the Soviet Union, reestablishing the German economy and military. The compensation promises at the Yalta agreement more or less ran into the sand.

Once again, Stalin, whose foreign minister had signed a nonaggression pact with Hitler, felt betrayed, and the inevitable result was the so-called Cold War. When the United States turned against its erstwhile ally, suddenly, despite the country's military and economic ruin, the alliance's significance lost its meaning in the Soviet Union; anti-Western feelings ran together with patriotism. In 1947 Truman launched a foreign policy that promised American support to any country threatened by external or internal Communist enemies, and the image of the United States as "the world's policeman" was born.

Germany and Eastern Europe ended up being divided between Western and Soviet interests. The Prague coup in 1948 annexed Czechoslovakia into the Soviet power bloc, and in both France and Italy, influential Communist parties were strengthened. In 1949 the USSR also became an atomic power, the Chinese civil war ended with a Communist victory, and the North Atlantic Treaty Organization (NATO) was formed. The ever-frostier political-ideological climate in the relationship between the superpowers made "balance of power" a key term, and the arms race took off. In the Soviet Union, the Iron Curtain came down. American propaganda invented the hue and cry "The Russians are coming!" and the image of communism as a threatening, multiarmed monster came to dominate American (and European) thinking for decades. Pressure breeds counterpressure; more than ever Soviet cultural life became a world unto itself.

From mid-1946 until his death in late 1948, Andrei Zhdanov was primarily responsible for the merciless ideological campaign against individual artists. But his restrictive cultural policy continued until Stalin's death in 1953 and, to a certain extent, even until the advent of glasnost, perestroika, and the collapse of the Soviet Union (the year before Khrushchev was removed from power in 1964, for example, he thundered against the "twelve-tone humbug" that had wormed its way into the music of certain socialist countries). Even at the Party's 1934 Writers' Congress with Maxim Gorky as spokesperson, Zhdanov had made "socialist realism" the ideological foundation of cultural politics. In the midforties, artists such as Prokofiev, Shostakovich, and the poet and novelist Boris Pasternak were increasingly denounced, and their colleagues had no choice but to join the chorus. Fear of professional and personal safety can make even the most upstanding artists weak on their pins. To a depressing degree, the situation was reminiscent of the show trials of 1936–38, only the spotlight was turned on the artists.

The confrontation between music and politics came to a head, and in April 1948 the Supreme Soviet called the country's most important composers—in addition to Prokofiev and Shostakovich, the symphonist Myaskovsky, and his students Aram Khachaturian and Dmitri Kabalevsky—to a "disciplinary congress," in which Zhdanov lectured for three days about "true Soviet art" and excommunicated "capitalist" music and "antipopular formalism." Prokofiev wrote a letter to Secretary General Khrennikov in which he carefully avoided a defensive position and explained—perhaps with his last piano sonata from the year before in mind—that he now aimed at "a clear and more meaningful tonal language. With some success, I have tried to liberate myself from formalism." Yet, as an example of Prokofiev's courage, Richter tells Monsaingeon that when Prokofiev was directly attacked by Zhdanov, he looked the politician right in the eye and asked indignantly, "What right do you have to talk to me like that?"

This may well be the kind of tall tale that Richter always hated when it was about him. Thikon Khrennikov was present, and in his 1994 memoirs he writes that Prokofiev's irritable exclamation was directed at a colleague with whom he was engaged in a loud discussion during one of Zhdanov's speeches. "There was actually something comic about the situation," Khrennikov writes. "Even Zhdanov broke off his speech and laughed." But once again creative Soviet memory is at work: Prokofiev was not even present. His illness had provided him with a convenient excuse to stay home.

Here, at the heyday of his career, Prokofiev was not only ill but also unable to work full-time and bereft of his former stubbornness, pride, and willpower. He was also marked by sad experiences. In 1930 his longtime friend the poet Vladimir Mayakovsky committed suicide. In 1938 another friend, the poet Osip Mandelstam, died on his way to a labor camp in Siberia. In June 1939 his friend of many years and collaborative partner, the controversial Jewish theater director Vsevolod Meyerhold, was arrested in the middle of planning rehearsals for his opera *Semyon Kotko*. The government had long persecuted Meyerhold. In the press, they attacked him again and again for formalism. When the sixty-six-year-old flatly refused to apologize for his experiments and even criticized cultural policy, he was arrested (and a couple of days later, anonymous thugs murdered his wife, a well-known actress, stabbing her seventeen times). Under cruel torture, Meyerhold was forced to "confess" to being an enemy of the people and then shot. Shortly after, Prokofiev had to compose yet another political cantata, a hymn to the "Great Leader" who had just exterminated his friend. The work, *Zdravitsa*, a musical toast to Stalin, is almost forgotten today (even in Russia it is difficult to deal with texts such as "Hail Stalin, father of us all"), but Sviatoslav Richter found exceptional qualities in this short, colorfully orchestrated work for choir and large orchestra.

Highly gifted colleagues such as Roslavetz and Mosolov, as early as at the beginning of the 1930s, had been designated class enemies and anti-Soviet composers, and they now were ostracized and forgotten in remote provinces. Upon his return to the USSR in 1938, the music engineer Leon Theremin was sent to a labor camp for several years. In a memoir from the year after Prokofiev's death, his colleague Aram Khachaturian remembers that "the Prokofiev we knew during the years right after he returned from abroad was, in many ways, completely different from the Prokofiev of the last ten years of his life."

The year 1948 was to be an *annus horribilis* for Prokofiev. In 1941, when he was evacuated because of the war, he had left his Spanish-born wife Lina and two children for a significantly younger Soviet woman. In January 1948 Prokofiev married his young girlfriend without divorcing the mother of his children. They had been married in Germany in 1923, but the marriage was never formally registered in the Soviet Union, and as a de facto unmarried foreigner Lina Prokofiev suddenly lost all legal protection. She was a woman of the world, spoke fluent Spanish, French, and English, and had friends in several Western embassies, which the Soviet Union always regarded with suspicion. A few weeks after Prokofiev remarried, she was arrested on the usual vague charges of espionage and spent the next eight years interned in a labor camp near the Arctic Circle. She did not see her children again until after the death of Stalin in 1953. Prokofiev apparently did not attempt to protest. He was powerless and more than ever in the line of fire himself. Only a few weeks later, film director Sergei Eisenstein, the admired friend with whom he had had a unique collaboration, died. Eisenstein had been a student of Meyerhold and had considered him a father figure.

In 1941, when Shostakovich was awarded the Stalin Prize for his Piano Quintet in G Minor, Prokofiev had criticized his colleague for being "too guarded" and for "never running a risk." But in his final years, plagued by illness—he died of a brain hemorrhage in the beginning of March 1953—he apparently attempted, to the best of his abilities, to reconcile his creative ambition with the demands of the Party. And the aesthetic police brutality was heavy-handed. Zhdanov lectured that "not everything that is easily accessible is genius, but a work of genius is always easily accessible." Ilya Ehrenburg recounts in his memoirs that he heard Shostakovich and Prokofiev cite Zhdanov's mundane philosophy of music: "The most important element in music is a melody that can be hummed!" Many influential intellectuals used this occasion to air their displeasure at "modern" music. With demagogical rhetoric, the system's spokesman, Thikon Khrennikov, put all Western innovators on the black list: "You can hardly mention a single significant composer from the West who is not infected by formalism, subjectivism, and mysticism." Famed composers such as Hindemith, Krenek, Berg, Britten, and Messiaen were tainted by "eroticism, sexual perversions, amorality and the shamelessness that characterizes 20th-century bourgeois heroes."

The whole foundation for this ideological mobilization, the concept that music for the people presumes a simplified musical content, rests on a dubious, if not entirely unmusical, assumption. The train of thought must have made its proponents blind to the undeniable fact that the most enduring, the most "popular" classical musical works are still works that cannot in any way be called simple—Beethoven's Ninth or his Fifth, Brahms's and Tchaikovsky's symphonies and piano concertos, operas by Mozart, Verdi, Strauss, and Puccini.

Historically, Zhdanov's way of thinking had roots in the conscious attempt that many Russian composers, even before the turn of the century, had made to avoid European standards and "speak Russian" by using melodic material from folk culture. But by making the naive idea of simplicity and popularity a moral-political requirement, Zhdanov narrowed and dictated the opportunities for the creators as well as their audience. In a democratic culture, the very existence of opposition ensures that misunderstandings can be corrected. The Soviet composer was now coerced by dictates from above; anyone who did not recognize the system's definition of easy accessibility was judged guilty in advance of being antipopular. The result was not a wave of beloved new music for the concert hall. In fact, very few of the countless Soviet musical works that aimed for state-authorized "popularity" achieved enduring popularity. In concert halls all over the world, many of the most popular and most often played "Russian-speaking" works from the twentieth century were written by the expatriate Russians Stravinsky and Rachmaninov.

The favorite invective of state cultural criticism, "formalism" (as is often the case with propaganda slogans), means almost the opposite of the word's normal use. Normally, it is an expression of "formal," academic habits and methods in opposition to musical inspiration and expressive spontaneity. But in the Soviet state's use of language, "formalism" meant unpredictability, probing freedom, and uninhibited creativity. The word referred to art that was complicated and difficult for the masses to access and was, therefore, unsuitable as a tool for developing an independent Soviet culture. The Soviet ideal was the academic Russian-classical tradition represented by Tchaikovsky's successors in Moscow (for example, Tanejev and Reinhold Glière) and in St. Petersburg (Balakirev, Rimsky-Korsakov, and Glazunov). It is a tradition that viewed even Mussorgsky as something of an outsider who had to be "adjusted." Both Rimsky-Korsakov and, later, Shostakovich reorchestrated his opera *Boris Godunov*.

The period from 1948 to Stalin's death in 1953 brought fallow years for Soviet music. Zhdanov himself was the victim of an assassination in 1948, but the effects of his cultural politics persisted for a long time. The fact that even Prokofiev apologized and that all of Shostakovich's public statements were humble, tame, and apologetic may seem flaccid and appeasing. But they were a simple expression of the instinct for self-preservation, a necessary defense against political stigmatization and witch hunts. And, one must remember, composers in the USSR, like musicians, were paid by the state, had wide-ranging privileges, enjoyed the same social status as government officials, lived separate from the workers they were expected to write music for, and had their music performed at the order and behest of the authorities. During the war, Soviet artists were evacuated to safe provinces on special trains for their own welfare. This system kept artists on a tether more effectively than any oppression under the czar. Regardless of talent, a state-sanctioned composer could live safely and comfortably if he obediently served the ideology of the government: art for the masses to the widest extent possible. By contrast, Zhdanov's edict had immediate deleterious consequences for the economic well-being of composers who were criticized, as Prokofiev, Shostakovich, and Khachaturian came to find out.

Of course, it is naïve to believe that experimental, noncommercial artists in the free West have always done better. In European countries free art is often supported by the state rather unconditionally, but in the United States the price of artistic/economic freedom often was (and is) silence; isolation; a lack of grants, performances, publication, or distribution; and therefore no fame or income. Exceptions such as Aaron Copland, John Cage, and Elliott Carter should not make anyone forget that Charles Ives made his living as an insurance executive or that Harry Partch lived as a hobo for long periods.

Zhdanov was uninterested in vagabonds. His critical eye soon took in music theory and music criticism, and hardly a single representative in these fields was immune to accusations of "Western influence" or of extolling composers who were under critical review. The problem is not the demand that art must be for the people, but the demand that *all* art should be for everyone. This artistic straitjacket (which reveals a poor understanding of what spurs artists to create art) necessarily led to massive quantities of compliant, humdrum art without any integrity.

Prokofiev had chosen sides when he returned to the USSR, not out of enthusiasm for Stalin or for the Soviet state's cultural policies, but because it seemed to him the wisest thing to do. In the West, he had to teach and perform as a conductor and a pianist to provide for his family. In the Soviet Union, he was paid well by the state. In addition, he did not hide his urge to compose in a simplified language for a large audience. Moreover, his many years abroad had convinced him that alien air was not good for his creativity. He missed Mother Russia not for nationalist or ideological reasons, but presumably because he had roots there. One friend heard him say: "I must hear the Russian language and the songs of Russia around me."

Even though Zhdanov's regulations did not, as they did with Shostakovich in 1936, entail a true prohibition of the music of indicted artists, in practice the effect was the same. The first of the two violin concertos Shostakovich wrote for David Oistrakh was finished in 1948, but the composer put the work on a waiting list for no less than seven years before he allowed it to be published. Several times in later life, he allowed new works to remain unperformed until he deemed the political climate suitable.

With his antiauthoritarian temperament, Richter could not easily be cowed or molded. Whenever possible, he continued to play the composers whom Zhdanov and Khrennikov criticized. But otherwise he kept entirely aloof from all this. "I never read the papers," the eighty-two-year-old Richter tells Monsaingeon. "In my view, they only serve to dirty the fingers. And so I didn't read Zhdanov's famous decree and took no interest in it."

Considering the tremendously negative effects this decree had for the two most important living composers in Richter's life, the remark seems almost cynical. It is likely that 1948 was the worst year these two composers had lived through. After Zhdanov's fierce criticism, Shostakovich was tormented with persistent thoughts of suicide. Prokofiev's music disappeared so thoroughly from concert programs that in 1950, in spite of the 1946 Stalin Prizes, he needed money for food; his young friend, the up-and-coming cellist Mstislav Rostropovich, indignantly took the matter up with First Secretary Khrennikov. When, almost forty years later, Richter remembers being "uninterested," there is an element of rebellion in his statement. It is, however, at the same time an expression of the apolitical musician's knack of suppressing what he finds most difficult to accept.

But there is a plethora of examples that Richter was anything but a fellow traveler. Together with Nina Dorliak, he performed songs by Rimsky-Korsakov and Prokofiev on January 28, 1948. The concert organizer wanted to cancel, but Richter insisted. They also performed Prokofiev's five songs to texts by the Symbolist Konstantin Balmont, who as a Russian exile in France was considered a heretic. After the concert, a happy Prokofiev embraced Dorliak with the words "Thank you for breathing life into my deceased works."

Nevertheless, Zhdanov's cultural politics formed the background for Richter's first and only true experience as a conductor before an orchestra. The hostile attitude toward Prokofiev persisted long after Zhdanov's death, and in 1952, now aided and supported by the immensely talented Rostropovich (who at that time was twenty-two years old), Prokofiev undertook another radical revision of his cello concerto, which had suffered a slightly sorry fate in 1938, with piano student Richter as the rehearsal pianist. This creative collaboration with Rostropovich had a decisive influence on the cello part. During the summer, the cellist stayed with Prokofiev in his dacha. In early 1949, Prokofiev had composed a cello sonata for Rostropovich and premiered it with Richter in December of the same year. Richter notes that Rostropovich resembled the composer so strikingly that everyone believed Prokofiev was his father! Despite illness and against doctors' orders not to work more than a few hours a day, the collaboration brought the best out in the composer.

In a conversation with Solomon Volkov forty years later, Rostropovich recalled Prokofiev's personality: "If he wanted to express his love for me, then he didn't speak, he lifted his hand (which was large and very long), and clapped me on the shoulder. It actually hurt. He underestimated his strength. But you could say that it was his best way of displaying friendship." After another reworking, the piece was titled Symphony-Concerto for Cello and Orchestra and became a high point in Prokofiev's final years, incorporating much of the younger Prokofiev's ironic bite, powerful gesture, bright colors, and unconventional use of instruments.

However, it proved difficult for Prokofiev to find a conductor who dared take on a performance of the work. The defiant and rebellious Richter came to his assistance. The reason for this has its entertaining side: he had broken a finger in a fight! Not that this "different kind of boy" had suddenly become violent. On a hiking tour outside Moscow with some friends, he came upon a young drunk sailor harassing an employee at a railway restaurant. He put himself in the middle and, with raw physical strength, hauled the man outside to calm him. The next day, a finger on his right hand swelled up. A doctor diagnosed inflammation. Richter had such severe pain that he had the finger X-rayed. There was a bone fracture, and the finger had to be put into a warm wax cast. "Thank God it didn't get stiff, for which there was a grave risk."

His first thought was to use the opportunity to learn Ravel's concerto for the left hand, but he began to think about the work no one wanted or dared to conduct. To support his case, he deluded the authorities into thinking that he might never play the piano again. "Pure blackmail," he admitted. But the authorities fell into the trap. His friend the conductor Kyril Kondrashin gave him tips on conducting, and on February 18, 1952, he conducted the premiere with the Moscow Youth Orchestra and the twenty-four-year-old Rostropovich as soloist.

The totally inexperienced conductor was, if possible, even more nervous than the young cellist, who was to take on an untraditional and incredibly demanding solo part. Many years later, Richter told his Japanese interpreter, Midori Kawashima, that Prokofiev had not attended the three rehearsals with the orchestra but suddenly turned up at the concert. Richter suggested that Rostropovich smile at him at the podium to calm his nerves. "When I went out on to the stage, I was dumbfounded to find there was no piano. For a pianist, a stage without a piano is indescribably strange, almost unbelievable. Lost in thought, I stumbled over the podium and just avoided falling down. I was completely beside myself. When the performance was over, I was so panic-stricken that I forgot to bring Prokofiev onstage to welcome the applause."

The work was warmly received by the audience, but the press was rather tepid. Prokofiev, who because of illness was no longer capable of conducting, later congratulated Richter: "Now I know I have a conductor for my works." Prokofiev continued to revise the work, perhaps in the hope of eliminating the "hardness" and "awkwardness" that annoyed the critics. The title "Symphony-Concerto" was added during these continued revisions. However, Richter could "never forgive" Prokofiev or Rostropovich for changes they made to the finale of the work. Rostropovich "got his way," Richter believes, and he bemoans the fact that the original version presumably cannot be reconstructed.

Richter's career as a conductor begins and ends here. When he was encouraged to conduct, he always replied, "Later!" Upon reflection, he did not think conducting held anything for him. "There are two things that I hate: analysis and power. A conductor can avoid neither the one nor the other. I do not want to analyze a score on behalf of others and impose my own view." At one point, he added with self-recognition: "A conductor must exude self-confidence. And, for me, that feels arrogant." A few days later at a concert with Kurt Sanderling and the Moscow Radio Orchestra, he performed the solo in Beethoven's choral fantasy for the first time. His injured finger had apparently healed completely.

Sanderling recalls Richter's very first attempt at conducting when he led the slow movement from Beethoven's Second Symphony at an orchestral rehearsal in Leningrad, long before the concert with Prokofiev. Sanderling does not believe the piano robbed the world of a gifted conductor. "He couldn't conduct at all, he was helpless. It is a myth that a good musician is always a good conductor." Many years later, Richter referred to this event, although in his view the "catastrophic experience" as a beginner was due to his exaggerated attention to detail.

In the years after Zhdanov's death, Prokofiev was an ill man. He was hospitalized numerous times. Richter visited him every so often at the hospital. Prokofiev was tremendously put out that the doctors had forbidden him to compose, and he hid paper napkins containing sketches under his pillow. "It is more of an effort for me to keep the melodies in my head than to write them down," he claimed. But Richter saw the writing on the wall. "It was difficult to square all this with the image one had of a giant of Russian music. One refused to face up to reality. Here was a man of enormous creative energy who was now utterly helpless." A month later, Slava and Nina visited him again, and he was better. As they departed and walked down the stairs, the composer waved good-bye with his foot. "There was something of the naughty schoolboy about him," Richter remembered. Prokofiev as *enfant terrible*, with his taste for the unexpected, for the controversial, for life as theater, may have encouraged corresponding aspects of Richter's personality.

Artistically, Prokofiev may have been the victim who was hardest hit by Zhdanov's crusade. He never heard many of his late, criticized works performed, and others had to be withdrawn immediately after their premieres. However, his final symphony, the Seventh—premiered less than six months before his death—was a success with both the audience and the critics. It was conceived as a reverie on childhood and had a nostalgic, almost idyllic tone, hardly something to which biased commissars would take umbrage. Nevertheless, he again made a few minor changes at the end of the symphony pursuant to dictates from above.

His final symphony might be seen as expressing the resignation and search for a compromise by an ill and exhausted artist. Prokofiev died a broken and humiliated man. However, to view him as an indolent fellow traveler without principles who gave in to the demands of the Soviet system is artistically and humanly senseless. All art risks becoming propaganda for good or for ill. Therefore, one must insist on the distinction between art created by individuals and that created by a despotic regime. To make art into a plain and simple byproduct of the political conditions that surround it is to reduce creativity to a formula. This was was what Stalin wanted. The fact that Prokofiev may have written his best music between 1936 and 1948 does not prove that political tyranny can lead to great art. It denotes, rather, willpower.

The date of Prokofiev's death has been subject to confusion. In older biographies and lexicons, it ranges between March 4 and March 7, 1953. The confusion arises from the fact that the seventy-three-year-old-Stalin died on the evening of March 5. The composer died suddenly in his small apartment near the Bolshoi less than an hour before the "Red Czar." The art magazine *Sovietskoye Iskustvo* reported later that Prokofiev's death occurred "on the same day as the tragic news of the great Stalin's death. As a consequence, the composer was buried in secrecy, and the death was first disclosed to the press a few days later." He was laid out in an open casket in the dark cellars of the Composers'

Union, where friends and family could say farewell, but all the flowers in the city were at Stalin's bier in the Kremlin. On March 7 a small retinue followed the composer's coffin through the city's empty streets to the churchyard. In the retinue was Dmitri Shostakovich.

Stalin's death was not unexpected. He had endured several strokes since the end of February. The power apparatus did not want another great Russian's death to preoccupy the public when "all of humanity was mourning the irreplaceable loss of our master and leader, the universal genius Joseph Vissarionovich Stalin."

"We had long ago lost the sense that Stalin was mortal," wrote Ilya Ehrenburg in his memoirs." We considered him an all-powerful, distant divinity." Richter was informed of the dictator's death while on tour in the Tbilisi area. The Supreme Soviet telegraphed him, demanding he return to Moscow immediately to play at Stalin's funeral. Despite the subtropical climate, a powerful snowstorm over the Caucasus made flying almost impossible. At the last moment, Richter, the only passenger, was put on board a plane filled from floor to ceiling with funeral wreaths.

The weather forced an interim landing near the Black Sea, and here, in the harbor city of Sukhumi, Richter heard of Prokofiev's death. After spending a cold night at the airport, he continued to Moscow the next morning, buried in flowers. "I thought of Prokofiev," he remembers. And Prokofiev must have thought of him. Among the works he left incomplete was the beginning of yet another piano sonata (number ten) and a concerto for two pianos and strings conceived for Tolya Vedernikov and Slava Richter.

Shostakovich

At the very last moment, Richter rushed from the Moscow airport to the Kremlin's Hall of Columns, where he was to play at the great leader's funeral. A sea of people had gathered to witness the ceremony. "The real reason they came was to be sure that 'he' was really dead," Richter jokingly tells Monsaingeon. At a wretched upright piano, he played not only the adagio from Beethoven's Sonata in C Minor (the *Pathétique*) but also the slow movement from Bach's Piano Concerto in D Minor. When the pedals of the instrument did not work properly, a musician from the orchestra helped him wedge a bundle of scores under them. Richter noticed that this created some discomfort among men in the gallery: "No doubt they thought that I was planting a bomb under the piano."

Richter had seen Prokofiev for the last time in April 1952, a few months after the success of his cello concerto, when the composer heard him give a piano recital in the conservatory's Great Hall. "As long as he was alive," he wrote in his essay on Prokofiev, "you could expect a miracle at any moment; he was like a magician who with the simple wave of his wand could produce the most fairy-tale-like riches."

Richter's relationship with the music of Dmitri Shostakovich was marked by a similar admiration, respect, and love, even though he was never close to Shostakovich the man. This may have to do with the fact that they were both very "private" personalities and that the composer was unusually shy, reserved, and testy. To Monsaingeon Richter recounts his first encounter with Shostakovich during his youth in Odessa: "I remember on one occasion being outside the Odessa Opera. It was dusk, and the street lamps hadn't come on. There was a man staring at me. He had white eyes, with no pupils. Suddenly, I realized that it was Shostakovich. I went weak at the knees."

In almost every respect, Shostakovich was Prokofiev's opposite. The relationship between the country's two most famous composers was a sort of armed,

One of the very few photos of Richter and Shostakovich together.

respectful neutrality, and many of their statements about each other were mea-sured, almost hostile. Condescendingly, Prokofiev called Shostakovich "our little Mahler." The party's ideological warfare made Shostakovich even more private and introverted, while the self-assured, extroverted Prokofiev reacted by seeking publicity.

Not until twelve years after the episode in Odessa when the war was over did Richter get a firsthand impression of the older Shostakovich, a man ten years his senior. A humorous high point in Monsaingeon's version of their conversations reveals the pianist's ironic memories of his encounters with Shostakovich.

In August 1945, the thirty-nine-year-old composer completed work on his Ninth Symphony, and the following year, he and Richter played the work in a version for four hands at a gathering in the composer's own home. After the two great "war symphonies," the Seventh and the Eighth, people expected a "victory symphony" from Shostakovich, but he confused, disappointed, and annoyed his followers by writing a short, almost cheerful symphony. Perhaps he wanted to play a joke on fate, since Beethoven, Bruckner, and Mahler had made the Ninth fatefully symbolic for a symphonist. Richter later described the work as full of "sarcasm, eccentricity, enthusiasm, and life," but he remem-bers the experience of sight-reading with the originator of the work as quite embarrassing. "He played the bass part, and so it was he who had the responsibility for operating the pedal, but he ignored it completely. And he played *fortissimo* all the time, including passages of pure accompaniment, I had to play even louder to bring out the melodies, without the use of the pedal to give it some sort of outline, I was fighting a losing battle, not least because I could hear him muttering to himself all the time: 'Toon . . . toorooroo . . . toorooroo . . . tooroorooroom!'"

The description of Shostakovich's dubious abilities as a musician should hardly be taken literally, even though others confirm that he sometimes had a tendency to gradually "run" and to unconsciously increase the tempo, which can be heard in the recording of his First Piano Concerto with himself as soloist. As a twenty-one-year-old, he was sent to Warsaw as part of a team expected to bring honor to the Soviet Union at the first Chopin International Piano Competition in 1927. However, he was awarded only a disappointing honorary diploma; David Oistrakh's later partner Lev Oborin won first prize. In his younger years, Shostakovich often performed his own works as a soloist. He was generally acknowledged as an excellent piano player, and friends testify he could play all of Beethoven's piano sonatas by heart until late in life. Conductor Nikolai Malko, who premiered Shostakovich's First Symphony, shows more understanding than Richter for a composer's special musicality. He wrote in his memoirs of the young composer's performance of this symphony on the piano: "Like most composers, he played with great consideration for the notes, and without greater expression. . . . He presented the music itself rather than an interpretation of it." Conductor Evgeny Mravinsky, who premiered close to half of Shostakovich's symphonies, told of an orchestra rehearsal in which the composer broke off in the middle of a very loud *tutti* and asked, "Why is the English horn playing an octave lower than written?" After a moment of total silence, the orchestra broke out in applause.

Richter provides more details in his unkind snapshot: "Prokofiev was violent. Shostakovich was always mumbling 'sorry.'" Yet Shostakovich could be very touchy. He never forgave Richter for not playing *all* of the twenty-four preludes and fugues in his major work for piano from 1950–51. Richter describes a persistent nervous oscillation between irritability and highly servile manners. A characteristic trait—perhaps a defense mechanism developed in a society in which people rarely said what they meant—is exhibited almost touchingly in an episode Heinrich Neuhaus relates. Neuhaus and Shostakovich were attending a disastrous orchestra concert. Neuhaus leaned over to Shostakovich and whispered, "Dmitri Dimitriyevich, this is awful!" Shostakovich replied, "You're right, Heinrich Gustavovich! It's splendid! Quite remarkable!" Neuhaus realized that he had been misunderstood and repeated his remark. "Yes," the composer mumbled, "it's awful, quite awful!"

As late as May 1969, together with David Oistrakh, Richter premiered Shostakovich's violin sonata from the year before. The two musicians hauled the composer on the stage for the applause, but the aging master was afraid of stumbling. Again and again, he whispered to Richter, "I don't want to make a scene. I don't want to make a scene." This droll situation has a sad background, however. At the beginning of the 1960s, doctors had ascertained that Shostakovich was suffering from a rare disease, a polio that resulted in muscle weakness and osteoporosis. On top of that, a serious fracture in 1960 made it difficult for him to walk for the rest of his life.

Shostakovich was known to hide behind a mask of aloof politeness. Kurt Sanderling relates that if he said "Wonderful, splendid, very beautiful, thanks so much" after a concert, one could be sure that he was not satisfied. "But if he said, 'At the beginning of the first movement, I would have liked the flute to be a little louder,' then you knew that he enjoyed it, that it had interested him." If people laugh about what might resemble a chronic spinelessness in Neuhaus's anecdote, the sinister background for this should be made known: January 1936 brought a brutal episode to the life, psyche, and career of the twenty-eight-year-old Dmitri Shostakovich. From one day to the next, he went from the heights of fame to being accused of "antinational formalist" tendencies that betrayed both Party and people. This veritable stroke of the ax had effects that spread like rings in the waters of Soviet musical life.

As early as 1932, he had finished his opera *Lady Macbeth of the Mtsensk District*. Even at the age of twenty-five, he had long been subjected to criticism from the authorities. However, a couple of years later, once it had premiered almost simultaneously in Leningrad and Moscow, the opera immediately became a magnet for the audience. In the first few months, it was performed thirty-six times; within two seasons it played ninety-four times in Moscow alone. The opera told a grim story of erotic obsession, violence, and death; the title's protagonist commits three murders, but Shostakovich transforms her into a victim by describing the world in which she lives as meaningless and everyone around her as idiots or inhuman. Some unusually realistic sex scenes unleashed violent debate (an American critic invented the word "pornophony"). Soon the opera would be seen in Cleveland, Stockholm, London, Prague, Ljubljana, Zurich, Copenhagen, and at the Metropolitan in New York.

Talk of the young composer-genius who aroused attention and engendered discussion even in the West attracted Stalin's curiosity. The party leader was very interested in art. He was an enthusiastic reader of novels and appreciated classical music, especially opera and ballet. On January 26, 1936, "the great leader and teacher" went to the Bolshoi Theater, escorted by, among others, Zhdanov, to see Shostakovich's opera, which now, in addition to the Nemirovich-Danchenko Theater, was also playing on the Bolshoi's second stage. Shostakovich was hastily summoned to attend the performance with these distinguished guests.

Three days later the composer was on a concert tour to Archangel. He bought the newspaper *Pravda*, the official party organ, in a kiosk and read on page three an anonymous review of *Lady Macbeth*. The article had the headline "Muddle instead of Music." The anonymity of the writer meant that this was someone from the upper echelons of the Party; music was not a common topic in *Pravda*. The article starts by reminding the reader that a composer has a duty to socialist realism, and in the description of Shostakovich's opera, the tone is violently accusatory: "Snatches of melody, the beginnings of a musical phrase, drown, emerge again, and disappear in a grinding and squealing roar. . . . The music quacks, grunts, growls and suffocates itself in order to paint the love scenes as realistically as possible. And 'love' is everywhere smeared in its most vulgar form. . . . It is music that is deliberately turned inside out. It is a twisted muddle instead of genuine human music."

Any attempt to defend oneself from an attack by the Supreme Soviet would be viewed as injurious to the state. The article's author could very well have been Stalin himself. And he may have had in mind something other than music that is easily accessible to people. A strict new family law to prevent divorces and strengthen national and family ties had just been approved. An opera about a wife's murder of her hated husband, more murders and a suicide, not to mention infidelity, sexual frustration, drunkenness, rape, and corruption, was totally at odds with healthy Soviet thinking. That the opera even showed a certain influence of Alban Berg's atonal opera *Wozzeck*—which Shostakovich had seen in Leningrad some years earlier—made it entirely unacceptable as Soviet art.

The article in *Pravda* concluded: "The power of good music to infect the masses is squandered for an unproductive, petty-bourgeois 'formalist' attempt to achieve originality through cheap clowning. This game of clever ingenuity could end very badly." The threat was evident. In the course of a few weeks, two additional attacks on Shostakovich were printed in the paper; he had become a virtual political liability. And the threat came just at a time when the gulag, deportation, prison camps, imprisonment, and liquidation of "conspirators" or "enemies of the people" belonged to the order of the day. Ilya Ehrenburg writes in his memoirs that "no one in my circle felt secure the next day; many had a small, packed trunk ready."

One can imagine the feelings of the twenty-eight-year-old composer. He knew that the Soviet dictator could eliminate him with the stroke of a pen. A number of his friends—poets, dramatists, actors, film people, and academicians—disappeared or were executed during these years. Many were awakened in the middle of the night and taken to the dungeons of Lubyanka Prison, where, through violence and torture, they were forced to "confess," just as the Inquisition had forced so-called witches and heretics to confess. Now, it was not just a question of Shostakovich's continued artistic activity; it was a question of his continued existence. Nobody came to his aid. People who had praised him a few days earlier now condemned him. All his colleagues saw the threat. Understandably, all of them thought of their own security and of their families, incomes, and careers. For musicians, the writing was on the wall: if the world-famous and celebrated Shostakovich could from one day to the next be humiliated, dethroned, and threatened, anyone could.

Shostakovich the man had been brought down to earth. The fear of reprisals or outright elimination never left him and undoubtedly led to lasting psychological harm. But Shostakovich the artist had no regrets; he did not throw his towel into the ring. "Even if you chopped off both my hands, I would write music with a pencil between my teeth," he wrote to a friend. Despite his apparent talent for music drama, despite his plan to make *Lady Macbeth* the first work of an operatic trilogy, he had composed his last opera.

In the four months after the first *Pravda* article, Shostakovich finished work on his huge, expansive Fourth Symphony, which was permeated by "formalism." The symphony was supposed to be premiered in December, but now, wiser from his wounds, the composer withdrew it after the general rehearsal (some believe that he was forced to), and a quarter of a century had to go by before its first performance. It must have been inconceivably painful to bury alive what he knew was his most ambitious symphonic effort to date. But the risk was too great, and instead he threw himself into music for the masses, music for the favorite art form of the "Great Leader," namely film.

Then, in the spring and summer of 1937, Shostakovich composed his "penance" amazingly quickly: the Fifth Symphony. Later his name appeared beneath a newspaper article in which he described his symphony as "a Soviet artist's practical, creative answer to just criticism" (and, in the West, this became a sort of subtitle to the work). But a ventriloquist is speaking here on the composer's behalf, or Shostakovich is lying from necessity, simply to ensure the continuation of his artistic work. He does not try to hide the fact that there is no published Fourth Symphony. Of course, he could have chosen to label the fifth as number four. The premiere with the Leningrad Philharmonic was scheduled for November 21, 1937, as part of the twentieth-anniversary festivities of the October Revolution (the Gregorian calendar had long before replaced the Julian in the Soviet state).

The Fifth Symphony was an unparalleled success, and within a few years, it was played by orchestras all over the globe. Today, it is quite common to read a plethora of secret musical codes into the work, "messages in a bottle," musical references to a time when most people in every concert hall would have friends and family members who had disappeared. This was true of Shostakovich as well. His uncle was shot; his older sister and her husband, his mother-in-law, and his brother-in-law were all arrested and interned in 1937. And with this knowledge in mind, one may hear tooth-grinding sarcasm in the Mahler-like scherzo and forced jubilation rather than a life-affirming triumph in the finale. Mstislav Rostropovich was present at the premiere and fifty years later related that the audience clearly experienced the music as "a message of suffering and isolation. . . . Anyone who believes that the finale is a glorification is a fool." Kurt Sanderling heard the first performance in Moscow a couple of months after the premiere and remembers that after the first movement, he "looked around nervously and wondered whether we would all be arrested after the concert. Most people in the audience knew quite well what the music was about. It mirrored precisely what was on almost everyone's mind." After the performance, it seemed the standing ovation would never end. For almost half an hour, the audience continued to shout and clap. It was a veiled protest, a political demonstration in borrowed plumes.

But in music, meanings can never be read precisely and unambiguously. Stalin and the power apparatus were apparently convinced that the symphony was "making amends" and that the vociferous finale meant optimism, praise, and ideological agreement. Or they pretended to be convinced. By completely controlling both the work's condemnation and its resurrection, the government demonstrated its power.

After this symphony, Shostakovich became a different person, an ambiguous figure. For the rest of his life, in a long number of commissioned works — "utilitarian music" for countless films and plays — he apparently remained loyal to the Party's wishes and demands. But at the same time, his music was viewed as a sort of running commentary on the artistic and human conditions in Soviet society. In a way that is often difficult to discern, he became a spokesperson for both the Soviet establishment and its underground culture. His status as the leader of Soviet music was undisputed, and he was celebrated in concert halls around the world. In the latter half of the war year 1942, his new

Seventh Symphony (the *Leningrad* Symphony), for example, was performed no fewer than sixty-two times in the United States. The sensation—the propagandistic fabricated images of the composer as a resistance man in a fire helmet, the story of the microfilmed score that reached the United States by air, and the pitched battle about who was to give the world premiere—generated enormous interest. Among others, Eugene Ormandy, Leopold Stokowski, and Serge Koussevitzky fought for the rights, but the seventy-five-year-old Arturo Toscanini and the NBC orchestra walked off with the spoils, and on July 19 the symphony was transmitted by radio in the United States. Three weeks later, it was performed in a besieged Leningrad, with Soviet artillery carpet bombing German positions to prevent an attack on the Philharmonic. Once again, a new symphony by Shostakovich was an event whose political undertones threatened to drown out the music itself, and gradually many people in the Soviet Union came to consider him the country's true, reliable writer of history.

When the cultural ideologue Zhdanov launched the campaign that led to the Composers' Congress and the "historic resolution" in January 1948, Shostakovich was in a different situation from Prokofiev for many reasons. He had experienced this sort of thing before. In addition, he was a child of the Communist school system. He had lived almost his entire life under the Soviet government and could not carry on conversations in any major language except Russian. Prokofiev, on the other hand, attended school under the czar, left Russia when revolution and civil war put a stop to musical life, and lived in the West for fifteen years. He felt cosmopolitan, spoke excellent English and French, and for obvious reasons did not feel tied to the country's political system in the same way as Shostakovich.

When Prokofiev declared himself "guilty," it was also in a less compliant tone than that of his colleague. In an 1948 letter to the official music magazine *Sovietskaya Muzyka*, Shostakovich admitted regretfully that "once again, I moved in the direction of formalism and have begun to speak a language the people do not understand. . . . I know that the Party is right. I am deeply grateful for the criticism." For the rest of his life, Shostakovich maintained a protective poker face; his public statements can only rarely be taken at face value.

Entirely deliberately, with a clear sense of the possibility of further reprisals, Shostakovich now concentrated on film music and the occasional patriotic work, postponing publication of important works he wrote in this period. These included not only the first violin concerto for David Oistrakh, but also the Fourth String Quartet and a bold song cycle (*From Jewish Folk Poetry*, with texts based on Yiddish folklore), which was first performed two years after

Stalin's death, with Nina Dorliak as one of the soloists. Shostakovich's contrarian attitude toward the state's power apparatus is apparent in this major work. He counted many Jews among his closest friends, and by all accounts Stalin's heavy-handed anti-Semitic persecution intensified after the war. Shortly before Zhdanov's pedantic lectures in January 1948, the most prominent Soviet Jew, the actor Solomon Mikhoel, was brutally murdered by Beria's MGB (later KGB). Mikhoel was the composer Moise Weinberg's father-in-law, and Weinberg may have been the colleague closest to Shostakovich. Soon after, the Jewish theater was closed, the only Jewish newspaper was shut down, and many Jews in public positions were fired. Writing Jewish songs precisely at that moment seems not a mere act of protest, but a death-defying stunt that negated any talk of Shostakovich as the submissive tool of the state.

Everything indicates that Shostakovich deliberately oscillated between different forms of expression: a "Party-friendly" music and a more searching, often more introverted music that better satisfied his artistic ambitions. There is no doubt that he wanted to compose music for the people, but he would not stoop to the lowest common denominator. After the Ninth Symphony of 1945, eight years would go by before the public heard a new symphony by him.

Shostakovich's earliest works bore the stamp of Prokofiev and the "new objectivity" that Paul Hindemith represented. These were tonal or neotonal, often grotesque parodies of Western tradition, but full of vitality and, at times, ferociously experimental (such as the metallic, hammering First Piano Sonata from 1928). An ironic bite and energetic diction go together with an alienated sentimentality in the nineteen-year-old composer's still immensely popular First Symphony from 1925, a work that unlike Prokofiev's first, the "classical," is a detached game with the conventions of music but at times a satirical caricature of a symphony with melancholy allusions to Mahler. The operas *The Nose* (after Gogol) and *Lady Macbeth* (which after the frontal political attack was revised in 1956, performed again as late as January 1963 after several vain requests by the composer, and renamed *Katarina Izmailova*, after the protagonist) were just as original, pointed, sarcastically orchestrated, and at times almost atonal. In earlier works, such as the First Piano Concerto and the satirical ballet *The Golden Age*, Shostakovich teases, parodies, and makes faces in a breathless, cabaret-like atmosphere in which polkas, waltzes, and galops parody "serious" music and bourgeois musical culture. These works apparently were composed with the greatest ease and are among his most untroubled and sprightly works.

Censorship and oppression, the tragic background of Shostakovich's long series of symphonies after 1936, all of which had roots in the nineteenth-century symphonic tradition, did not prevent them from winning a place in today's orchestral repertoire, which, seen as a whole, makes them the most frequently played symphonies from the twentieth century after Mahler and Sibelius. This fact must make many composers in the free West, who have full artistic freedom, ask themselves difficult questions. Shostakovich, under enormous psychological pressure, was able to reconquer the history-fraught symphonic genre. It is difficult to reject Leonard Bernstein's claim that Shostakovich's symphonies mark the end of the historical career of the symphonic genre. There are deeply felt personal outbursts in the monumental Eighth or the contrast-rich Tenth (possibly a musical expression of his personal anger at the recently deceased Stalin), irony in the Ninth, and sarcasm followed by thoughts of death in his final symphony (the Fifteenth). And in the sixties, he wrote the Thirteenth and Fourteenth Symphonies, both "song symphonies" and both using texts more or less openly critical of the system, side by side with the colorful simplicity on a wide symphonic screen of the "filmic" Eleventh and Twelfth Symphonies.

Shostakovich is less defensive and often more reticent, melancholy, and introverted in his chamber music; the fifteen string quartets, in particular, distinguish themselves as his most "private" works after 1936. Something similar is true of his chamber music for piano; the splendid, Jewish-inspired Second Piano Trio and two late sonatas, a violin sonata and a viola sonata, played an essential role in Richter's repertoire. Shostakovich began his most important contribution to the piano literature, the twenty-four preludes and fugues, in all twelve major and minor keys (of which Richter played sixteen), after having participated in memorial ceremonies in Leipzig in 1950 for the two hundredth anniversary of Bach's death.

In his coerced revision of *Lady Macbeth*, Shostakovich played down or removed the most realistic expressions of fleshly desire but maintained, for the most part, his original music. Several times, he chose to collaborate with the controversial young poet Yevgeni Yevtushenko—in the cantata-like Thirteenth Symphony with bass solo and male chorus—even using poems against anti-Semitism. This does not draw a portrait of a fellow traveler, either. In 1962, in connection with this symphony, the composer lost his respect for his favorite conductor, Mravinsky, when, apparently in fear of reprisals, Mravinsky declined to take on the premiere. The work is based in part on poems by Yevtuschenko, poems that looked at the Nazi genocide of Kiev's Jews during the war from a contemporary perspective and which, in many respects, could be viewed as a critique of the regime and of Stalin's time. The authorities tried to prevent the performance, which once again turned out to be a combined political and musical event.

The most incontrovertible proof of Shostakovich's equivocal relationship to the power apparatus and his contempt for the dogmatic Soviet cultural politics, however, is a satirical operalike sketch (*Anti-formalist Rayok*), which he began as early as May 1948 and then apparently worked on at intervals for several years. A *rayok* is similar to what in the West is called a peep show. Shostakovich's favorite composer, Mussorgsky, had composed a *rayok* in 1870 in which he mocked music critics. The piece—parodically subtitled "The Struggle between Realism and Formalism in Music"—ridicules Zhdanov's simplistic view of music; in the caricatured text he himself wrote, Stalin the cultural ideologue and his successor Shepilov—though with slightly transparent pseudonyms—are portrayed as pompous fools. The music—for voices and piano—makes ironic use of well-known melodies and cultural hits that "are easy to hum." Of course, the piece was kept secret; only his family and close friends knew about it. A performance of it had to wait until fifteen years after his death.

Yet, from the perspective of social criticism or Realpolitik it hardly makes sense to see Shostakovich as a dissident; when the Party limited his artistic freedom and put him on the defensive, he did not protest, or only mildly. And the disgust he felt for Stalin's crimes and for Stalinism hardly distinguishes him from the vast majority of Soviet citizens; Soviet propaganda did not fool the populace. But behind the backs of the power brokers, Shostakovich undoubtedly expressed his reaction to the attacks and abuse of power in the wordless language of music. Many Western critics in later years have insisted on looking at his life's work as an ongoing, wordless commentary on the regime's inhumanity, but this reduces and betrays the true depths in his music and makes it one-dimensional. His powers of creation constantly went beyond the aesthetic framework usually considered politically correct. And when younger generations chose him as an icon, his music gave them irrefutable arguments for expecting a corresponding freedom. Whether he would have been an even greater composer without the artistic shackles that often characterized the form and content of his music, no one can know. The difficulty in penetrating his personality and the unique conditions that produced his music render considerations of what his music *could* have been empty guesswork.

Shostakovich's putative autobiography, *Testimony*, which the young journalist Solomon Volkov published in the West in 1979, four years after the composer's death in August 1975 (ostensibly dictated to Volkov by the protagonist himself), with its hair-raising descriptions of Stalinist despotism provided even more fodder for the mystery of Shostakovich's real relationship to the regime and made an explosive contribution to Cold War rhetoric. Until then, it had been customary to look at Shostakovich as a scapegoat, the victim of a smear campaign who later submitted to the demands of the regime. In reality, he was far less yielding than many of his colleagues. His oeuvre is not flooded by odes, oratorios, and cantatas praising Stalin, peace, the Red Army, revolutionary holidays, national heroes, party bosses, or female cosmonauts.

The autobiography testifies to a man who put his name to statements in which others glorified the government in the official press and mocked the "monotony and chaos" of the Western avant-garde. It attests to a man who had no illusions about the crimes of Stalin and the Party apparatus, but also to a man who—after Khrushchev came to terms with the Stalin era in 1956—helped and supported progressive musicians and colleagues. He always helped others when he could (he used the enormous sum of 100,000 rubles, the award money for his 1941 Stalin Prize, to help family, friends, and acquaintances living in poverty). Above all, the book testifies to a life filled with enormous psychic costs. "Isn't history really just a whore?" Shostakovich asks his ghostwriter.

Volkov's book transforms the former Soviet idol into a martyr, into a "dissident," less overt and ready for battle but in the same weight class as, for example, Alexander Solzhenitsyn. Yet, late in life, Shostakovich cosigned a declaration that stamped Solzhenitsyn and physicist Andrei Sakharov as socially harmful elements, declarations that other artists refused to sign. His reasons are unclear. In the last ten years of his life, he was plagued by weakness and constant health problems. He always had to conserve his energy in order to continue composing. His temperament was anything but that of a fighter. He indulged in a sort of escapism, almost an indifference to the surrounding world, and his music increasingly touches on the topics of darkness and death, or perhaps it simply mirrors the always apologetic, oblique, and accommodating man Richter remembered.

The book shocked Soviet intellectuals. It was immediately condemned as a falsehood, "a lie from one end to the other," even by friends and students of Shostakovich. In the West even today, there is a bitter feud between its proponents and opponents. Volkov refuses to produce the evidentiary material, which he claims to have in his possession. The 1998 book *Shostakovich Reconsidered* defends Volkov against his critics in a tone that often reminds one of a vociferous argument between neighbors. But in 2004 *A Shostakovich Casebook* presented very-difficult-to-refute arguments for the claim that the dictated autobiography is a fake.

Not even Volkov claims to have written down precisely what the composer said to him. He states he took notes "in a sort of personal stenography" and that he later reshaped these notes into longer chapters. As a basis for a four-hundred-page monologue put in the mouth of Shostakovich, this seems dubious. A memoir in the first person written by someone else must necessarily be ambiguous when the person speaking is speaking postmortem and thus is denied the possibility of retort. And the reader of this book must recognize that the same problem arises with confusing frequency in Richter's story—Monsaingeon, Meyer-Josten, Milstein, Chemberdzhy. No one can act as a ventriloquist, regardless of how close he or she may have been to the other person. And what was said with respect to Monsaingeon's film of the aging, ill pianist is also true here: a human being marked by psychic wounds and with bitter reckonings to make cannot be expected to present a balanced description of events over the course of a long life. Whoever reviews the past in the light of later experiences cannot avoid reminiscing and making things up at the same time. And regardless of how much care goes into the references and notes of a conversation, one can only rarely determine with any certainty when a thought or sentiment is expressed as a lifelong conviction and when it is simply a casual remark.

But Volkov's Shostakovich is a consistent human figure who cannot be rejected as simply a figment of the imagination. No one can deny that the book may contain much that depicts the composer correctly and faithfully; many find it improbable that Volkov would be able to "invent" and sustain Shostakovich's nervously jumpy, ironic use of language, and his idiosyncratic modes of speech, events, anecdotes, and points of view, which only those closest to him knew. And most people recognize the book's more general description of artistic conditions in the Soviet Union as accurate. Many artists who were close to the composer—musicians such as Emil Gilels, Kyril Kondrashin, Rudolf Barshai, and Kurt Sanderling, and authors such as Yevgeni Yevtushenko and Andrei Bitov—have declared themselves convinced of the book's authenticity. According to his colleague Andrei Gavrilov, Richter was also inclined to believe it. And as part of this assessment, it must be said that these musicians had always seen Shostakovich's music as an autobiographical expression of his hatred for Stalin and the system's brutal oppression of "undesirable" art.

It is unlikely that an irrefutable piece of evidence for the purported autobiography as an authentic document of the composer's own voice (or the reverse, as a fictionalized account) will turn up. But that this debate persists more than twenty-five years after the book's publication is evidence of its indisputable value as a document of musical history and as a vehicle for the intense growth of interest in the composer's music.

On the basis of Volkov's book—although very unlikely to be an echo of Shostakovitch's own voice—Richter's one-dimensional picture of Shostakovich widens. He describes an awkward side of the tetchy, nervous, fearful temperament that one encounters in almost every photograph of the composer: the suspicious, nearsighted look behind thick glasses; the narrow, tight, rarely smiling mouth, strained at the edges; the tormented boyish features; the haunted expression; the pallid face. It is the picture of a man who oscillated between courage and fear, self-assurance and doubt. Courage in art need not necessarily mean human courage. Perhaps it is the picture of a man who came to despise certain aspects of himself because he was forced to be loyal to the artistic shackles he hated. And perhaps it is a telling picture of what may have been the Soviet intelligentsia's tragic dilemma: an impossible choice between exile and nostalgia on one hand and inner emigration on the other.

In his memoirs about the end of the 1920s, Nikolai Malko describes the young Shostakovich as a "Mephisto," a cheerful wag with a caustic, sarcastic, and provocative tongue, a fearless, Siegfried-like party lion who loved boisterous discussions and late-night social gatherings. In connection with the aging Stravinsky's visit to his homeland in the fall of 1962 (for the first and only time in fifty years), Minister of Culture Furtseva invited select composers to a dinner at the beginning of October. The guest of honor sat with the minister on one side and Shostakovich on the other. Stravinsky's assistant and famulus Robert Craft participated, and in his diary he notes: "He [Shostakovich] is the shyest, most nervous human being I have ever met. He chain-smokes, chews not only his nails but his fingers, twitches his pouty mouth and chin, wiggles his nose in constant adjustment of his spectacles, looks querulous one moment and ready to cry the next. He stutters too, and his hands tremble. . . . He has a habit of staring, then of guiltily turning away when caught. . . . But the thoughts behind those frightened, very intelligent eyes are never betrayed." That these two descriptions deal with one and the same person can make Rainer Werner Fassbinder's 1974 film *Angst essen Seele auf* (*Fear Eats the Soul*) haunt the subconscious.

In 1981 Shostakovich's son, the conductor Maxim Shostakovich, sought political asylum in the West and settled in New York. He is ambivalent about Volkov's book, but he does not deny the book's image of Shostakovich as "a secret critic" of state authorities. "My father was a patriot, he belonged to his people—which one should not mix up with an *apparatchik*," he says in a conversation with Boris Schwarz. "My father was forced into a mask of loyalty." He claims that the composer's many "official" statements "were always sent to him from the Composers' Union fit to be published."

The similarities between Richter and Shostakovich—despite their differences in personality and circumstances—are clear in their attitudes to the political reality surrounding them. On this point, Shostakovich's example can shed light on Richter's firm rejection of anything touching on the political. Like most Soviet intellectuals, both had contempt for the brutality of the Soviet regime and the government's cultural politics, but they did not actively oppose it. They just wanted to be left alone to work. This was not a political choice between conformity and revolt; it was simply a matter of artistic and personal survival. In her memoirs, the soprano Galina Vishnevskaya cited what she remembered as Shostakovich's habitual reaction to the government's injustices. It seems likely that Richter might have expressed it in the same way: "Don't waste your energy. Work, play. You live here, in this country. You have to see things the way they really are."

As mentioned, a true friendship never developed between the pianist and the composer. Shostakovich was known as a reserved, introverted person, even with his lifelong friends. According to Volkov, Shostakovich devoted more attention to other Russian giants of the piano, particularly the eccentric genius Maria Yudina and the much-loved Vladimir Sofronitsky. Sviatoslav Richter is not even mentioned in *Testimony*.

But there is no doubt that Richter admired Shostakovich. "I finally learned to love and, I think, also to understand his music. For me, the Eighth Symphony, the Piano Trio, and the song cycle *From Jewish Folk Poetry* are among the most sublime and inspired works of the twentieth century." Nina Dorliak is said to have reported that when Shostakovich was to visit them in their Moscow apartment, Richter exclaimed, "Imagine Tchaikovsky coming for a visit!" (Dorliak had close friends among Shostakovich's family.)

Nevertheless, Richter apparently did not learn to love or understand Shostakovich as a man. "I had difficulty getting used to his presence; I always went weak in the knees. He was too jumpy and clinically depressed. A genius, but completely mad, like the rest of us. But why do I say 'like the rest of us'? I'm not mad, I'm the most normal person you could imagine. I just mention that in passing. Perhaps I might have wanted to be mad."

Richter's cousin Fritz Reincke does not quite agree. In an attempt to describe Svetik's unpredictable, restless personality without typecasting him, he takes refuge in a German saying: *Jeder muss masslos verrückt sein; oder er ist masslos langweilig* (Everyone must be totally mad; otherwise he's totally boring).

PART **III**

The Heartbreak

Among the mysteries, fabrications, and suppressions that are a part of the Richter story, none is deeper and darker than the story of how his father and mother disappeared from his life. "In our country, everything was hushed up," he tells Monsaingeon. "It isn't hard to guess why. As far as my father is concerned, no one has ever dared to describe events exactly as they happened."

His mother obviously did not. Her memoir (*From My Life*) ends abruptly when her son goes to Moscow and applies for Neuhaus's class. She loses contact with him when the war reaches Odessa. With a single sentence, she summarizes the last twenty-five years of her life: "A heavy destiny lay before us, we had to endure years of cruel suffering."

Unfortunately, Richter does not tell everything either—in part because he is unaware of the precise details. He knew that his father was arrested and shot by the secret police before the Germans and the Romanian Fascists reached Odessa in 1941, and he believed it happened a few weeks after he had visited his parents for the last time (and had practiced Prokofiev's Fifth Piano Concerto in his childhood home). Stalin's "butcher," Lavrenty Beria, the unscrupulous head of the NKVD from 1938 on, had thousands of Odessa citizens with German ancestry arrested and interrogated. Many were executed, suspected of being spies for the occupation power. The accusation against Teofil was based on a single witness statement from an NKVD agent. There was no proof, and the conservatory's principal testified that Teofil Richter was completely apolitical.

In 1954, when Beria was sentenced and executed, the NKVD was reorganized as the KGB, the Committee for State Security. (The Soviet secret service was a complicated system of partly overlapping units; the original Cheka became the GPU, and later the NKVD and the MVD. Under Beria, it was under the Ministry of State Security, the MGB.) A 1998 certificate from Kiev, presumably from the KGB's archives, mentions the name, birthdate, position, and address of "Rikhter, Teofil Danielovich." It reads: "Arrested August 25, 1941 by the Odessa regional NKVD, charged with counter-espionage. Sentenced to death by the naval military tribunal on October 3, 1941. Executed by firing squad on the night

One of the last photos showing the Richter family together. Could
Anna and Theo have had premonitions of a sinister future?

of October 7, 1941. Rehabilitated on February 1, 1962, upon decision from the
military panel of the Supreme Court of the USSR in absence of *corpus delicti*."

The document further states that the death penalty had been carried out
at the five-mile mark on the road to Ovidiopol, by a garbage dump. The same
night, twenty-four people were executed there. The next day, the NKVD sent
garbage trucks to where the bodies were buried.

The date indicates that the execution took place more than six months after
Richter's last visit to Odessa; the fact that he believed it happened "a few weeks
later" (in the Monsaingeon interview he mentions "in June 1941") makes it
unlikely that he was familiar with the particulars. He heard of his father's death
in Tbilisi in the early fall of 1943, on his first concert tour to Georgia. The "rehabilitation" of Teofil Richter in 1962 was part of a wave of bureaucratic rehabili-
tations instigated by Khrushchev as an expression of his critique of the Stalin
era; murdered people were "acquitted," others were set free, and their families
received a symbolic financial compensation. The fact that Teofil made the list

may have had some connection to the international media's interest in Richter's family following his reunion with his mother in the fall of 1960.

But the sad drama does not end there. As the apolitical Richter saw it, the real villain was clearly Sergei Kondratiev, a well-educated man who had studied law, geology, and music in St. Petersburg, taught at the Odessa Conservatory, and, for a brief period, was a private tutor in composition and music theory for the teenage Slava in Odessa. With a bitter irony, the eighty-two-year-old Richter indicates that, in a way, he himself is to blame that this man became a fateful player in his life. On the recommendation of an elderly musicologist in Odessa (the man whose library was made available to Richter and Yakov Zak when they played four hands together), he had looked up Kondratiev. Kondratiev was a highly respected teacher; one of his most gifted students had a ballet performed at the theater in Odessa. One day, when Slava visited him, he found him lying on the floor, gasping for breath, with something stuck in his throat. The fifteen-year-old rushed to help. "If I had not been present on that occasion, I'd not have been guilty of saving him. Kondratiev, who was the source of so much misery for me and my father, would have gone to meet his maker without causing us any harm."

Anna Richter's otherwise detailed memoirs tiptoe ever so lightly (with only three lines) over her son's relationship with his stepfather. Her writing is so out of step with her normal diction that one might suspect a guided hand: "Missing from the present record are details of the time when my subsequent second husband taught Svetik and substantially helped promote his career. This omission will be rectified later." The promised rectification of course never happened.

Kondratiev was of German ancestry, the son of a high-ranking officer under the czar. His original name (according to Richter's cousin Walter Moskalew) was Alfred von Ketterer. Why he chose the name Kondratiev is unknown. Nothing indicates a familial connection with Tchaikovsky's close friend Nikolai Kondratiev, a rake who died of syphilis in 1887, or with the folk music scholar and composer Sergei Kondratiev, who died in Moscow in 1970 at the age of eighty. But it is clear that after the Revolution, Alfred von Ketterer went underground and changed his name, presumably to avoid persecution and possible execution. A friend, a well-known singer, helped him escape from Moscow to Odessa and used his influence to get him a fake passport and work at the conservatory there. He had a reputation as a knowledgeable and interesting teacher. In his diary, V. A. Shvetshe, a student, wrote of his first encounter with him in 1942: "The door was opened by a small, compact man in a chocolate-colored morning robe. His round face made me think of the last portrait of Maxim Gorky. He moved very

Anna reads for the ill (faking?)
Sergei Kondratiev in Odessa.

nimbly, and it amazed me that this man had been bedridden for years. Was the 'illness' simply a ruse to avoid something? He invited me into a splendid living room with a beautiful grand piano and lots of books and paintings."

Apparently, Slava Richter was disgusted by Kondratiev from the beginning, even though, at that point, he had no reason for these intense negative feelings. Kondratiev was very friendly toward him, but Richter viewed him as false, unnatural, and stilted, as well as extremely talkative. "He never stopped talking, and it's no doubt because of him that I'm not much of a chatterbox myself."

When the war broke out, the rival even moved in with the Richters (Teofil Richter's tolerance must have been astounding). Anna and Teofil were to have been evacuated from Odessa before the war reached the city, but Kondratiev claimed to be suffering from a tuberculosis of the bones. He was bedridden for twenty years, "getting up only when the Germans arrived. It was a pretense," says Richter. "Mother waited on him hand and foot, and my father, of course, knew what was going on." Richter's mother presumably refused to be evacuated so as not to leave her allegedly ill lover in the lurch. Other sources, however, indicate that Kondratiev was pro-German and was expecting the arrival of the Nazis. The gentle, accommodating Teofil Richter's decision not to leave his wife and get to safety cost him his life.

After Kondratiev and Anna Richter were married in a church, presumably at the end of 1943 or in early 1944, they had no choice but to go with the occupation forces (now the Nazis' Romanian allies) when they withdrew from the town the following year. In the hands of the Soviet authorities, they would have had a death sentence hanging over them as renegades and enemy collaborators.

Richter could never forgive his mother for her deception and the desertion of his father and him. She robbed him of any sense of security, home, and family life, a tragedy from which he never recovered. But he aimed his most serious charges against Kondratiev. He believed that Anna's future husband was responsible for the anonymous letter sent to the NKVD informing against his father. "He hoped to get rid of my father. Of course, it was easy to denounce other people at this time on the flimsiest pretext." Richter admits, however, that he finds it hard to believe Kondratiev could sink so low. Considering that Beria had a large number of Odessan citizens arrested for no reason other than their German background, the charge seems loosely based. The role of the Soviet *Hamlet* most likely belongs to Richter's imagination.

Von Ketterer changed his name again, this time to Richter. "I never understood how my mother could have let him do this," the son avows. After being interned first in Romania, then in Hungary and Poland, Anna and Sergei succeeded in obtaining a travel and residence permit in Germany, apparently by exploiting contacts from Teofil Richter's fateful time as a teacher of the German consul's children. They wound up in Stuttgart, where von Ketterer, alias Kondratiev, alias Richter, hoped to get a position at a conservatory. When that failed, they settled in the medieval town of Schwäbisch Gmünd (a historic center for gold- and silversmithing), about thirty-five miles east of Stuttgart. It is unclear whether Kondratiev changed his last name when they married in Odessa or later in Germany, but it is clear that he pretended to be Teofil Richter's younger brother. In Germany Richter met people who claimed to have seen his "father" ("you can imagine my anger!"). But Kondratiev's secondary role as Richter's father is presumably the result of a misunderstanding among people, local gossip about the Russian emigrants with the famous son, something that Kondratiev can hardly be blamed for; he was undeniably Richter's stepfather.

At the end of the 1950s, Anna Richter, who had long suffered from asthma, also began to have heart problems, and she was treated by a southern German doctor, Georg Egert. In a slim 1966 book on Richter, Egert quotes his mother about his father's death: "Along with six thousand others from Odessa, he was under suspicion for collaboration with the Germans, and on orders from Beria, he was arrested. He was tortured and later executed. The only concrete charge against my husband was that, in 1927, he had taught at the German consulate in Odessa." (This is a memory lapse or, perhaps, an attempt to tone down the connections with German officials in Odessa. According to Richter, his father taught at the consulate for a number of years "from the beginning of the '30s"; the young Richter played dirges for the consul's guests at a memorial for Hindenburg as late as 1934.)

Egert reports as fact—and again with Anna Richter as a source—that "after her husband's death, she married his younger brother Sergei." The information was later repeated in countless dictionaries, articles, and so on. Anna and Sergei, of course, were in cahoots about the deception (but in her unpublished memoirs, Anna does not refer to her new husband as Teofil's brother). One cannot overlook the possibility that this may have been a ruse to save their lives.

When Richter was asked about his parents in the years after the war, he always answered, "They're both dead." And that is how the story was told until news of mother and son's reunion became fodder for the Western media. But the truth is that Richter was informed about the matter immediately after his mother left Odessa with Sergei Kondratiev. He hid this knowledge not as an act of repression but because of the intensity of his emotions (he withholds the truth even with Monsaingeon and repeats simply: "It was only much later that I understood what had really happened"). Throughout his life, he must have found it unbearable to talk about this painful episode. For Richter, the loss of love was irrevocable.

Among the very few who know the whole story is his lifelong friend Vera ("Vipa") Prokhorova. She relates:

> For Sviet, his mother was the very symbol of love, femininity, and the noble and moral aspects of life. Before our family met Anna Richter, he said: "You will love her." When someone made a good meal, he praised it and then added, "But my *mother* . . . !" He admired her without bounds for her ability to create the ideal domestic atmosphere and fill the home with the joy of living. And for having brought the family through dire straits and war, for having walked across Odessa to care for the (allegedly) invalid Kondratiev, and for having been an unusually good seamstress and thereby helping to support the family. She visited him in Moscow only a month before the war, and he had planned to visit his parents along with his fellow student Tolya Vedernikov on June 23. The German invasion happened the day before, and everything had to be canceled.
>
> We heard from his childhood friend, the pianist Yakov Zak, that his mother did not work as a seamstress during the occupation of Odessa. She feared that it could be viewed as collaboration with the occupying powers and that it could harm him. Before he went to Tbilisi in 1944, he wrote a long letter to his mother, and he hoped to find a courier. After Odessa's liberation, later the same year, I met one of Anna Richter's friends, a Czech woman, who had the impression that Anna was waiting impatiently to receive word from her son. The woman's husband was an engineer, and he was among the first to

go into Odessa after the liberation. He promised to visit Anna Richter, to bring the letter and bring a letter back.

Two weeks later, he returned. I hadn't heard from him at all and looked him up with a premonition. He was working in his garden. "Bad news," he said. "Anna Richter left Odessa with Kondratiev and the occupation troops." I was startled. And we waited in horror and despair for Richter to return from Tbilisi.

A former student of his father's, an older lady who had helped his family during the hunger crisis, brought him the dreadful news. She said of his reaction: "I've never seen anyone change physically in front of my eyes in that way. He was like a snowman who melted. He sank onto the sofa and sobbed deeply for hours." The woman sat with him all night. In the morning, he was silent and pale but collected.

We picked him up at the station. He almost fell out of the train, merely mumbling: "Vipa, I know everything!" It was an inconceivable blow to him, morally, mentally, and physically. For many months, he didn't say a word about it. Later, I met Anna Richter's closest friend in Odessa. She told me that Anna Richter had come to her and said: "I am leaving." The friend was startled: "What are you saying? Slava could be arrested, perhaps shot!" But she wouldn't listen. She was pale and seemed disturbed. She had a small trunk with her. She just repeated, again and again, emptily, "I have to go."

Then almost twenty years went by. Richter knew that his mother was in the West, but any opportunity to search for her was precluded. We do not know whether he felt motivated to do so, but it is unlikely. Not until 1960, and under very special circumstances, did Richter see his mother again. Nor did she apparently make any attempt, during her years in Germany, to contact—or even obtain information about—her son. She told Georg Egert that she happened to hear him play on Radio Moscow and that she wrote to a female acquaintance in West Berlin, asking her to get hold of some of Richter's Soviet recordings through friends in East Berlin.

The American journalist, photographer, and author Paul Moor, who lives in Berlin, was dispatched by *Time* magazine to cover the first International Tchaikovsky Competition in Moscow. He had met Richter in Prague in 1956, had written an article about him, and wanted to meet him again. However, for a correspondent from the West, it was not easy to obtain permission to meet the Soviet legend. When an acquaintance finally brought them together, the pianist immediately invited Moor to visit him the next day (he must have trusted that the KGB would approve). With difficulty, Moor found Richter's apartment, which was next to Nina Dorliak's (they were partly connected). It was decorated with artworks on the walls and two baby grand pianos placed side by side, a German Steinway and an Estonia.

Before Moor left Richter, Steinway's representative for Eastern European countries arrived to inquire about the condition of the pianist's grand piano, and this chance encounter made history. The two men left Richter's apartment at the same time, and on the street the Steinway man told Moor that he knew of a woman in West Berlin, a certain Frau Braun, who had received a letter from Anna Richter. Identifying herself as Richter's mother, Anna Richter had asked Frau Braun whether she could get hold of some of his recordings and send them to her. She understood that the recordings had now become available in East Berlin. This incredible coincidence provided Moor an opportunity to track down the sender. Equipped with the address "Stadtgarten 2," he visited the Richters in Schwäbisch Gmünd later that year with an offer to deliver a letter to the son in Moscow.

Moor visited Anna and Sergei (now Sergius) in a modest apartment that looked like a Sviatoslav Richter museum. Everywhere he looked, the walls were decorated with photographs of Richter from babyhood to his mid-twenties. Moved by this visit, Anna Richter wrote a few lines. The letter shows how conscientiously she avoided saying anything that might cause her son problems if it wound up in the wrong hands. She wrote in German, without a return address, without a family name, and without mentioning to whom the letter was addressed. The brief message begins "Mein über alles Geliebter!" (My most beloved!) and ends with "Deine dich liebende Anna" (Your loving Anna). Anna Richter was sure her son would recognize her handwriting.

Moor wanted to secure a thoroughly reliable courier, and while covering the Chopin competition in Warsaw, he saw Heinrich Neuhaus's name among the competition's list of jurors. Who could be more trusted than Richter's old teacher to make sure the letter was delivered into the right hands? Moor recalls the chain of events with an ironic smile; meeting with Neuhaus in Warsaw actually surprised him. He had been told that the pianist suddenly had fallen ill; Anna's letter, therefore, was still in his office in Berlin. The situation was further complicated by the delay to which almost all postal traffic between West and East was subjected during the Cold War. Fortunately, the letter was sent by air express from West Berlin in time, and the elderly Neuhaus carried out his discreet mission.

When it was clear that Richter had received permission to perform in the West (he played his first concert outside the East Bloc in May 1960 in Finland), Anna decided that she had to see her son again. In 1960 the Russian-American impresario Salomon Hurok engaged Richter for a grand tour of the United States

Anna and Kondratiev listening to a Richter recording in Schwäbisch Gmünd.

from the middle of October to the end of the year; friends and family collected money, and the Richters bought plane tickets to New York. After Richter's debut at Carnegie Hall on October 19, mother and son saw each other again for the first time in more than nineteen years. But the pianist was very dissatisfied with his performance in a program of five Beethoven sonatas ("clusters of wrong notes") and put off the meeting. The next morning, he slipped unseen past his Soviet minders and got into a taxi to Flushing Meadows.

The prodigal son does not remember the reunion as a happy event. He told his friend Vera Prokhorova that this visit was a trial for him, that he almost fainted when he saw Kondratiev again, and that he could barely recognize his mother. "She was like a mask. It was like a dream or some kind of theater." In his conversations with Monsaingeon, he merely refers, with obvious irritation, to Kondratiev's behavior at a farewell party held at the end of his U.S. tour, a party at which the relatives on his mother's side who lived in America were present (none of them were professional musicians): "He spent the whole evening over supper explaining Rimsky Korsakov's treatise on harmony!" And

Prokhorova understands his feelings: "His mother's deception was the great tragedy of his life. He felt that he had lost something he had loved, honored, and respected more than anything else. An ideal. What was left was a sort of phantom. A ghost. No longer a human being. A doll, sweet and smiling, but without a soul."

During this first concert tour of the United States, Richter was constantly surrounded by curious members of the press. The story of a mother and son's reunion after so many years apart soon spread from paper to paper, both in the United States and in Europe.

Richter and Nina Dorliak cultivated their acquaintance with Paul Moor, who, of course, now had a special status in Richter's life, in an unusual way. When Richter (who hated to fly) went to the West, he almost always traveled by train through East Berlin. And it became a tradition to invite the Berliner Moor along and use the time spent waiting at the railway station to exchange news about friends and acquaintances. At the beginning of July 1961, Richter was on his way to London to give three piano recitals and two concerts with the London Symphony Orchestra and the friend of his youth, conductor Kyril Kondrashin, all within eleven days. His program was dizzying: Liszt's two piano concertos (which he also recorded) and the Dvořák concerto, sonatas by Prokofiev, Schumann, and Schubert, Schumann's Fantasy in C Major, and a number of major works by Chopin and Debussy. The concerts were given to full and enthusiastic houses at the Royal Festival Hall and the Royal Albert Hall.

At the East Berlin railway station, Richter and Dorliak told Moor that before leaving Moscow, they had received one-week transit visas from the West German consulate there to go to Schwäbisch Gmünd and visit Anna Richter in her own home. Moor offered to meet them at the station in Stuttgart and drive. At the beginning of August, the couple arrived on the Orient Express from Paris, and, accompanied by a man working for Deutsche Grammophon, they drove to the nearby provincial town. It was Richter's first encounter with his "second homeland." Until then, he had been in Germany only in transit. Moor expected the visit to be emotional, but despite his almost fluent German, Richter behaved like an ordinary tourist, a Soviet citizen in a foreign country.

Schwäbisch Gmünd is a typical, idyllic, medieval German town with only about sixty thousand inhabitants and beautiful surroundings of forest-covered mountains. The city's stately marketplace testifies to a glorious past and attracts many tourists in the summertime. There is a small park, Stadtgarten, in the city's western corner. Anna and Sergei lived on the south side with a view of the well-kept park and a small Rococo pleasure castle. Today the houses on that

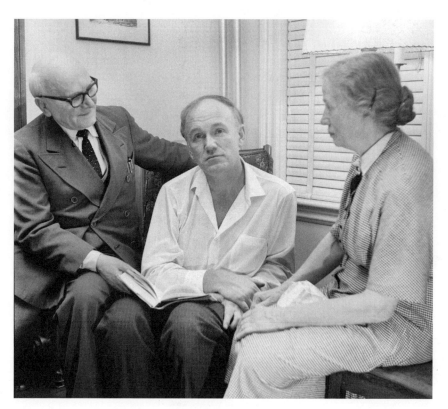

Kondratiev, Richter, and Anna. A picture more telling
about complicated emotions than many words.

side of the road no longer exist, having been replaced by a modern conference
and cultural center of glass and concrete.

Moor recounts that the reunion seemed warm and joyous. It was his impression that Sergei Kondratiev/Richter worshiped Slava. But Richter tells Monsaingeon of the immense anger he felt when he arrived at his mother's residence and discovered the inscription "S. Richter" on the door. Out of respect for his mother, however, he did his best to appear as the loving son.

"My mother had completely changed," Richter tells Monsaingeon. "He [Sergei] had cast a spell on her with his inane chatter, never leaving her alone for a moment, never letting her get a word in edgeways, even when she was with me, but prattling on all the time." The diplomatic Nina Lvovna tried to keep the stepfather busy with small talk, but he never allowed his wife out of sight. His logorrhea clearly got on Richter's nerves. Richter, to get away, frequently disappeared for long walks in the little town (which a tourist can cover fully in a couple of hours). He had an old dream of taking his mother to Wagner's festival house in Bayreuth, and his friend, the record producer Jacques Leiser, from the French division of EMI, arrived with tickets to *Tannhäuser*, one of Teofil's favorite operas. With Nina Dorliak and the others, they attended the work in a production by Wagner's grandson, Wieland Wagner. A photograph taken in front of Wagner's operatic palace shows that, for once, mother and son were able to escape the talkative stepfather. He had remained in Schwäbisch Gmünd. But Richter discovered that when he was finally alone with his mother, she hardly spoke at all.

Leiser used the opportunity to introduce Richter to Dietrich Fischer-Dieskau, who had leased a house in the town for the duration of the festival (a few years later, the two celebrities were to begin a unique collaboration). On the way back to Schwäbisch Gmünd, the group visited the picturesque medieval town of Rothenburg on the Tauber River and the Romantische Strasse. Here, German Romanticism, history, and cultural heritage are distilled in a city that despite heavy bombing during the two world wars remains one of the most impressive medieval towns in the world. Once again, Moor observes that Richter seemed not to have any feeling of *Heimat* (motherland) that usually arises in people of German origin. Nothing indicates that he identified with the German people or their history. The little town's idyllic charm did attract him later, however, as attested by several vacation greetings from him or Nina Dorliak written on stationery provided by the local hotel Eisenhut. Moor also notes that Richter was completely uninterested in current affairs; he left Germany just as Walther Ulbricht ordered the Berlin Wall to be built, without considering it for one moment.

The tension in the whole situation became clear to Moor on August 12, 1961, while he was putting Slava and Nina on the train in Stuttgart, when he obtained Richter's permission to provide an account of the events of the previous week, namely the story of an affectionate mother and a "lost" son who are reunited. "Yes. But on one condition," Richter demanded. "Nothing about emotions. For there are none!" Might Richter's ambivalent relationship to his German origin also be the cause of this heartbreak? Not until December 1971, in Bonn, did he give his first recital in Germany.

He paid his second visit to Schwäbisch Gmünd in December 1962 between two concerts in Paris, less than four months before Anna's Richter's death. His mother was hospitalized; on April 13, a few months later, she died of a heart attack. But he had to travel back to the French capital early the next morning, and his mother begged Sergei not to talk too much and for too long. "Promise me that you'll let him go to bed no later than one-thirty." Richter narrates: "But he twittered on until six in the morning. I was flat out and had long since stopped listening, but he still went on and on. Always the same rubbish that I'd

Anna and Kondratiev waving goodbye to Nina and Slava
at the Stuttgart railway station.

heard a thousand times before. Music, current events. On and on. A complete
maniac" (one wonders why the world-famous musician did not simply go to
bed when he needed to).

Richter had seen the despised Sergei earlier in the year, on the day he was
to perform for the first time in the most legendary of music capitals, Vienna.
He had spent the entire day traveling from Florence, was exhausted, and had a
demanding program in front of him. Sergei Kondratiev, alias Sergius Richter,
showed up unannounced with Nina Dorliak to attend the concert. And Kondratiev told him that his mother was seriously ill, that she had been hospitalized after a series of heart attacks, and that there might be reason to fear for
her life. Richter hated him for delivering this information in passing, only a few
hours before an important concert. His solo concert of Schumann, Chopin,
Debussy, and Scriabin was not a success—"a disaster," according to Richter.
So he cannot have been entirely without feelings for his mother. And Vienna's
feared critics did not indulge him. *"Abschied von der Legende* [Farewell of the
Legend]," he read in the newspaper.

When Richter and Nina Dorliak attended the Salzburg Festival with Paul
Moor a few years later, Kondratiev suddenly showed up once again, uninvited
and unannounced. But now Richter refused to see him. Kondratiev could no

longer enjoy his position as the stepfather of a world celebrity. Thus, his role in the Richter case was definitively played out. He died in 1973.

Concerning the subject of homosexuality, Moor mentions that Richter had a lover, an Austrian actor who was with him and Nina Lvovna during this trip to Salzburg. "We all stayed in a hotel on the outskirts of the city. It was apparent they were lovers; none of them hid anything. Richter had met the actor when he first performed in Vienna. When I met him, he had already visited Richter in Moscow, installed at a hotel. When you were together with them, they seemed like three close friends!"

On April 11, 1963, Richter recorded Schubert's *Wanderer* Fantasy for EMI in Paris. The Soviet government now felt so secure about his ties to his home country that he was allowed to travel without his "secretary," that is, his shadow. A few days later he attended his mother's funeral in Schwäbisch Gmünd accompanied only by the record producer Jacques Leiser. Nina Dorliak was prevented from attending and had called to ask whether Leiser could accompany Richter. The pianist was not dressed in mourning clothes. Leiser relates that he was in a very bad mood, more irritated than grieving. At the funeral, Kondratiev played a prelude on the organ, and Richter hissed at Leiser, "How can anybody play so unmusically?" To his friend Vera Prokhorova, he wrote: "My mother died for me a long time ago. I can't feel anything. She has disappeared. She was just a mask." The betrayal could never be atoned for.

A clip in Monsaingeon's film captured the event. In it, Richter seems almost absent.

Later, Richter never spoke about his mother to anyone, except occasionally to Prokhorova and his aunt Dagmar. "Our relationship was based on perfect confidence," she underscores. And she attributes to him the idea that his mother may have been subjected to some form of hypnosis, that she suffered from an unconscious need to follow, like a rat behind the Pied Piper of Hamelin. "Perhaps he was just trying to find some sort of comfort. But he referred to a train trip in his childhood in which he saw his mother follow a man who had looked at her long and intensely, and she almost got off at the wrong station, as if she didn't see or hear anything. Perhaps it was a sort of comfort."

A Pianist on the World Stage

For a long time, it seems, life in Moscow fulfilled in most respects the expectations young Slava Richter had about life, despite his lifelong compulsion to experience new things. At the Neuhauses, he met many of the most significant artists of the day, and he hungrily snapped up the city's numerous cultural opportunities. When he arrived in Moscow in 1937, Stanislavsky and Nemirovich-Danchenko, two of the Russian theater's most significant figures, still worked at the famous Art Theater (MCHAT), which they had founded in 1898. Stanislavsky died in 1938, but by then he and his colleague had established an opera house that became a required alternative to the tradition-bound Bolshoi. Here, the seventy-nine-year-old Nemirovich-Danchenko staged the Moscow premiere of Shostakovich's *Lady Macbeth*. And here, the theater-loving pianist saw new operas, such as Prokofiev's *Semyon Kotko* (before the commissars called it "incomprehensible" and demanded it be closed after a few performances). At the Art Theater, he attended not only works by Pushkin, Chekhov, Turgenev, and Gogol, but also many dramas by Shakespeare and Beaumarchais' *The Marriage of Figaro*. He saw Chekhov's widow, the actress Olga Knipper, in Chekhov's *The Cherry Orchard* and *The Seagull* and became close friends with her. And, of course, he saw new Soviet-proletarian drama, the "socialist realism" that Stalin's self-chosen cultural adviser, the aging poet Maxim Gorky, had advocated. Not everything was equally good, he remembers, "but when staged by Stanislavsky and Nemirovich-Danchenko, practically anything made an impression."

On the whole, the ever more celebrated Soviet musician who in 1949 received the Stalin Prize and in 1952 the "People's Artist" prize did not seem obsessed by dreams of international fame. After 1948 he began to give concerts outside Moscow more frequently, alone or with Nina Dorliak—in the Baltic countries or in Czechoslovakia. The first foreign capital he visited was Prague ("along with Venice, Paris, and Vienna, one of my favorite cities"). At that time, the Baltics were a part of the Soviet Union. But Moscow was the magnetic pole of his activities, and the vast majority of his concerts took place there.

After 1953 foreign concert tours became ever more frequent. He went on a concert tour of China (and toured there again in 1957), and in 1954 he spent a month in Hungary, gave a series of concerts in Budapest, played another series of concerts in Prague, and the next year had Poland and Romania on his travel calendar. In the summer of 1956, he toured Czechoslovakia. In 1957 he curtailed his concert activities significantly, but in February 1958 he once again returned to Hungary and added Bulgaria to the list; at a concert in Sofia on February 24, he played Mussorgsky's *Pictures at an Exhibition*, and despite a flu epidemic (the audience sounds as if it is suffering collectively) and antiquated technology, the radio recording from this concert has achieved cult status. In Budapest in October 1958, he played Bartók's Second Piano Concerto for the first time. In 1959 Moscow almost disappeared, temporarily, from his concert calendar, and in 1960 his foreign activities exploded when he finally got the green light to perform in the West. But he continued to give concerts in the Eastern Bloc countries outside the Soviet Union. In the 1960s and 1970s, for example, he gave a concert at least every other year in Budapest and sometimes in other Hungarian cities.

During the 1950s a long series of his Moscow concerts were recorded by Russian radio and were released on numerous records, issued primarily by the state company Melodiya. At least a third of these radio recordings, however, are still unavailable for general listeners.

Stalin's death was a historic turning point. Everyone realized that an era had come to an end, but no one had any idea whether this gave reason for hope or fear. The political situation in the USSR changed slowly but perceptibly. Stalin left a political power vacuum behind, and a bitter power struggle ensued. Georgy Malenkov was a plausible successor, but he was soon replaced by Nikolai Bulganin. The head of security, the executioner Lavrenty Beria, the second most powerful man in the Kremlin since 1938, proposed a program of de-Stalinization. But Nikita Khrushchev's influence grew, and in December 1953 he had Beria sentenced and executed. In February 1956 the Twentieth Party Congress became yet another dramatic turning point: in a seven-hour speech (which was not approved in advance by the Central Committee), Khrushchev boldly criticized Stalin's regime of terror and warned against the cult of personality of which Beria more than anyone had been the architect. Of course, everyone knew of Stalin's despotism, but to criticize him from the speaker's chair of the Party was unheard of. In the intellectual circles, poets such as Yevgeni Yevtushenko and Ilya Ehrenburg sensed a "thaw" (the word is the title of a novella by Ehrenburg), and for many of them, Khrushchev's speech was an eye-opener. It loudly proclaimed that Stalin's crime had not merely been a "personality cult" but torture, concentration camps, and mass murder.

Formally, Bulganin's leadership continued until 1958, but Khrushchev was the de facto leader. He removed, among others, the reinstated foreign minister Molotov in 1957. In the foreign policy arena, Khrushchev had his hands full in the following years. The Central Committee had to deal with demonstrations in Poland, resistance in Hungary, a breach with China and Albania, the Lumumba crisis in the Congo, the Berlin conflict (which, in 1961, led to the erection of the Berlin Wall), and a confrontation with President John F. Kennedy, the Cuban missile crisis in October 1962. But this hectic activity helped soften the domestic political climate. Critics of the system were still condemned, but the vague charges, cursory civil procedures, and ad hoc executions of the Stalin years were gone. A rural, bald as an egg, rotund, outgoing, and cheerful man, a "popular" politician who did not compel reverence or fear, had replaced the distant divinity with a sinister mustache. But Khrushchev's appearance could be deceiving. Behind his joviality and spontaneous outbursts hid a cunning and coldly calculating politician. When Imre Nagy introduced a government without a Communist majority in Budapest, promised free elections, and wanted to pull out of the Warsaw Pact, Khrushchev's reaction gave no indication that the Soviet iron fist had loosened its grip. In early November 1956, Soviet tanks moved into the streets of Budapest. The revolt cost twenty thousand Hungarian lives, ten times as many fled to the West, and Nagy was executed.

In March 1957 yet another Composers' Congress was held, now with the politician Shepilov in charge, and again with the maneuverable Tikhon Khrennikov on the sidelines. Shepilov, however, had neither Zhdanov's political power nor his authority; he acted as a sort of mailman between the Central Committee and the Composers' Union and soon disappeared again. In the years before his fall in 1964, Khrushchev himself formulated all official cultural and political guidelines. Of course, he de-Stalinized the country and admitted that Stalin had made serious mistakes, but he warned anyone "who attempts to use these mistakes as a shield against the control of literature and art by the Party and the State." Stalinist cultural ideology remained intact.

On October 4, 1957, the Soviet Union launched the *Sputnik* satellite, the first man-made object in space, and about three years later, Yuri Gagarin was the first human being sent into orbit around the earth. The United States was caught napping, and the space race began. The relationship between the superpowers developed into a fierce battle for prestige and leadership, with technology, sports, and music as the preferred battlegrounds.

In early 1958, the United States and the USSR entered into an agreement for a mutual cultural exchange. In May, Eugene Ormandy visited the Soviet Union with his Philadelphia Orchestra; as mentioned, he accompanied Richter in Prokofiev's Fifth, and he encouraged then Soviet minister of culture Nikolai Mikhailov to give the West the opportunity to become acquainted with the pianist, whom many in the West had heard of but almost no one had actually heard. In June, Leopold Stokowski became the first American conductor to lead Soviet orchestras in Moscow and Kiev in a program that, among other works, included Samuel Barber's *Adagio for Strings*. This melancholy, gently flowing piece — the slow movement of a string quartet, in fact — was received with thundering applause and had to be given *da capo* (even today the piece is something of a popular icon, used in countless movies). In a few years the Soviet musical audience had become acquainted with some of the United States' best conductors and orchestras, among them Charles Munch with the Boston Symphony Orchestra and the New York Philharmonic under Leonard Bernstein.

In the spring of 1958, the first International Tchaikovsky Competition was held in Moscow, a world event that was then repeated every fourth year. A Russian violinist won the violin competition. But competitions are unpredictable; the piano competition was sensationally won by a young pianist from Texas, the charismatic Van Cliburn. Despite his aversion to any form of competition, Richter served as a jury member (under the chairmanship of his colleague Gilels). Neuhaus was also on the jury, and he remarked afterward about the winner: "I don't particularly like his Chopin. But I like *him*." Cliburn had studied at Juilliard in New York with the legendary Rosina Lhévinne, who was originally from St. Petersburg. He was viewed as a continuation of the Russian piano traditions, and the tall, boyish, charming, modest, and somewhat shy pianist won everyone's heart. Richter says, "He was miles better than any of the others. By giving a zero mark to all but three of the other candidates, I'd decided to eliminate the others and leave only him. The public had in any case fallen madly in love with Van Cliburn, and they were ecstatic when he won." The persistent story that Richter awarded Cliburn 100 points out of a possible 10 is a fabrication. His ballots still exist, and they show that he awarded the three other participants 15, 23, and 24 points. To Van Cliburn, he gave 25 out of a possible 25.

The young American became an idol in the USSR; dozens of Russian women wrote poems and love letters to him. And in his homeland he was welcomed with a shower of confetti on Broadway, a ticker-tape parade on the scale of Lindbergh's in 1927. As Boris Schwarz remarks in his indispensable research on Soviet music and musical life, Cliburn may have been more instrumental in the thaw and "international understanding" that occurred than high diplomacy ever was. The LP of Tchaikovsky's First Piano Concerto, which Cliburn recorded with Kyril Kondrashin (as part of the prize), became a common household object in the United States, an indispensable icon in every educated home and a megasuccess for RCA. Four years later Van Cliburn was ready with a piano competition in *his* name (in Fort Worth, Texas), and the mutual cultural exchange continued; the first-prize winner was Neuhaus's student Radu Lupu. At the end of the 1970s, Cliburn halted his concert activities for a number of years, and even though he resumed his career in 1989 with a comprehensive tour of the USSR and received great attention from the press, he only rarely appeared on the concert stage. Nevertheless, his status as the most famous American pianist of the twentieth century seems uncontested.

In 1955 Emil Gilels became the first Soviet musician to perform in the United States after the Iron Curtain came down. The financially powerful American impresario Sol (Salomon) Hurok sponsored the tour. Hurok was Russian born, had close ties to the USSR, and had previously collaborated with the state concert agency Goskoncert in representing Soviet musicians in the United States. Gilels's performance of Tchaikovsky's perennial First Piano Concerto created huge headlines. He recorded the concerto with Fritz Reiner and later returned again and again to North America. Shortly after, David Oistrakh amazed the Americans with samples of Soviet interpretive art and virtuosity, followed by Mstislav Rostropovich and violinist Leonid Kogan. Their tours were triumphs, and people had their eyes opened to the fact that the Soviet educational system had not only preserved the proud Russian musical traditions but had developed a uniquely broad range of musicians at the highest level. Richter's generation speaks for itself. But there was more tangible proof. In a speech to the Party Congress in 1961, the new minister of culture, Ekaterina ("Madame") Furtseva, reported that "in the last five years, 39 international musical competitions have been held. Soviet musicians were awarded 27 first prizes and 35 second and third prizes at these competitions."

Her pride was palpable, and between the lines she clearly implied that the prizes were won by the "system," not by a series of highly gifted individuals!

Emil Gilels's legendary remark (cited again and again) when he was praised for his playing in the United States ("wait until you hear Richter!") showed respect for a colleague, but was, in the mouth of a pianist of such colossal status and with such a hypersensitive ego, probably a politically correct gesture aimed at the Soviet home audience. In any case, the anecdote's origin cannot be determined with any certainty; some attribute it to the conductor Eugene Ormandy. Sol Hurok now went to Moscow every year to negotiate North American tours with Soviet musicians. And rumor had it that every time he asked for Richter, but every year he was told that Richter was indisposed!

When Paul Moor visited Richter in his apartment during the 1958 Tchaikovsky competition, the pianist admitted that jury work was pure torture for him — "I never sat on a jury before, and I never want to do it again!" But Moor's inevitable questions about when he would be willing to perform in Western Europe or in the United States just elicited that innocently naughty smile and the teasing turn of the head with which Richter's friends were familiar: "But I have to be invited first!" Moor was thunderstruck. Western concert organizers would stand in line to book Richter. But the pianist left him in no doubt that the subject was exhausted: "That sort of thing is a matter for the Ministry of Culture." And the semiofficial Soviet music establishment routinely repeated the rumor of Richter's fragile health. The health risk, it was said, would be too great if he traveled too far from Moscow's climate and the city's doctors. But in Moscow, Moor met a young Chinese violinist who enthusiastically told him about Richter's sensational success in China the year before. And China is significantly farther from Moscow than London, Paris, or New York.

Over the long run, the situation had become politically untenable. The longer people waited, the more their curiosity increased and myths flourished. Spurred by the new, energetic minister of culture Furtseva, Khrushchev himself got involved, and after some hesitation, it was agreed, in connection with a renegotiation of the cultural exchange agreement, that Richter, too, should be heard in the United States (some sources hint that the agreement included an out-and-out trade for American recording know-how and German-made equipment). Khrushchev's policy to reach out to the West presumably also played a role. In September 1959 Khrushchev made his historic visit to the United States; for the first time ever, a Soviet head of state visited the other superpower, and he was received with enthusiasm and applause. Soviet authorities decided to test Richter's loyalty and allow him to perform in the neighboring country of Finland. Presumably, they considered Finland safe, a country that would hardly run the political risk of granting Richter a resident's permit.

Then, in May 1960, Richter had what amounts to a dress rehearsal of his tour to the "golden West" with three recitals in Finland, two in Helsinki, and one in Turku. On the program were sonatas by Beethoven. His first historic concert outside the Eastern Bloc took place at the Sibelius Academy in Helsinki on May 10, and a Finnish critic commented: "Strange that a Communist country should breed the era's most arrogant individual instrumentalist." Among those who attended the concerts from abroad were Jacques Leiser, a French record producer and artistic agent at the French department of the EMI/HMV

Jacques Leiser, Richter's friend and collaborator for more than thirty years, 2006.

company. He was to become a close friend of Richter and played an important role in his career in the West. About the beginning of this friendship, Leiser relates:

In Prague in the late fifties, I discovered a rather unknown recording with him of the Schumann *Fantasiestücke*, opus 12, made by DGG. That was before he was known in the West. And I just fell apart, I was paralyzed, his playing knocked me out. At the time, I was working as a record producer and artistic representative for EMI. I went regularly to London, and I mentioned this recording to the HMV (EMI) artistic director, who had never heard of Richter. A conservative man, he saw no reason to hurry. Richter would come to Europe, he could wait. I feared that would be too late, and suggested that they should send me to Moscow to track down Richter. He looked at me as if I suggested they send me to the moon!

Then I went for the 1960 Chopin competition in Warsaw. I signed up Pollini, and I met Neuhaus, who was on the jury. Neuhaus spoke fluent French, and he tipped me off about Richter's upcoming concert in Helsinki. That concert was not publicized, the authorities were worried. Richter had no children and was not a member of the Party. They thought he might escape to the West. I stormed back to London with this news. They did not have to send me to Moscow, Helsinki would do. But Walter Legge, the principal record producer, heard about this. He was quite domineering, he had antennas all over, he was going to go. He was the director, I did not have such authority. But fortunately the annual meeting of all the representatives of the EMI took place during the same period, he [Legge] had to stay in London. So I went.

Leiser wanted to be sure of getting hold of Richter before the concert in Helsinki. But where was Richter? Telephone calls to the city's larger hotels produced no results. Rumor had it that he was staying at the Russian embassy for "security reasons." But the embassy had access only to a rather dilapidated piano. It seemed likely that he would practice at the Sibelius Academy.

There were countless practice rooms, and I simply had to open every single door and say "excuse me, I am sorry" until I found Richter. He immediately said: "*Kommen sie herein* [Come in]." I presented myself as representing EMI, the company which recorded Rachmaninov and Shalyapin, and without any formalities I told him bluntly that we wanted to record him. He just said: "*Mit grosse Freude* [With great pleasure]." During the concert on the next day, I spotted the Phillips people in the hall. They were the arch-competitor, but later we, in fact, collaborated on Richter recordings in Italy. I produced, and they provided the equipment. A unique situation! A German journalist approached Richter and wanted an interview. But Richter simply answered: "You attended my recital. That's my interview!"

The pianist put all the Soviets' worries to shame; he returned to Moscow as planned by train and without any side trips. The idea of defecting had hardly occurred to him. And there is no indication that he ever considered emigrating. He was an inexhaustibly restless traveler and became a veritable globetrotter, but throughout his life he felt like a Soviet citizen who belonged in Moscow. This was true even later in life, when he spent only a few weeks a year there. Like most people, he loved his homeland just the way it was, for good or ill. Memories, feelings, friends, colleagues, and his "own" audience bound him to a city that, for him, had no semblance to the gloomy image the Western media drew. This was a Moscow whose traditions, habits, art, and culture meant for him what the fairy-tale writer Hans Christian Andersen—also a dedicated traveler—expressed when he wrote of Denmark, "Here I have my roots, from here my world extends."

Shortly afterward, Sol Hurok issued a press release: "The Ministry of Culture in Moscow has just telegraphically confirmed that Sviatoslav Richter will spend ten weeks as a guest artist in America." The road to the Promised Land lay open. But Richter was unenthusiastic: "I will perform in Western Europe with pleasure, but I have no need to travel to America." By a Freudian slip, he almost missed the train, "but no such luck!" There was no way around it. Via Paris, Richter went by train to Le Havre in Normandy, and from there he continued by the steamship *Queen Mary* to New York. He traveled by plane only when no other means of transportation was available. "I don't smoke, I don't drink, and I don't fly," he liked to say. But this was hardly more than a guiding principle.

Richter did fly when there was no way to avoid it, he sometimes smoked ciga-
rettes (often by holding them between thumb and forefinger), and he drank
with pleasure and insight; at times he even imbibed vodka in the energetic way
that is a well-known part of the Russian lifestyle.

On the trip, he was escorted by two officials, guards, or "gorillas," as they
were secretly known among Soviet musicians; they are called "chauffeurs" or
"secretaries" in the travel documents. Richter understood that these people
were only doing their job. They were helpful in unfamiliar, foreign climes, but
they had to make sure he did not defect. And he admits that their very presence
could be tiresome. It sometimes happened that he had to endure a bawling-
out like a defiant schoolboy when he succeeded in getting away for hours at a
time, as on one of his cherished walking tours or while sightseeing at art museums or architectural sights that interested him. Richter gradually grew used
to being under surveillance on his trips, but "unlike what people may think,
I'm not entirely insensitive. I hated the constant pressure. By withdrawing into
myself, however, I was able to struggle against my disgust."

His negative, prejudiced expectations of the United States would soon become
a self-fulfilling prophecy. He believed that the United States is a "banal place."
"American orchestras are of the very first rank, as are its art galleries and cock-
tails," but he detested the noise, the advertisements, the "cheap" culture, and
the American version of English (a language he did not speak). His antipathy
toward a country he knew nothing about in advance, his insistence on seeing
everything in black and white, may seem a bit comical. But many Western European intellectuals in exile from Nazism had similar problems with seeing this
"confounded mass society" from anything but their own cultural standpoint.
Even a thinker such as the philosopher and sociologist Theodor W. Adorno
rejected American culture in advance. His feeling of alienation made him incapable of seeing culture as anything other than industry: jazz, fashion, Mickey
Mouse, and chewing gum.

Richter also assesses his artistic efforts in the United States negatively: "I played
poorly!" However, the reason was hardly the American way of life, but rather the
fact that he was "terribly nervous and in a state of almost permanent panic."
His stage fright is understandable when one realizes that he had to live up to
the legend created by rumor and hearsay. And any pianist who steps into Carnegie Hall (which Tchaikovsky himself had inaugurated in 1891) hears the echo
of piano giants who performed there over time: Paderewski, Rachmaninov,
Hofmann, Horowitz, Rubinstein, and so on. His cousin Fritz Reincke recalls
that for days before his first concert, he could neither eat nor sleep. Richter

thought that it may have had to do with the fact that, suddenly, he could freely choose the piano he wanted to play. He was quite unused to such choices and the ruminations that freedom of choice could bring with it. "You should play on whichever piano happens to be in the hall, as though fate intended it so. Everything then becomes much easier from a psychological point of view."

It is indeed difficult to know from recordings of the concerts what annoyed him so intensely. His six October concerts at Carnegie Hall can be heard on LPS from CBS/Sony, but they are difficult to procure, are sold in used-record stores for monstrous sums, and leave much to be desired in terms of their sound technology. Only recently have they been transferred to CD by Doremi, Legendary Records (as volume 10 in the series Sviatoslav Richter Archives). This story is yet another labyrinthine Richter fable with elements of incompetence, noncooperation, and Soviet cultural politics.

At the end of the 1950s, Goskoncert established a company that managed all recording rights and negotiated contracts (under the name of Mesdunarodnaya Kniga, or "International Book"). Goskoncert had contracted with the American company Columbia Artists when Emil Gilels and David Oistrakh came to the United States as the first Russian musicians. But Sol Hurok took over that market.

At that point, after a career at Columbia Artists as, among other things, tour manager for Jascha Heifetz, Schuyler Chapin was head of Columbia Masterworks (Columbia Records, a part of CBS). He read in the *New York Times* that the storied Richter was finally coming to the United States, represented by Hurok's agency. Hurok had a general agreement with RCA Victor, the competitor, but Chapin saw the opportunity for his own company to contract directly with Mesdunarodnaya Kniga to record and issue Richter's New York concerts. He succeeded in securing the rights, but the Russians demanded a cash advance of no less than $65,000, a gigantic sum in 1960.

Nevertheless, a young, ambitious American whom the Russian company had made coresponsible for the concerts in New York (a charlatan, according to Chapin) insisted on organizing the recordings himself. As a result, a stagehand was given the task of operating the standard equipment at his disposal, entirely without the record company's technology and practical know-how, and the result was technically unsatisfactory. Chapin doubted that Richter wanted the recordings to be made public. Nevertheless, a telegram from the Soviet embassy in Washington, ostensibly from Richter himself, gave the green light. But Chapin suspected that something was wrong (why the embassy? why a telegram? why not a phone call from the pianist himself?) and asked violinist Isaac Stern, an acquaintance of Richter, to investigate the matter discreetly.

"Isaac came back to me with a letter from Richter, in Russian," Chapin says in New York. "He wrote that he had been nervous, that he was very dissatisfied with his playing." Even though it is unlikely that he had heard the tapes, Richter begged Chapin not to disseminate the recordings.

Schuyler Chapin—whose success and experience in the music industry are legendary (few, if any, have worked so closely with so many of music's most prominent names: Heifetz, Horowitz, Stravinsky, Gould, Cliburn, Stern, Stokowski, Ormandy, Bernstein, Kubelik, Szell, and so on)—had to go to the chairman of the board and acknowledge that even though a shocking amount of money would presumably be lost, it would be morally irresponsible to issue the recordings. "It was an episode that made me feel very guilty. A lesson," he admits with an annoyed grimace. "Later I never tried again to play Mr. Know-it-all!"

A couple of LPs were already in print, but it was Chapin's impression that the project had been called off. Even today he cannot explain how the recordings got on the market (and later commanded sky-high prices among collectors). Fortunately, the tour's final Carnegie Hall concert, on the day after Christmas, was soon made available on a good recording from RCA Victor (and now on two CDs with the title *Richter Rediscovered*).

The pianist was extremely dissatisfied, although he in no way disappointed the wildly exorbitant expectations of the audience or the critics. He was even annoyed at the expectations themselves. He believed that when newspapers, television, and hype trumpeted a particular expectation, the experience lost some of its freshness. People were prevented from listening freely. A year later, in London, the influential critic Peter Heyworth agreed with him; it was absurd that he had to walk around "with the sign *World's Greatest Pianist* hanging around his neck." From the beginning, Hurok had branded Richter as the "greatest pianist of the century."

Richter, the secretive "super-Gilels," the storied artistic legend, the mysterious private person who was a political topic of conversation, suddenly could be seen and heard in the land of the free. "A living enigma is good advertising," wrote the German critic Joachim Kaiser with an irony that ignores the fact that Richter was always an extremely private person; for example, he almost never gave interviews, either in the West or in the East. But it is evident that the media-created smokescreen was a welcome hiding place for Richter's Schumann-like evasive and self-protective personality, and that he was content with the role of inscrutable sphinx.

Joachim Kaiser was also the author of the book *Great Pianists of Our Time*, a standard work that has achieved the status of a Bible of the piano or "the

Richter, in a photo by his cousin Walter Moskalew, practicing Tchaikovsky
on an upright piano during his first visit to the States . . .

pianist's Michelin." He was not in attendance at Carnegie Hall but heard
the recordings and wrote about a "high point" in the first concert, on October 19—Richter's interpretation of Beethoven's *Appassionata*: "The beginning
in *pianissimo* had magic, powerful outbursts came with wild abandon. Richter began the finale in a fantastic, exaggerated quick tempo. His tempo was so
fast that he could hardly have played the *presto* of the conclusion faster. The
whole piece became a single *accelerando*." But as anyone with access to the
recording can attest, this is wrong. Richter plays quickly, but not faster than
many of his colleagues (Beethoven stipulates *Allegro, ma non troppo*—"not too
quickly"). He plays the coda's ecstatic *presto* at least a third faster—so quickly
that it led to a couple of the mistakes that annoyed him so immensely. But the
implication that Richter plays faster and faster—"runs away"—is nonsense;
the movement has an inexorable but never forced stringency and razor-sharp
precision.

... and looking satisfied.

Richter's U.S. success was in the bag, "entirely undeserved," as he believed. In newspapers from New York to Washington, Chicago, Boston, Philadelphia, Montreal, Detroit, and many other cities he visited, he saw himself described as a "member of the royal family of pianists" and the greatest pianist of his time: "For years, we'd expected the Russian pianist who would overshadow everyone else"; "Richter is the best I have ever heard"; "It's true! He is the pinnacle of the world's pianists." The *New York Times* saw a veritable Caesar of the piano ("he came, he saw, and he conquered"), and the paper's feared critic Harold C. Schonberg wrote, "It is without doubt the most singular triumph this writer has ever witnessed." *Newsweek* wrote expansively of his tour as "the legend of an incredible personal triumph." And the magazine added that even the critics who looked upon Richter's subjectivity with skepticism "capitulated unconditionally to the poetic spirituality and technical boldness of his playing."

Cousin Walter and Richter. Practicing is over.

But Richter was not for sale; he could not be bought by the endless curtain calls, flowers, or cries of bravo, much less the effusive praise of reviewers. "They understand nothing!" he claimed. Because he felt he did not deserve their superlatives, these were without value to him. Only twice in his later life, in 1965 and in 1970, did he return to the "banal" United States, each time with thundering success.

His first concert in the United States took place in Chicago, "the only American city I like," he wrote to a friend; in his autobiography, Yehudi Menuhin mentions that in Richter's opinion the city was possessed of an unpredictability he always wanted from life, "a feeling that every time I left the hotel, *anything* could happen." With Erich Leinsdorf and the city's eminent orchestra, he played Brahms's Second Piano Concerto—a work that, with its shifts between weighty, powerful gestures and gentle emotion, almost became a trademark for him in the 1950s and 1960s. And after the concert, the work was recorded for RCA. But Richter felt stressed by Leinsdorf's quick tempos: "one of my worst records, even though people still praise it to the skies. I can't bear it. . . . *A tempo di allegretto*—you bet! Leinsdorf took it at an *allegro*, constantly pressing ahead."

It may be true that Leinsdorf, also in the first movement, conducts more quickly than the music's weight calls for. But Richter's interpretation seems anything but a failure, and the American record audience disagreed with him. For many, this recording became a sort of talisman. It achieved the status of a commercial hit, almost in the same class as the twenty-two-year-old Glenn Gould's *Goldberg Variations* a few years earlier; for months, it was at the top of the sales charts.

Richter did not remember Leonard Bernstein fondly either. On December 18, they performed Liszt's Concerto in A Major and Tchaikovsky's First with the New York Philharmonic. But Bernstein kept pushing the tempo forward in Tchaikovsky, and Richter felt compelled to follow him. "Half the time he was up in the air," Richter says ironically (Bernstein was known for dancing and hopping on the podium).

Kurt Sanderling, one of his favorite conductors, has a simple explanation for his annoyance:

> Richter often said, "I'm very dependent on conductors. If they do things I don't like, I unfortunately do the same thing myself." He needed conductors with whom he was on a wavelength. We have played a lot together, he liked to play with me. The only time I could not follow what he was getting at was in Rachmaninov's Second Concerto. He admitted that it was a work he played a bit crazily. He was usually very faithful to the score. He played very strictly, but in this work he played virtually every measure with a different rhythmic sense, and I couldn't follow. We were technically together, but not musically. But again and again we have had a splendid collaboration.

Yet, the ten weeks in the United States left Richter with some pleasant memories as well. The variable American landscape impressed him during the long car trips between urban areas. And his encounters with other important musicians gave him pleasure—at least occasionally, as with Vladimir Horowitz and Arthur Rubinstein, the most admired and highest paid instrumentalists of their day. Both had long been American citizens (and both were used to the label "world's greatest pianist"). It was also true of Eugene Ormandy, who, on the evening he played the Brahms concerto and Dvořák's solitary, rarely heard concerto, ingenuously asked, "Slava, why don't you stay here with us, in America?" (When the pianist Rudolf Serkin offered to get Richter an apartment in New York, he replied, "My countrymen value you highly; if you wish to leave the United States, I can find an apartment in Moscow for you in less than fifteen minutes!") And it was particularly true of the admired head of the Boston Symphony Orchestra, Charles Munch, who conducted the Brahms concerto and Beethoven's Piano Concerto in C Major. At the rehearsal, Richter was so moved by the wonderful accompaniment that he spontaneously kissed the maestro's hand. His "secretary" was appalled. "How can a Soviet artist sink so low as to kiss the hand of a foreign conductor?"

When, according to reliable sources, the story of the reunion of mother and son filled the papers, the same state-authorized traveling companion, a certain Byelotserkovsky, took the opportunity to ask whether he would like his father to be "rehabilitated" (as mentioned, Khrushchev had instigated an extensive rehabilitation program of Stalin's victims). Richter replied, "How can you rehabilitate him when he is innocent?" Nevertheless, the rehabilitation occurred in 1962 (an unconfirmed story claims that Khrushchev himself contacted Richter and obtained the same answer). Moreover, Minister for Culture Furtseva authorized Byelotserkovsky to invite Anna and Sergei Richter to visit the USSR, with a view toward settling there. But the couple contented themselves with a promise to think it over. Alfred von Ketterer, alias Sergei/Sergius Kondratiev/ Richter, had many reasons to ignore the invitation.

In the USSR, the idea of the trinity of the working class, the peasant collectives, and intellectuals to secure the continued development of communism and thus the "creative possibilities and talents of all humanity" once again got wind in its sails. Artists began to breathe more easily. However, the case of Boris Pasternak's great epic novel *Doctor Zhivago* constituted a tremendous setback. The long-criticized Pasternak had given up trying to get a Soviet publisher to issue his book, but he had many admirers outside the Soviet Union. He sent the novel, chapter by chapter, to the West. In 1957 the book came out in Italian and, a year later, in English, French, and German. It created a sensation. However, in Pasternak's homeland, this was seen as treason. When Pasternak became the first Soviet writer to receive the Nobel Prize for Literature in October 1958, he first telegraphed his thanks the Swedish Nobel Committee but was then subjected to colossal political, collegial, and public pressure. Although no one had read the book (his depiction of the revolutionary period contained nothing treasonous), he was called "Judas" and a "calculating scribbler" and was threatened repeatedly with banishment. Under pressure, he refused the prize, which led to tremendous international condemnation of the Soviet government. Pasternak was thrown out of the Writers' Union, and he had to write an apology for *Pravda*, in which, for all practical purposes, he renounced his book. The novel had to wait more than thirty years for a translation into Russian. This affair resulted in a considerable cooling of the cultural thaw, which turned out to be of short duration. Despite his critique of the "cult of personality," Khrushchev soon began to make all the decisions himself.

We can only guess why Richter had to wait longer than most of his colleagues to obtain a travel permit. There is no doubt that he was reticent. As a cultural export article, he was clearly as well suited as anyone. Yet the government may have believed that with his family in Germany (and, from the mid-1950s, also in the United States), the risk of defection was too great. And since he had no children, parents, or a wife, there were no obvious "hostages" the KGB could use as collateral for his return. Moreover, his homosexuality (of which the authorities were of course aware) and his outspoken defense of Pasternak (whom he had met several times with Neuhaus) may have had a certain dilatory effect. When Pasternak, enfeebled and humiliated, died of lung cancer in May 1960, his funeral attracted not only hundreds of people but also Western media attention. Many musicians attended the funeral, and Richter played on an upright piano.

Yet, "de-Stalinization" continued. In 1961 Stalin's embalmed body was removed from the Lenin Mausoleum on Red Square. The Twenty-second Party Congress adopted a resolution condemning Stalin's break with Lenin's heritage, his abuse of power, and his oppression of the people. The autumn of 1962 was marked by new cultural rapprochements between East and West. Famous names such as Stravinsky, Menuhin, and the New York City Ballet, headed by the Russian-born George Balanchine, came to Moscow. Even the Cuban missile crisis did not put a spoke in the wheels of this rapprochement. The ballet danced Stravinsky and Prokofiev in Moscow, and the Leningrad Philharmonic performed in New York just as the showdown was ending. Richter's international career reached new heights. The grand political drama, the test of wills between Khrushchev and Kennedy, did not concern the apolitical pianist. At any rate, he does not mention it at all when he reminisces with Monsaingeon.

The year after his tumultuous success in the United States, Richter performed in Europe's most prestigious concert halls in London, in Paris, with Karajan in Vienna, with Celibidache and La Scala's orchestra in Milan, during the fall of 1962 in Turin, in Rome, Bologna, Florence, Venice, and, again, several times in Paris. Wherever he went he was praised as a musician in a unique class. And his repertoire in the early 1960s was overwhelming, both in breadth and in depth:

at least a dozen of Beethoven's sonatas, many of the sonatas of Schubert and Prokofiev, and sonatas by Scriabin, Haydn, Schumann, and Hindemith; piano concertos by Beethoven, Liszt, Brahms, Dvořák, Chopin, and Tchaikovsky; etudes, scherzos, and ballades by Chopin; preludes by Debussy; preludes and fugues by Bach and Shostakovich; suites by Handel; and, of course, dozens of piano pieces by Chopin, Schumann, Scriabin, Prokofiev, Debussy, and Ravel. The only one of his "house composers" who was (almost) absent during these years was Rachmaninov.

In 1961, when Richter performed in London for the first time, Jacques Leiser arranged, at Richter's own request, a recording of Schumann's Fantasy in C Major and Beethoven's Sonata in D Minor (*The Tempest*) at EMI's famous Abbey Road Studios, which became his first studio recording in the West.

On his first concert tour to Italy, Leiser acted as his chauffeur. Richter played Schubert's *Wanderer* Fantasy many times along the way, and in April 1963 he and Leiser went to Paris to record the work in the studio. According to Leiser (who, by the way, has recently finished writing his memoirs),

> he had the flu, he wasn't well, and he struggled with it. But the EMI people were satisfied; they would just splice the bits together. He went to Vienna, and I made sure that they would send me the test pressing. When I heard it, I said to myself: "Who is that playing?" I thought they had put a wrong label on the LP. But they had just been splicing like crazy, creating something out of the laboratory. They spliced it to death, note perfect, but no Richter! I called him, took a deep breath, and told him. There was a long silence. "I will come back in three weeks and do it again," he said. It was not as easy as that. The French EMI had no stereo, so it meant bringing equipment and technicians from London once again. The EMI director thought Richter was crazy, wanting to redo it. He thought the recording was splendid and wanted to play it for Richter. But Richter did not want to hear it. We went to the studio, and he played the *Wanderer* five times without a stop! The technicians hardly had time to change the tapes. After that, he started the Liszt B-Minor Sonata, but then they just stopped him. . . . The recording got the Grand Prix du Disque. But nobody except Richter knew the real story! If EMI had discovered that Richter had decided to redo the recording without even listening to the test recording, I would surely have been fired.

The Nomad

Khrushchev was overthrown in October 1964. The willful, temperamental, and challenging leader had dared to suggest doing away with certain perks such as gourmet foods, fancy clothes, and so on, which leading members of the Party enjoyed; and with the pretext of the failure of his economic reforms, he was removed. He had aimed for "peaceful coexistence" and increased technological and economic cooperation, particularly with West Germany and the United States. His successor, the fifty-nine-year-old career politician Leonid Brezhnev, continued the foreign policy of détente. Brezhnev skillfully balanced an outward-looking policy of collaboration and security and an internal ideological crackdown on "revisionists" and reform Communists. In August 1968 he put a definitive end to Alexander Dubček's "Prague Spring" and set in motion what the West called the Brezhnev Doctrine: the Soviet Union's claim to have the right (or duty) to intervene in other socialist countries when "external or internal forces hostile to socialism" tried to reestablish a capitalist system. The wording was almost a mirror image of the 1947 Truman Doctrine.

At first, Brezhnev's takeover meant a certain relief from the ideological-political pressure on art and artists. Brezhnev apparently did not view the role of art with the blend of interest and concern that had characterized his predecessors. Stalin had been an ardent consumer of art, and even though Khrushchev hardly listened to a single new symphony from beginning to end (and later admitted that he had never read a single line of Pasternak's *Doctor Zhivago*), he impulsively and heavy-handedly argued about art, basing his views on tactical considerations or personal taste. Brezhnev reiterated the dogma that capitalism stood in the way of art, whereas Marxism set it free; the notion of a socially useful art remained unchanged. But he expressed himself only rarely on art and only in very general, ideological terms. The author Andrei Bitov remembers that "when he [Khrushchev] was gone, the power apparatus no longer raised its voice in discussion; so there was no more 'criticizing'; after his time, accounts were settled with each artist, and they were wrapped in cotton when they flailed, so no bruises would show."

The Soviet Union spent enormous and ever-increasing sums to support art, literature, and music; to document its role in the service of the people, the Composers' Union instigated a veritable cultural mobilization at the beginning of 1971. Thousands of concerts were arranged all over the country, in industrial areas, in rural areas, in metropolitan areas and villages, in factories and collectives. And Brezhnev once again stressed that the primary purpose of art was to help society develop in accordance with Communist principles. "The Party and the people will not tolerate any attempt to weaken the efficacy of our ideological weapons," he wrote. And the composers' ideological head, Tikhon Khrennikov, admonished: "In order to be victorious, we must strictly obey the Party line and guide our youth."

As usual, Sviatoslav Richter stayed aloof from politics. It is evidence of his special status in Soviet musical politics that he apparently was not drawn into the 1971 musical-cultural offensive. At that point, he was considered an international flagship, an export article whose efforts should be focused on the international arena. The Brezhnev era was the period in which his status as a Soviet world star was cemented the world over. Cities such as London, Vienna, Paris, Salzburg, Amsterdam, Rome, Florence, Geneva, Basel, Dresden, Brussels, Warsaw, Budapest, and Edinburgh appear again and again on his travel calendar. In 1964 he toured Canada for a month and a half. In April and May the next year, he once again performed in the American metropolises of New York, Boston, Washington, Philadelphia, Chicago, Ann Arbor, Los Angeles, and San Diego.

During the fall of 1966 he gave dozens of recitals all over Italy. He spent March and April 1967 on a comprehensive tour of France. These two sun-drenched countries with proud traditions of art, literature, and history had become highly valued haunts for him during the summer—both for concerts and for relaxation. Richter loved France. Living with Nina Dorliak, who had French roots and spoke fluent French, gradually helped him learn the language fairly well. He had many friends in France and appreciated French elegance and civilized conventions, and he was highly interested in French literature, architecture, and art. But Italy was even closer to his heart. As a rule, he preferred to vacation there, and Italy became the country outside the Soviet Union in which he gave the most concerts. As a man of the theater, he was attracted to Italy's *spettacolo*, the theatrical, operatic scenes on every street corner. He gave concerts there almost every year from 1962 on, in small towns, in large towns, in metropolises. No music-loving Italian could claim not to have had the opportunity to hear Richter during those years.

Richter and aunt Dagmar at Lago Maggiore in the Italian Alps, 1977.

If one were to compare another piano legend, the great Vladimir Horowitz, with Richter, one could describe Horowitz as "pianistic" and Richter as "orchestral." Throughout his life, Richter played orchestral music on the piano, and in contrast to Horowitz, he was extremely active as a chamber musician and a lied accompanist. It always nourished him to play with colleagues, and with world-renowned names such as the Borodin Quartet, Benjamin Britten, David Oistrakh, and Dietrich Fischer-Dieskau, he not only enjoyed great musical collaborations but made friends for life. In the last part of his life, he played numerous concerts with his close Moscow friends—the couple Oleg Kagan and Natalia Gutman and the viola player Yuri Bashmet.

Richter had known Oistrakh since his childhood in Odessa. When he met him for the first time as a twelve-year-old, he thought Oistrakh was "an unusually pleasant fellow." And he noted that "later, I saw him often on the stage and always admired the pure power and beauty of his playing. He is certainly the greatest violinist I ever heard. It is really a shame that we only started playing together late in life, after Lev Oborin's death . . . those two were a wonderful duo."

In a book of conversations by Victor Yusefovitch, Oistrakh's son, Igor, explains that his father was a man with a great sense of obligation. While the pianist Lev Oborin was his permanent partner, he refused to play with anyone else. It was not a question of jealousy but a feeling of loyalty known by most musicians. But there had always been great mutual respect and admiration between Oistrakh and Richter. Prokofiev in his day had suggested that they perform his dark Violin Sonata in F Minor (which they later did several times).

After Oborin's death, Richter turned to Oistrakh and suggested a collaboration, and the violinist, seven years his senior, accepted on the spot. The two enormously peripatetic artists often found it difficult to schedule appearances together. In spite of this, a number of concerts were booked. Richter and Oistrakh performed together for the first time in 1964 at the festival in Tours and later in Lyons, Paris, London, Salzburg, New York, Philadelphia, Leningrad, and repeatedly in Moscow. In addition, Richter performed several times as a soloist, with Oistrakh on the conductor's podium, playing, for example, Grieg's Piano Concerto.

It is no exaggeration to say there was a spiritual affinity between the two musicians from Odessa. They found a perfect balance almost immediately, mentally and instrumentally, and they had in common the firm conviction that interpretation must always be based on a careful, dedicated reading of the composer's score. Igor Oistrakh tells that his father was often amazed at Richter's colossal energy and his indefatigable desire to rehearse the same passages over and over again, even when Oistrakh was completely satisfied. They played Schubert's Duo in A Major, Brahms's Sonatas in A Major and D Minor, and César Franck's Sonata in A Major, in addition to a number of Beethoven's sonatas. Bartók's First Sonata and, of course, Prokofiev were also part of their repertoire. The premiere of the sonata Shostakovich wrote especially for them was a particularly memorable event in their collaboration.

In 1964 Richter performed for the first time at composer Benjamin Britten's summer festival in the small English fishing town of Aldeburgh in Suffolk, directly east of Cambridge. As early as 1947, Britten's partner, the tenor Peter Pears, had suggested that the two do "a modest festival, a few concerts with our friends." After its start in 1948, the festival slowly grew. Their circle of friends and the audience gradually grew so large that the festival threatened to burst out of its modest physical framework. However, beause the town was bounded by the sea, a river, and marshes, the festival was safe from uncontrolled growth. The reason for the festival's attraction was simple: great musical experiences in beautiful natural surroundings a long distance from the metropolises of musical life. The setting was a piece of old England in which the audience could enjoy the strand, the sea, the fishing boats, and the fresh air during intermissions; here, one could not only listen to world-renowned performers, but could also run into them around a street corner.

Britten wrote a longer series of works for his festival and began a tradition of composing music for minor operas and plays, often with a conscious popular appeal, for the annual event. Works such as *Let's Make an Opera*, *Noah's Ark*, *Curlew River*, and *A Midsummer Night's Dream* came into being in this way. Despite its modest size, Aldeburgh had good, if modest, concert halls available: the Jubilee Hall, the Blythburgh Parish Church, and, especially, the Maltings in the nearby village of Snape, a great agricultural edifice in which barley had once been turned into malt. The Maltings became a beloved concert hall. When it burned down in 1969, private sponsors had it rebuilt before the following year's festival.

Britten's huge impact on the broad musical audience has to do with a rare combination of a simple, singable melodic style, an emotionally charged musical dramaturgy, and a transparent form. He had grown up in the English choir tradition, and he is one of the twentieth century's greatest musical dramatists. In the Soviet Union of the 1950s, Britten's music was probably performed more often than any other Western contemporary composer. He and Richter had met each other before in Moscow, and the opera lover Richter admired Britten's music tremendously. After Richter's first visit to Aldeburgh, they became close friends, although their professional obligations and constant travel often made it difficult for them to see each other.

The Aldeburgh Festival had a fixed place in the calendar in the second half of June immediately, before the French summer festival that Richter's friend Jacques Leiser had initiated. This did not stop Richter from returning there year after year. In 1964 he played sonatas with his friend Mstislav Rostropovich and Schubert variations for four hands with Britten. In 1965 the festival attracted a host of the world's most sought-after musicians. In addition to himself and Rostropovich (and, of course, Britten and Pears), there were Dietrich Fischer-Dieskau, Julian Bream, Zoltan Kodaly, and Witold Lutoslawski. With Britten as conductor, Richter and the English Chamber Orchestra played Mozart's Piano Concerto in B-flat Major and Schumann's rarely heard concert piece *Introduction and Allegro Appassionato*, which Richter esteemed highly. With Brahms's song cycle *Die schöne Magelone*, he began a collaboration with Fischer-Dieskau on June 20, which later resulted in a series of concerts and recordings with this hotly demanded dream team.

On June 22 Richter and Britten performed two of the literature's major works for four hands, Schubert's Grand Duo and his Fantasy in F Minor. Like Richter, Britten felt a deep kinship with Schubert's muse. The respected English critic Peter Heyworth wrote in the *Observer*,

> It wasn't easy to see what common ground there would be between Britten's
> rhythmic-linear energy and Richter's idiosyncratic tempos and brooding

sensibility. The first two movements of the Grand Duo were not uplifting. Britten played with exaggerated respect for the great pianist that led the way, and Richter's tone was hard and no-nonsense as it sometimes is before he calms down. But in the scherzo, a miracle happened. Without warning, all the problems of balance and style disappeared. . . . The music streamed out in a flood of inspiration. . . . I was so absorbed by the F minor Fantasy that I cannot even recall the performance. Which, I suppose, speaks of its quality.

A year later, Richter gave two piano recitals, again with assistance from Britten: short duos, now by Mozart and Schumann. He played two of his star turns, Schubert's last and Liszt's only sonata and sonatas by Mozart, Scriabin, and Prokofiev. In 1967, with Peter Pears, he performed songs of Britten and Debussy and played Mozart's D-Major Sonata for Two Pianos with Britten in addition, of course, to a solo program. A few days earlier, he had played Britten's youthful piano concerto for the first time, with the composer himself conducting the New Philharmonic. He had then rushed to Tours to perform with, among others, Fischer-Dieskau and, for the first time, with David Oistrakh at his own French summer festival. After this intense period, a few years elapsed before Aldeburgh appeared again on his itinerary.

In 1964, a few days before Richter and Britten performed the Schubert, their friend Mstislav Rostropovich had played Britten's new Cello Symphony, with the composer conducting. It is hardly a coincidence that the work's title leads one's thoughts to the Prokofiev concerto that Rostropovich and Richter premiered in 1952. It was composed for Rostropovich, who had given the first performance of the work three months earlier in Moscow. Rostropovich had become a very close friend of Benjamin Britten. The composer wrote several of his most important works for him (in addition to the Cello Symphony, a cello sonata, and a solo work) or with Rostropovich's wife, the soprano Galina Vishnevskaya, in mind; and he was a regular returning guest at Aldeburgh. After Britten's death in 1976, Rostropovich (who had left the USSR) took over the artistic leadership of the festival for a period. In a 1989 conversation with Solomon Volkov, Rostropovich remarked that the four people who had meant the most in his life were Prokofiev, Shostakovich, Britten, and Solzhenitsyn. "Britten had a strong, charismatic personality. He glowed from the inside as if he were a saint, literally a saint. . . . Britten gave one—I'll say it just this way—human friendship and tenderness."

Richter must have felt something similar. "In Britten, speculative power is always combined with human feelings," he noted. The friendship between him and Britten lasted until the composer's long-term illness and early death, even though after 1967 Richter revisited the Aldeburgh Festival only once—in 1975 (the year before, he had been on the program but canceled because of the flu). But many greetings and letters from him (or from Nina Dorliak) testify to the impatient longing for a reunion and to a strong feeling of solidarity, and the letters often express enthusiasm for Britten's works, which he heard on records or watched on television. If he and Nina were in England, and the friends were not on concert tours, they visited Pears and Britten's home, the Red House in Aldeburgh.

And Dorliak told them they could at any time use her apartment when they were in Moscow. They communicated in German or a bit of French (Britten spoke what he called "Aldeburgh German"). In 1966 Britten got a telegraphic cry for help from Richter: "Dear Ben. Bitte, bitte, write a little cadenza for me for Mozart's Piano Concerto in E-flat Major, no. 22. There isn't one by Mozart. Forgive me." Britten granted his friend's wish and composed two cadenzas for this amazing concerto, which is among Mozart's most ambitious. Mozart had undoubtedly composed a cadenza for his own use, but even though most of his own cadenzas have survived the ravages of time, it was not the case here. In August Richter telegraphed from the French Riviera: "Dear Ben. Have played concert with your cadenza twice. Thanks with all my heart."

After his performance at the festival in 1967, Richter played Britten's Piano Concerto a dozen times in the late 1960s and 1970s, both in the Soviet Union and in the West, with, among others, Rudolf Barshai at the podium. He (or Nina) often mailed or cabled short, affectionate greetings to tell him how it went and how it was received. He was sorry that the recording they did together in December 1970 was not successful. "Britten was only a shadow of himself—he was ill—and there was only a single rehearsal. How sad!" Britten suffered from chronic problems of the heart musculature, as Richter was to experience a number of years later.

In June 1975 Richter once again played two concerts at the festival, this time Beethoven, Tchaikovsky, and Rachmaninov, and twice he attended the now fatally ill Benjamin Britten's last opera, *Death in Venice* (after Thomas Mann's novella), at the Maltings. As always, he appreciated the composer's music, but he thought the staging, which apparently pleased the composer, was "a total disaster . . . pseudo-realistic, unwieldy and hard to grasp." Later, in August–September 1983, Richter the theater enthusiast was to get to the core of Britten's musical drama when he made his debut as theater director at the Pushkin Museum in Moscow by staging Britten's two chamber operas, *Albert Herring* and *The Turn of the Screw.*

A similarly large chapter in the story of Richter as chamber musician is his collaboration with the person he repeatedly described as "the greatest singer of the twentieth century": Dietrich Fischer-Dieskau. They met for the first time in Bayreuth in August 1961, when Richter had invited his mother to Wagner's festival house to attend *Tannhäuser*. Then, they performed together in 1965 at Britten's festival in Aldeburgh. And this musical collaboration continued to the extent that their busy calendars allowed.

In his memoir, *Zeit eines Lebens* (The Time of a Life), Fischer-Dieskau wrote with great enthusiasm about their musical and personal relationship. Fischer-Dieskau was also an eager and gifted amateur painter—which, of course, provided common ground for the two musicians. When on rare occasions Richter had the opportunity to visit Fischer-Dieskau privately, he commented on the singer's paintings "with great technical expertise," as Fischer-Dieskau wrote "To describe a human being like him in forced brevity is quite impossible. He gave of himself gladly and withdrew into himself with the same ease."

Fischer-Dieskau took on the job of dubbing Richter's voice in the German version of Monsaingeon's film, and it gave him an opportunity to contemplate what the pianist really meant when in the film he mentions "difficulties" while they performed Brahms's Romances for the first time in Aldeburgh:

> For many years, I had been intimate with the work, of course, and I had my own view of a faithful reading of the score. It may have amazed Richter that a singer would have such firm suggestions for an interpretation ready, even with respect to the piano prelude and afterlude. But we only needed a single rehearsal, before the dress rehearsal, and everything went off without the least hitch and with a wonderful result. He may have told his wife Nina Dorliak about his amazement, to me he said nothing. And at none of our later concert preparations was there the least insecurity between us. I always found his most outstanding quality—in addition to an almost self-evident, phenomenal piano technique—to be his ability to maintain the dynamics exactly as the composer had instructed. This endowed his delivery with something archaic, indisputable.

The great singer, however, made demands Richter found difficult to honor, as is apparent from Richter's notes: "Dieter's insistence on every single vowel and consonant got in the way of the music's free flow. . . . If he has to sing consonants such as, for example, "str" or "pr," he insists that the pianist play with a very slight delay. His diction is clearly phenomenal, but it alters very slightly the music's natural rhythm." When Richter later worked with the excellent German tenor Peter Schreier, it pleased him that Schreier subordinated the words to the music. "This is the exact opposite of Fischer-Dieskau, who, for his part, sets out from the text. For me, it is a strange approach, and I lose some of my freedom of performance when I accompany him."

In 1964 Richter left a lasting mark on the Western concert world with the festival the Fêtes Musicales en Touraine. But the initiative came from Jacques Leiser (who, as mentioned, was Richter's agent and record producer for an extensive period, and who remained his friend for almost forty years). Leiser talks about the background:

> I was working for EMI in France, and we had a reorganization in 1964. The English section of the company wanted to control everything. They offered me a job in London, but I refused. So, I was out of a job for nearly a year. I went to Moscow several times to discuss upcoming recordings with Richter, and he asked me what I would want to do. I mentioned working with a music festival, as my job had brought me to all the major European festivals. And he just said: "Why don't you start a festival?" I tried to explain that this was not as easy as it might seem to him, but he said: "You need only three things, the artists, the site, and the money. You find the place and I will come with my friends and colleagues. Then, surely, you will find the money." I thought about it, and we decided that it should be not too far from Paris, but I doubted that a suitable hall could be found. "Just find it!" he said. So I started driving around, collecting information, looking for a hall that would seat about a thousand people.

The Loire River runs through the wine region called La Touraine (known as "the garden of France") with a wealth of cloisters, châteaux, and other historical monuments and sights, but the halls in the area were either too small or acoustically unsuitable. On a drive through the region, Leiser contacted the music union in Tours, the ancient pilgrimage city in the Loire Valley, a hundred miles south of Paris in the direction of Bordeaux. They suggested that he look at a historic barn from the 1220s (Grange de Mesley), only ten miles west of Tours and surrounded by wheat fields. The building was full of hay, and Leiser was in doubt about the acoustics, but he took some pictures and sent them to Richter. "He was wildly enthusiastic," Leiser says; "he literally flipped out."

The unique building complex, originally connected to the Marmoutier Cloister in the vicinity, consists of a huge barn ("when I came, there was hay, and chickens running around everywhere," Richter remembers), a bunch of stalls, a large courtyard surrounded by a castle wall, and a portal with a very monumental tower. The 120-foot-long wooden building was modeled on a church basilica; the ceiling was borne by four rows of oak columns, reaching forty-five

The old storage building/concert hall at Grange de Mesley.

feet in height. There was space for music of almost any sort, and after the necessary alterations, the acoustics were acceptable, except that the wooden floor, which was laid directly on sand, squelched some of the resonance. Fully exploited, the floor area provided room for up to fifteen hundred listeners.

Richter saw immediately that there were ideal possibilities for an annual summer festival in these beautiful natural surroundings—just like Britten's Aldeburgh—a festival where people could perform together with friends and colleagues, far from the "official" concert halls and production centers of classical music. When, the year after, he was introduced at the Maltings in Aldeburgh, he must have sent proud thoughts to La Grange. Here he could, to a certain extent, avoid the long-term planning he detested. Programs could be changed without great ado. If necessary, concerts could be announced from one day to the next. The effort needed to meet the tough demands of the concert-making business could instead be invested solely in the music itself.

Leiser organized a gala concert with Richter at the opera in Tours, and he made sure that people, particularly potential benefactors, could get back to Paris the same night by a special train. Interest in the concert was great. It was the first time a famous Soviet pianist played outside Paris. This got the mayor of Tours involved. He offered financial backing. Leiser says: "Richter wanted me to be the artistic director. But things did not turn out that way. The local music people wanted to get in on this, intrigues, French-style, you know. I did not pay attention; I thought that my leverage was Richter. But he was already committed, Minister Furtseva had been invited, there was no way he could cancel. So I had the rug pulled from under my feet. It was a hard blow for me after putting so much energy into it. They never even acknowledged my name in the program." The festival is still going strong today. And in the official accounts of its history, Richter stands alone as its founder and mastermind.

The next year, on June 23, 1964, immediately after his first visit to Aldeburgh, Richter played music by Prokofiev, Scriabin, and Ravel in the converted grain silo, and the Fêtes Musicales en Touraine became a reality. Even in the first year of the festival, such international names as Rudolf Barshai (with the Moscow Chamber Orchestra) and soprano Rita Streich performed there. Until illness seriously hampered him, Richter returned at the end of almost every June to this French idyll, where nature and culture compete for attention—always escorted by Nina Dorliak and each time playing with friends and colleagues. Once the festivities were over and the musicians left the countryside, the medieval storage building reverted to its usual functions.

What was true of Britten's Aldeburgh was true here: the festival was "small," but obviously it was also "big." Richter's worldwide reputation almost immediately catapulted it into the first rank of European musical events. Few places have attracted such a succession of world-class names for so many years to such a remote place, often working with Richter or with each other. In 1967 he played with David Oistrakh for the first time. He continued his collaboration with Fischer-Dieskau here, and in the following years colleagues such as Arturo Benedetti Michelangeli, Claudio Arrau, and Christoph Eschenbach were guests at La Grange. Pierre Fournier, Christian Ferras, Paul Tortelier, Jessye Norman, Alfred Brendel, Maurizio Pollini, Cathy Berberian, Barbara Hendricks, Pierre Boulez, the Amadeus Quartet, and countless other celebrities also performed in the rural surroundings. In addition, Richter's closest personal music friends, members of the Borodin Quartet, Rudolf Barshai, Oleg Kagan, and Natalia Gutman, viola player Yuri Bashmet, and pianists such as Lisa Leonskaya and Eliso Virsaladze, gave concerts. The piano was always at the center of these musical activities. Even Horowitz was invited, although he declined; but he sent his favorite pupil, Byron Janis. For hundreds of people, a musical pilgrimage to the Loire Valley became a recurring part of their summer calendar. Over the span of a quarter of a century, a wide range of concert recordings with Richter were made there.

Naturally, Richter was the uncrowned king of the roost. The festival management did what it could to make him feel comfortable and "in form." He always stayed at the nearby La Tortinière, a Renaissance-inspired castle from the 1860s with a spire, blue-slate roof, park, and five-star restaurant—a place where film stars and French presidents vacationed. And he enjoyed the freedom of giving concerts where no one could predict what he would play or when. He often surprised his audience with a sudden, unannounced concert or with cancellations. Umberto Massini, the Italian editor of the periodical *Musica*, recounts: "When Richter was to play, you could sense a vibration in the air in the moments before, a disquieting electric charge like just before a summer storm. It was released when *il maestro* appeared on the stage at La Grange and was greeted by a collective sigh of relief and thundering applause." Richter himself often attended concerts but always arrived at the last minute and sat in the very back row as the musicians took the stage and the lights were dimmed. At the end of the concert, he left the hall as soon as the last tone died down. He knew that any personal interest in him might spoil the audience's appreciation of the music. And he hated being an object of curiosity when he was not onstage.

It is difficult to imagine the introverted hater of any form of planning leading such a demanding organizational jigsaw puzzle as an international music festival. But it was crucial that Richter put his name and prestige on the line as a guarantor of the concerts' quality. His role as festival manager did not consist of endless meetings with sponsors, politicians, concert agents, or marketing people. He was content to propose the theme of the festival and to invite whomever he wanted.

He was involved with the festival until its twenty-fifth anniversary in 1988. And he was persuaded to celebrate its birthday by displaying some of his pastels. But he assigned the role of de facto festival manager to the innovative and internationally experienced cultural entrepreneur René Martin.

Yet, Richter's activities as originator and artistic leader of music festivals do not end here. In 1981, together with Irina Antonova, the influential head of the great Pushkin Art Museum, he began the annual December Nights at the famous museum in Moscow. The idea was a series of concerts with chamber music playing off art and, sometimes, theater as well. Every year the festival was organized around a thematic idea in which music and art came together. Titles such as "Mozart's Times," "Pasternak's World," "Russian Art and Music," "Tchaikovsky and Levitan," and "Rembrandt and Beethoven" indicate the scope of these activities. Almost every year, Richter performed solo soirees, as a chamber musician with his friends, or as a lied accompanist. Here, too, he staged two Britten chamber operas in 1983 at a festival dedicated to English

Richter on stage, 1970.

music and classic English painters. This festival, too, lives on after Richter's death in 1997, now as the December Nights of Sviatoslav Richter.

Richter dedicated the first three months of 1970 to his third concert tour of the "vulgar" United States; he never visited the country again. His annoyance at the American way of life increased when on February 1, in a concert with David Oistrakh at Carnegie Hall, he encountered anti-Soviet demonstrations. Yehudi Menuhin, who was in the hall, writes in his memoirs (*Unfinished Journey*) that a young man suddenly stormed onto the stage in the middle of Brahms's Violin Sonata in D Minor and shouted: "The Soviet Union is no better than Nazi Germany!" "The music halted and Oistrakh left the stage, but Richter sat on at the piano, observing with interest the thin, taut, fanatical young fellow still screaming protests against the Soviets' treatment of Jews." Later, however, the apolitical Soviet citizen felt upset and wronged on behalf of his colleague. Oistrakh was Jewish, and the experience may have contributed to Richter's refusal of all American invitations.

It was at this point that Richter experienced health problems for the first time beyond those what most people encounter. Back in Moscow, he sought the help of a young doctor, Irina Voevodskaya. Over the years, a relationship

Irina Voevodskaya, Richter's "court doctor," 2006.

developed between her and the pianist, made up of equal parts of professional aid and friendship. He complained about shoulder pains, dizziness, and continual exhaustion. In Richter, Voevodskaya met a man who was unused to illness, a man with a strong immune system and a high threshold of pain. Ahead of him were massive obligations in Italy, Spain, and France. In September and October, he was supposed to go to Japan for the first time. Voevodskaya noted a slightly elevated blood pressure, but clinical tests showed no alarming deviations from the norm. Dorliak resisted the drugs she recommended to Richter; she would accept only massage and, possibly, acupuncture. Voevodskaya quickly realized that Dorliak had a special hegemony over anything to do with Richter, and she discovered that Dorliak stopped giving Richter the prescribed pills as soon as there was the least sign of improvement.

Gradually, Voevodskaya became Richter's personal physician. If she needed clinical assistance from specialists, she selected them herself. But Dorliak was always fiercely and personally involved in any treatment. If she was not satisfied with the doctors, the consultations ended abruptly. This meant that there was often a lack of context and direction in the treatment. One doctor had little opportunity to know what another had done or prescribed. Dorliak had a box in which she kept medical documents, lab results, X-rays, electrocardiograms, foreign journals, and so on. But an overview was impossible (and, at one point, the box disappeared without a trace, according to Voevodskaya). Richter was totally uninterested in his medical treatments. He considered it a matter for the professionals. Voevodskaya quotes from a postcard Richter sent her, written during a trip abroad: "Hi, dear little doctor. How's it going? I am like a ball in the hands of the international doctors. I move from hand to hand. And now I've ended up with one that has Nina Lvovna's great affection."

Before one of Richter's trips to Japan in the 1970s, Voevodskaya consented to his imaginative request that he be anesthetized during the long plane trip (he hated flying), so that when he woke up he would find himself at his hotel in Tokyo. This was highly unusual, indeed. On the plane Voevodskaya was in charge of the anesthesia, and everything went according to plan.

Japan was to be one of the favorite travel destinations for Richter the nomad in the last quarter of his life. Despite the difficulty of getting there, he toured the country no fewer than six times after his first visit in 1970. He believed that his understanding of Japanese manners and lifestyle was due to the fact that he probably had a bit of Asian blood in his veins on his mother's side of the family. Japanese audiences adored him with an unrestrained rapture, which reminded him of his audience back home in Moscow. His warm regard for the piano division of Yamaha Corporation, which always made sure that he had topnotch instruments available, may also have played a role in this. The piano technicians from Yamaha who accompanied him all over Europe and Japan from the beginning of the 1970s—Teruhisa Murakami, then Koh Segawa, and in his last years Kazuto Osato—were all close, highly valued friends and coworkers who did not only secure optimal instruments but often acted as drivers and readily assisted him with the most mundane tasks of daily life. His indispensable Japanese interpreter, Midori Kawashima, also became very close. She had a degree in Russian literature from a Tokyo university and was known for her work with Japanese subtitles in Russian films. She had been an interpreter for many other well-known Russian musicians and had spent more than half of her life in the USSR.

According to Kawashima, Richter admired the medical arts of the East, often let himself be treated by Japanese masseurs, and was convinced that acupuncture had a unique curative effect. The Japanese language also fascinated him, and he was quick to learn Japanese words. He was not satisfied with the tourist's *arigato* (thank you) and *sayonara* (good-bye), but learned polite phrases such as *kekko-deshita* (thank you for an unusually good meal) and even invented special meanings for Japanese words. *Gomi* means garbage, or filth, but Richter said *gomiko* and used this for everything that was bad: a concert, a recording,

Richter and Nina Lvovna at a formal Japanese meal.

a film, clothes, and so on. When he fell behind in his piano practice, he said, "I am a *gomiko*!" Thanks to his Russian friends, the word almost became a fad, and it even spread to Europe.

Kawashima can also testify to Richter's legendary memory. He performed across the length and breadth of Japan; she says that he remembered the names of all the cities on the concert calendar and all the restaurants he had visited. Dorliak reproved him. She believed he was taxing his strength by storing such trivialities in his mind, but he claimed that it demanded far more energy to empty his memory. He quickly became more knowledgeable in Japanese geography and history than many of his Japanese friends, and he exploited every opportunity to take in the country's sights—temples, ruins, burial places, museums, and nature.

A characteristic episode was his visit with Kawashima and his Japanese manager to a restaurant, where a Japanese specialty was served consisting of very small fish that were eaten alive with soy sauce. Richter the pantheist, however, could never eat a living animal; he could not kill. So the chef was asked to serve "small fish that have just died," and the Japanese quietly shook their heads.

Today Japan may well be the place on the globe where Richter's mythological status is the most indelible.

In the mid-1970s Alban Berg's Chamber Concerto for piano and violin with thirteen wind instruments came to play a very special role in Richter's career (the work is dedicated to Arnold Schönberg and makes use of Schönberg's twelve-tone method). In 1972 he played the work for the first time in Moscow with Oleg Kagan (and Rudolf Barshai on the podium). It was also the first time he performed with the young violinist, who became one of his closest musical colleagues until Kagan's early death in 1990. At the time Kagan was married to Richter's friend the pianist Lisa Leonskaya (later he married Natalia Gutman). Together they played—and recorded—a number of violin sonatas, mainly by Mozart and Hindemith but also by Brahms, Grieg, and Ravel.

Richter still did not feel he was entirely on the right wavelength with Berg's difficult, tightly woven, and unusual music. At La Grange in 1975, he heard the work with Christoph Eschenbach and violinist Saschko Gavriloff as soloists. And it fascinated him so deeply that he wanted to fathom its mysteries. This resulted in a typical Richter notion and became one of the rare examples of pedagogy in his career. He got the idea that, with its unusual instrumentation, the piece could be rehearsed methodically and carefully by a wind ensemble under the aegis of the Moscow Conservatory, an ensemble he put together himself, consisting of teaching assistants and older students. Oleg Kagan again took on the violin solo; conductor Yuri Nikolayev began working with the thirteen wind instruments; and once the technical and intonation problems were somewhat solved, Richter joined in the work. The rehearsals often took place in his and Dorliak's apartment at Bolshoya Bronnaya. Richter found that everyone worked hard and concentrated (he believed that this may, in part, have been because all participants were fed during rehearsals at his apartment).

In May 1976 the musicians were ready to perform the work. They played it no fewer than five times in Moscow and, in late summer, several times in the provinces. The idea was kept alive, and it became a long-term project, stretching over four years; some people claim that they had approximately one hundred rehearsals. If any of the ensemble's members graduated from the conservatory along the way, new members came in. On his trips abroad, Richter kept in close contact with the musicians, at times even by telephone (which he despised), to make sure that the rehearsal was kept up. When he was in Moscow, it was rehearsed once again.

In 1977 the group performed the work several times in Leningrad, and later in December of that year, they played it in Belgium, Germany, and France and recorded it in a studio for EMI in Paris (Richter remarked that "this is the recording I am most proud of," although he did not find the instrumental balance in the recording ideal). Critics in France and Italy reviewed the recording enthusiastically. But to Richter's annoyance, it proved difficult to sell and quickly disappeared from the catalogue. The work was performed again in Athens in August 1978 and in Warsaw in September 1980. In all, there were about thirty performances over four years, always with Kagan and Nikolayev. A musical project of this nature and stature must be called unique.

The most prominent examples of Richter's attraction to the nomadic life and his antielitist view of his role as musician are his incredible automobile excursions through Siberia in the latter half of 1986, first from west to east and onward from Kabarovsk to Japan, and then from east to west all the way back to Moscow. In Japan he gave a dozen concerts, recitals, and sonata soirees, including one of chamber music with the Gutman-Kagan pair and with Yuri Bashmet. In Siberia there were sometimes daily concerts, often more than one in the same town, a veritable tour de force. Including the spring concerts, this amounted to at least 150 recitals in one year! For most people, the fifty or so different Russian and Siberian towns that appear on his itinerary will be exotic and unknown: Veliyke Luki, Naumovo, Rshev, Orekovo-Suyevo, Lakinsk, Susdal, Cheboksari, Kasan, Ufa, Chelyabinsk, Kurgan, Chita, Taishet, Abakan, Sushenskoye, as well as many better-known cities, such as Irkutsk, Pskov, Ulan-Ude, Krasnoyarsk, and Nishni-Novgorod. He played in towns with all sorts of pianos, in all sorts of halls, for all sorts of listeners. And everywhere people were grateful that the world-famous pianist had come so far off the beaten path—often for modest fees—to create musical experiences that were otherwise unavailable in these distant regions. Valentina Chemberdzhy, the author of *On Tour with Sviatoslav Richter*, followed him eastward for a few days in September and westward for a few weeks in November. Richter did not return to Moscow until just before Christmas. And, as previously mentioned, much of the book is yet another version of "Richter in his own words" told by someone else. But Chemberdzhy writes matter-of-factly and believably, and often she is allowed to quote directly from the notes Richter jotted down every day in a thick notebook.

"At heart, I don't like to be very long in the same place, no matter where," he said. "Geography, new sounds, new impressions—that, too, is art. So, I am happy when I leave a place for somewhere unknown. Without that, life would be uninteresting for me."

One day in September, Oleg Kagan showed up in Irkutsk. Together, they gave several recitals on this leg of the tour: violin sonatas by Brahms, Grieg, and Ravel. Kagan had brought with him an offer for Richter from the German conductor Kurt Masur (later head of the New York Philharmonic) to stage Wagner's *Tristan und Isolde* at La Fenice, the opera house in Venice. Richter the opera lover was both proud and happy, but after a few days he gave up the idea as "utopian." He had no doubts about his ability to take on the task, but he did not believe that he could find enough rehearsal time. His friends Gutman and Bashmet joined him for some days on the tour to play sonatas—now with cello and viola, perhaps as a sort of "dress rehearsal" for the concerts they would later give in Japan.

One mysterious omission in Chemberdzhy's book is any mention of a person who escorted Richter on his long Siberian tour, the man who for the last years of Richter's life presumably was closer to him than anyone except Dorliak, the engineer Viktor Gerasimovitch Zelenin. Zelenin met Richter in the 1970s, and even though he was about half as old as the pianist, they developed and cultivated an extremely close friendship that lasted until Richter's death. Why Chemberdzhy, with a wave of the wand, has removed him from her story is a mystery. Richter's Japanese interpreter Midori Kawashima—who always escorted him when he was in Japan—was also in the entourage on parts of the Siberian tour.

Despite the physical and mental efforts required on these incredibly long car trips, Richter the nomad was undoubtedly in his element. His hatred of airplanes had mostly to do with the vacuous, humdrum nature of plane trips. In a car, he could stop to eat, rest, look around, and experience new things. This was hardly fear of flying in the usual sense.

One can almost get the impression that 1986 was the year in which Richter wanted to test his outer limits, both physically and mentally. From the end of March to the beginning of May, he gave more than twenty solo concerts in just as many cities all over Italy. At the end of May, he planned what in the sports world would be considered a world-record attempt: in the famous Teatro Bibiena in Mantua, he would give six solo concerts in ten days with a huge program, including music that was new to his repertoire. He was to play Chopin's four ballades, his Polonaise-Fantasy, almost all the Chopin etudes, Schumann's Toccata, *Blumenstück*, some fugues, and his Paganini etudes, Brahms's first two piano sonatas, Beethoven's *Diabelli Variations* and his great Sonata in A Major, opus 101, plus other minor pieces by Beethoven, a whole evening of music by Hindemith, and an evening with Haydn sonatas. Decca had sent a team of technicians from London to record all six concerts.

But the recording was only partly successful. Richter was forced to acknowledge that he was tired, and he complained of feeling unwell. He canceled the Hindemith concert and was several times on the point of giving up and going home. He was far from satisfied with his performances, and behind closed doors, he repeated some of the program for Decca's microphones. But the recordings, many hours of music, were put aside in the company's archives for many years, and only a modest portion of the huge material (primarily Haydn and Brahms) ever reached record stores' shelves.

Only a couple of weeks after this depressing experience, Richter was to go to Copenhagen to receive the annual Sonning Prize and play at the award ceremony at Tivoli's concert hall on June 15. The Danish music prize was first given to Igor Stravinsky in 1959, and several of Richter's closest colleagues and friends also received it: Benjamin Britten in 1968, Shostakovich in 1973, Fischer-Dieskau in 1975, and Rostropovich in 1981. Some may find this honor a bit late in coming, but the occasion actually formed the background for an appearance by Richter in Copenhagen (where he had played only once, nine years earlier). Lars Grunth, Tivoli's head of music for many years, relates with sardonic humor the many obstacles in the planning: "Richter had suggested two concerts with an orchestra, Schumann's Concerto and Stravinsky's *Capriccio*. When I asked what conductor he preferred, he answered without hesitation, 'Pierre Boulez.' I considered that improbable, but to my surprise Boulez reported that he was available and could come." The year before, Richter and Boulez had performed the Stravinsky work at the festival in La Grange de Mesley, and Richter claimed that he had wanted to play "this wonderful Capriccio" his entire life but had never dared. And these concerns apparently did not disappear; he never succeeded in persuading himself to play the work again. The Copenhagen plan came to nothing.

Lars Grunth explains:

I sent a contract to Boulez, and Richter informed us that he would play only if Boulez conducted. But then Richter seemed to vanish into the earth. No one was able to track him down, and as time went by without an explanation, Boulez had to stop keeping the date open. When we were finally able to contact Richter and had to report to him that Boulez had to step down, he suggested a sonata recital instead. But it was still incredibly difficult to contact him. Every time we heard from him, it was through a new middleman. Once again, he vanished without a trace, and we were able to track him down in Mantua only through the Russian embassy. It was now just a few weeks before the concert, and any idea of a concert with an orchestra had to be given up.

Richter wanted to play the works by Beethoven that he had played in Mantua but insisted that he had to consult his female dentist in Vienna before the concert. To the concern of the organizers, it was reported that he would not fly and that he was too weak to ride for long periods in a car. Time went by. Not until a few days before the concert was a suitable driver found who could take him from Vienna to Copenhagen. But the allegedly infirm Richter demanded that the trip take place in virtually one stretch, and he arrived in the Danish capital in plenty of time.

Tivoli's music director continues:

When I was going to help him with the lighting in the hall, he insisted—quite unexpectedly—on having the hall darkened entirely. He said he would bring along his own floor lamp, which would illuminate the music rack. He agreed to go onstage with the lights on. Then all the lights would be turned off. A page turner also had to be engaged (his Scandinavian agent Gösta Schwark was married to the pianist Assia Slatkova, and she took on the job). We had told Richter that the award ceremony would take place after the concert break; but when the chairman of the prize committee stood ready, Richter realized that he would be awarded the prize onstage. Under no circumstances would he do that. It was impossible, he said. If we demanded it, he would not play at all. The audience in the brimming hall was amazed when he finished his Beethoven program without going through the award ceremony. And so—for the first and only time in the history of the prize—the check was presented to him after the concert, in the dressing room, after an ultrashort award speech. He just stuck the check for DKK 100,000 in his back pocket.

Clearly, however, Richter was proud of this Danish honor, and the press was effusive: "Richter plays different roles, and it is their interchange that makes it so extraordinarily interesting. He modulates between characters, the way others are content modulating between keys." "The telling pause in which the entire hall listens breathlessly." "A Beethoven you have never before experienced, and probably never will again." That may be why Gösta Schwark was successful in getting him back to Copenhagen (and Stockholm) only three weeks later with a Schumann program. No other musicians at Richter's level would have been able to handle it on such short notice, and here ends the story of Richter in Denmark almost before it had begun.

Richter ultimately paid a high price for the constant stress, the endless car trips, and the often cold Siberian concert halls and hotel rooms in 1986. Even the "iron man" had to recognize that the body has its limits and that one cannot tax it without paying a penalty. His health began seriously to hamper things. Only a year later, a diminished heart function—presumably angina pectoris, a calcification of the coronary artery—began to give him problems. In Munich in March 1987, and a couple of months later in Helsinki, he had to undergo extensive treatment; during the fall, he played only a few concerts. Nevertheless, in July–August 1988, he threw himself into yet another physical tour de force with more than two dozen concerts in as many cities in the southern USSR, the area from the Ukraine eastward to Khirgistan. He continued with the

Trans-Siberian Railroad to Vladivostok, sailed to Sapporo, Japan, and played another two dozen times in a succession of Japanese cities. At that point, he was still tackling some of his *métier*'s most physically demanding challenges: Liszt, Brahms's *Handel Variations*, and Chopin's etudes.

Again he suffered from serious heart problems. At the university clinic in Zurich, in the summer of 1989, he went through his first heart surgery, a bypass operation followed by a long rehabilitation program at the clinic. He convalesced for the rest of the year. Nevertheless, at the beginning of 1990, the seventy-four-year-old pianist was again ready to resume battle. Hundreds of concerts and hundreds of thousands of fans still awaited him.

Piano, Pianist, Music, and Audience

Once, a piano in the home symbolized a musical communion with the self; the piano was not just a status symbol for the bourgeoisie and, later, the middle class. It was the special place where playing and listening were one and the same, a user culture more than a consumer culture. Just think of the teenage Richter's passionate, solitary physical-mental involvement with the great Romantic operas. Before the electronic age, the piano was a necessary prerequisite for a repeated encounter with the great works of music history, especially orchestral music. Only very few could expect to hear, for example, a symphony by Beethoven more than a few times in their lifetime. But in adaptations for four hands, they could be experienced again and again.

The piano underwent a metamorphosis, with Franz Liszt as the archetype of the virtuoso who controlled the instrument, seduced his audience, drew a crowd, and created mass hysteria. Well into the last century, nevertheless, the piano preserved its character as a private, anonymous place, a mirror for the mind's unchallenged world of imagination. That is no longer the case. Of course, the piano is here to stay; more pianos and grand pianos are produced than ever before, now also in China, Thailand, Australia, Korea, and Brazil. And today Japan is a leading player on the world market. But the role of the piano has completely changed in consumer society. Today anyone can hear Beethoven at any time. It is now unusual for the ordinary music lover to play the music him- or herself. The two realms are separate (and if they happen to occur in the same person, the instrument is more likely to be a guitar or a synthesizer). Very few people play operas or symphonies on the piano. The "interpreter," or the professional, long ago sidelined the piano-playing amateur musician. Today listeners are moved when they hear music, but they rarely "move" the music themselves.

If certain aspects of concert culture may seem anachronistic, the great tradition of the pianist's lonely test of strength apparently still has something to offer a contemporary public. Here, like theater and sports, nothing—not CDs, television, videos, or DVDs—can replace the physical encounter with the living person on the stage. The troglodyte Glenn Gould saw nothing but a bullfight arena: "the typical concert-goer is attracted by gladiator battles; I don't care for him as a type, I have no confidence in him, and I do not want him as a friend." But he was blind to the fact that when music comes into being in the concert hall, it is not about losers and winners, not about death, but about life. When a listener experiences, say, Beethoven's *Appassionata* in a concert hall, he or she invests a piece of lived time with a beginning and an end, and this time is shared with others. In the course of only a few minutes, the music unfolds a life cycle in sound, but it does not consume life; it symbolizes and affirms it.

The musician, and especially the piano soloist, who is completely alone with his audience, must love (or learn to love) the role of performer, the limelight, the tension, the expectant, demanding audience, the applause, the encores, the curtain calls, the adoration. And he or she must become accustomed to stage fright, dilapidated pianos, lonely hotel rooms, fatiguing journeys, forced society, and too little sleep. The concert business demands competitive skills and the ability to deliver the goods. The only alternative is to perform in audiovisual media—TV, film, video, or DVD—or to be content with playing for oneself, which does not tally well with most people's conception of what a musician is.

Listeners today have become passive consumers, whether they listen in a concert hall or through loudspeakers. The optimistic Gould imagined that "in the electronic age, music will be an integrated part of the individual's life, not simply an ornamentation of it." He believed that electronics would liberate the individual's engagement and put an end to the artist's monopoly as "soloist." "Audiences will be artists, and their lives will become art," he wrote. But had he lived to the end of the twentieth century, like Richter, he would have had reason to be disappointed. Concert audiences did not change; most of them still view the concert hall as a place where something is done to them, not as a place where they *themselves* must do something (in John Cage's simple way of putting it). The soloist must by necessity adjust to this expectation in the audience.

In a famous conversation in which Gould interviewed Arthur Rubinstein, one aspect of this problem appeared in its most blatant form: a soloist who entirely eschews a live audience for the solitude of the recording studio, and a soloist who quite literally wants to "own the listener's soul." Of his listeners, Gould (who had long since abdicated his role as a concert pianist) said, "I did not want any power over them, and I certainly was not stimulated by their mere presence." "We are absolute opposites," said Rubinstein. "If you would have followed a pianistic career for many years as I have—over sixty-five years—you would have experienced the constant, constant contact with the crowd that you must in some way persuade, dominate or get hold of." Clearly, Rubinstein is speaking as an entertainer in the best sense of the word. He is a stage artist who is always angling for the listeners' attention and who is able to personify the eternal or the mundane, a performer whose art is in continual dialogue with the audience to which it is directed.

We can only guess where Richter would place himself on this scale. Of course, he would be closer to Rubinstein than to Gould, but certainly not obsessed by the need to "dominate" anyone. He wanted to share his unique experience of the music he played with others, but to him an audience was hardly the anonymous mass Rubinstein describes as "the crowd." Rather, it was a selection of individuals each of whom represented what Søren Kierkegaard called "You individual." These individuals are left to themselves and to their own experience. They should not be seized by the collar, persuaded, seduced, or entertained. The music is enough in itself, a bid for the individual's imagination and emotion. Whether Richter's audience numbered in the thousands in a most magnificent concert hall or fifty in a Siberian factory was a matter of indifference for him. And what they felt, whether they loved or hated him, whether they liked his playing or his personality, was completely irrelevant. "Grabbing their attention" was for Hollywood or showbiz. Richter was his own harshest critic; only the music and its merciless demands held sway over him.

But, of course, a man who gives nearly four thousand concerts in more than fifty-five years must like being onstage and establishing close contacts between the music and the listener. "The only thing that means anything to me is that people come not from a snobbery but from a desire to listen to the music," he emphasized. Whether one can assess his indifference to the audience as arrogance is a matter of opinion. What mattered was that he *played*, and when he did, one could listen, if one could get tickets. In his eyes the enthusiastic and adoring crowd of listeners became a necessary evil. "All the praise that rains down on me only serves to spoil my relationship with the audience," he grumbled.

To Jürgen Meyer-Josten, he said: "I am not so altruistic that I only play for the listener; no, I play first and foremost for myself. If it goes well, the listener may also get something out of it. A well-known musicologist once asked me, 'Why are you always surrounded by these invisible walls when you play? Don't you care about the audience?' My answer was, 'No, it does not concern me. I simply don't notice it.'"

However, this severe remark should not occasion comparisons with the introverted Italian Arturo Benedetti Michelangeli, a phenomenal pianist who also said, "I do not play for others, only for myself." Like an aristocrat, Michelangeli felt he was above his audience; his performance onstage hinted at something like contempt, and he sought (and usually achieved) an immaculate, sparkling perfection that sometimes risked draining the music of any corporal, physical, and communicative immediacy.

In his book *How People Change*, psychologist Allan Wheelis (as quoted in David Dubal's *The Art of the Piano*) relates his experience of how the encounter with the public drove Richter to retreat into himself: "His face is grim, there is anger in the set of his jaw, but not at the audience. This is a passion altogether his own, a force with which he protects what he is about to do. If it had words, it would say, 'what I attempt is important and I go about it with utmost seriousness. I intend to create beauty and meaning, and everything everywhere threatens this endeavor. The coughs, the latecomers, the chatting women in the third row, and always those dangers within, distraction, confusion, loss of memory, weakness of hand, all are enemies of my endeavor. I call up this passion to oppose them, to protect my purpose.' "

In a famous photograph from Tours showing the two maestros in conversation, there is an obvious affinity between Richter and Michelangeli; there is hardly another photo where the frosty Italian is smiling broadly and warmly! Richter admired his great colleague but saw him as a fanatic whose compulsion for perfection sometimes kept him from finding a natural expression for his love of music. For Richter, perfection was unattainable and therefore an inhuman ideal. However, "I don't want to judge a great artist," he remarked. But he did not treat Michelangeli's favorite student, Maurizio Pollini, with kid gloves: "Ice-cold and all too self-assured. No poetry, no sense of improvisation." When in June 1975 Pollini suddenly had to beg off the festival at Grange de Mesley, Richter invited the young Hungarian Zoltán Kocsis as a replacement. Kocsis performed a few days after Michelangeli, and Richter remarked (to the Hungarian poet János Pilinszky): "Michelangeli is certainly the best pianist of our time, but Kocsis is already a greater artist." And even though he described his young colleague as "wild and temperamental, like a child," he invited Kocsis to collaborate on a Schubert program for four hands a few years later.

Apparently Michelangeli's feelings for Richter were just as mixed. But the Italian's collegial feelings were almost always uncharitable. Jacques Leiser, who beginning in 1963 was Michelangeli's personal agent, recounts that when asked which pianists he appreciated most, Michelangeli replied: "*Sono tutti morti!* [They're all dead]." In the beginning of December 1964, Richter played Grieg's Piano Concerto with Lorin Maazel at the Paris Opera, and Leiser persuaded a reluctant Michelangeli to come along. Only a month and a half later, Leiser had arranged a comeback for Michelangeli in Paris (where he had not performed in many years), and, by chance, he was to play the same work in the same venue. He had just toured with great success in the Soviet Union, and Leiser managed to get a place for them in the Goskoncert's loge.

During the Grieg concerto, Michelangeli was restless and ill at ease. "I noticed that he was making grunting sounds," Leiser relates, "but I tried to ignore them. After the performance, Richter came back onstage and played the last movement *da capo*. Then Michelangeli stood up with a loud '*Basta!* [Enough]' and disappeared from the loge." Leiser followed him, distressed. He had promised Richter that he would bring the Italian backstage after the concert. The two pianists had never met each other. After an espresso at the bar while Richter played, Michelangeli calmed down a bit. Reluctantly, he consented to go along but mumbled, "*Ho niente da dire* [I have nothing to say]." Leiser begged him; he told him he did not have to talk to Richter but could merely shake hands with him. "Richter received him with a warm smile, but Michelangeli was like a statue, like the statue in *Don Giovanni*." Then Leiser and Michelangeli had dinner with the artistic head of Phillips and his wife (who spoke fluent Italian). "While I was absorbed in conversation with my colleague, I suddenly heard a deep sob, and I realized that his wife was crying. Michelangeli had apparently said something quite horrible. That evening made me years older," Leiser says with a sigh.

The perfectionist Michelangeli was known and criticized for canceling concerts on short notice when he was not convinced he could achieve perfection. Richter was also known to cancel when he did not want to play. However, he denied ever having canceled when he was not sick. But whether *sick* here means "plagued by physical infirmities" or simply "indisposed," incapable of handling the ferocious expectations, the spinning wheels of commerce, or the agony of stage fright is unclear. At one point repeated cancellations earned him the nickname "the Maria Callas of the piano." He was a devoted admirer of the great diva, whom he had heard live only once, at La Scala ("a miracle . . . impossible to live up to"). Obviously, the comparison emphasized Richter's own star status. He insisted that he always tried to make up for cancellations later. But that was often cold comfort to a disappointed audience.

The moral aspect of this issue can be assessed very differently. To claim a musician has a right to cancel an obligation when he does not believe he can do the music and the audience full justice makes sense. But, as was often true with Richter, a strong element of the need for freedom and willfulness also plays a role. With frankness, the ninety-three-year-old Kurt Sanderling reveals his own view:

You could never know what he wanted to play or *whether* he wanted to play at all. In Moscow, it happened—I cannot document it—that he canceled a piano soiree four times and performed only on the fifth scheduled time. The audience apparently forgave him but not the organizers. They were left with empty concert halls. I don't know how he behaved in the West, but when he came to us at the Berlin Symphony, shortly after I had moved to the DDR [East Germany], he played once and canceled three times. Then, I didn't invite him again. I simply couldn't do that to the audience.

He was very sensitive. Perhaps more sensitive than one has a right to be as a performing artist. I believe that you have obligations to your audience. If people have traveled to hear my concert, I cannot simply report that I have a headache. And he did that, perhaps too often. Even though you are a great artist, you have obligations to your audience. Because he behaved this way, he may not have been as beloved as he deserved.

About Richter the person there can be no disagreement: you can only admire him; he was a deeply fascinating person. All the things he knew! But in this respect, he was a split person. You shouldn't judge people, but I can only see it as a character flaw. "I'm not in the mood, so I won't play today!" As long as you live integrated in a society, you have obligations. I cannot say, "I am great when it suits me, and when it doesn't suit me, I am nothing." For me, there was a defect in his personality in this respect. Which, of course, does not alter the fact that he was a great and unique artist.

I didn't know him in his later years or had only sporadic contact with him. He didn't care for Berlin. He always traveled by train through the DDR, and the first station was Frankfurt an der Oder. He got off there and played, and simply went through Berlin. In Poland, the concert agency complained that he would only play outside of Warsaw. How do you explain this to your audience?

Sanderling's colleague Rudolf Barshai sees the matter differently.

Richter was one of the most serious people I have ever met. He was incredibly demanding of his collaborators, but above all of himself. It is true he canceled concerts. After Valentin Berlinsky replaced Mstislav Rostropovich as cellist for the Borodin Quartet, we played with him often. I remember that we had rehearsed a Brahms recital incredibly thoroughly. He simply went on and on, he wouldn't stop. The day before the concert, however, he felt ill, but he did not actually cancel. He postponed the concert. He always tried to perform a canceled concert at a later date.

Once, we were together in Budapest before one of his piano soirees. Throughout the night, I heard him practicing Ravel's *Alborado del grazioso*, the same passage x number of times! His concert was a triumph, but he took Ravel off the program. . . . His attitude was simple: All or nothing!

After Richter began to give concerts in the West, the major music centers of Berlin and Warsaw were rarely on his calendar. He made no secret of the fact that his choice of concert venues was guided by personal preference, not any feeling of obligation. He returned again and again to the railway station of Rolandseck in Bonn. Here he often performed for free—for example, for his friend Johannes Wasmuth's charitable program for poor children. The city's venerable Beethoven Hall was, on the other hand, a rare exception. And reprehensible or not, this issue is an integrated part of the Richter story. He despised any long-term planning with all his heart, although it is an inevitable part of the modern music business. Today it is not unusual for famous musicians to have their calendars filled three to four years in advance. The idea of knowing today what you are going to be doing, for example, on a Wednesday in May in four years' time would frighten people other than Richter. "If I have a work ready and want to play it, then I do it wherever I can, at the local school, it doesn't matter, and for free. . . . I may be on form today, but who knows what I'll feel like on such and such a date in the more or less distant future?"

In the commercial concert business, this point of view speaks the language of the *enfant terrible* and has led to many misunderstandings. At one point, it was said that Richter preferred smaller halls to larger ones or that he no longer had any desire to play concerts with orchestras. But the explanation was far more down to earth: large halls and competent orchestras must be booked far in advance. Someone like Richter, who hated long-term planning and always wanted to see new places, would necessarily have had to play without orchestras in smaller halls.

"When I arrive in a country, I prefer to open a map and show my impresarios the places that have certain associations for me or that excite my curiosity, and, if possible, that I have not yet had a chance to visit. We then set off by car, followed by the pianos. And then I may play in a theatre or chapel or in a school playground in some remote corner of, say, Provence," he tells Monsaingeon. "Or a concert every other evening announced by the local police officer, in some little village that just has a pretty little church or a school." Several times, he toyed with the idea of free concerts. If it created problems for the sponsors, well, he would just put a black top hat out in the middle of the stage, and people who wanted to contribute could do so (a suggestion that hardly won him applause among agents and organizers). He told Chemberdzhy that he once tried to provide free tickets, "but scalpers simply bought up all the tickets. I so much wanted to play for free in order to be free of snobs and the well-to-do."

If the truck with the grand piano was not with him, he played on whatever instrument he could get ahold of, a Blüthner, Bechstein, Estonia, Hindsberg, Förster, Baldwin, Haase, Yamaha, or, perhaps, a Soviet "Red October," "Moscow," or "Yenisei," regardless of the qualities or deficiencies of the instrument. He recalled terrible pianos deep in the heart of Russia on which he believed to have played "extremely well." His favorite story is about a concert at the Soviet embassy in Paris. The local piano tuner pronounced the embassy's grand piano "completely unusable," and Richter canceled the concert. But at five o'clock in the afternoon, the ambassador called: "The audience is arriving. What shall I do? Shoot myself?" Richter took pity on him and played anyway, convinced that the concert was going to be a catastrophe. He played, among other things, a sonata by Brahms. "It was probably my best concert of the season. You have to believe that you'll walk on water. If you don't believe it, you'll go under."

This apparent forbearance with the practical-technical sides of his profession, however, is by no means the whole story about the pianist and his work tool. In the book *Music Makers on Record*, the Indian-born record producer Suvi Raj Grubb, who was the assistant of Walter Legge, the legendary head of EMI/His Master's Voice's famous Abbey Road Recording Studios in London, relates an episode in connection with Richter's recording in November 1969 of Prokofiev's Fifth Piano Concerto with Lorin Maazel:

> I was warned that Richter had to be treated with extreme tact and that he was very sensitive as to whether the keyboard was completely level. I went to great effort with a spirit level to make sure that it was completely even. Richter arrived, returned my greetings gloomily, walked over to the piano and played an ascending scale: the bubble was not exactly in the centre, but only a couple of millimeters to one side. We put a thin piece of cardboard under the left leg. Then the bubble moved some millimeters in the opposite direction. After several attempts, we put two sheets of cigarette paper to make the bubble hit the exact centre! Again, Richter played a scale, now descending. He declared himself satisfied, and the recordings began.

Sometimes Richter himself brought along a spirit level to test the precise position of the keyboard.

Presumably, it had to do with the fact that he gave many concerts in halls that were also used for plays, and, therefore, the stage floor slanted slightly downward and toward the audience. Hence, one or more wedges or blocks had to be put under the legs of the piano. And if his minute care may sound eccentric, most pianists will concede that even a slight gradation changes the geometry, even the very feeling, of spaces on the keyboard in a disturbing way.

In August 1967, at the music festival in the vacation town of Menton on the French Riviera, Richter had a piano tuner made available who was to have a decisive significance for him, Teruhisa Murakami from the Yamaha piano company in Tokyo. Richter suggested that he come along to a small town in the vicinity of San Remo, where the day before his recital in Menton the pianist was to "try out" his program of Beethoven and Schubert. The rented Steinway in the little hall had seen better days, but Richter was quite satisfied with Murakami's preparations. However, he mentioned that he found the attack a bit too light. When Murakami was about to tune the instrument in Menton the next day, he got nervous. The audience that evening would include luminaries of the piano world such as Emil Gilels, Wilhelm Kempff, and Byron Janis, and celebrities such as Maria Callas and Grace Kelly were also expected. In a Japanese publication (*What Good Sound Is*, 2001), Murakami writes: "I lowered the keyboard a paper-thin amount (0.2 millimeters) and extended the distance between the hammers and strings by 0.1 millimeter. This was within the limits of changes that a piano tuner can make. I adjusted the mechanics of the piano in this way, so that Richter would feel the keystroke as heavier." After the concert, Richter embraced him with the words "wonderfully tuned!" A journalist overheard the remark, and it made newspaper headlines. Offers to Murakami streamed in.

Precisely at that point, Yamaha's new concert grand (Yamaha CF 275) had arrived by ship in Germany, Italy, and France and had slowly begun to spread throughout the European market. On January 30, 1969, Richter was to play a Mozart concert together with I Solisti Veneti in Padua. He was not happy with the instrument at the Verdi Hall and suggested a Yamaha. He had become a Yamaha fan. In the summer of 1969, he returned to Menton, where Yamaha had become the official instrument of the festival. Thereafter, he played in Bonn, Essen, Hanover, Cologne, and Wiesbaden, among other places, always accompanied by Murakami, his younger colleague Koh Segawa, and a Yamaha concert grand piano. A year later Richter used a Yamaha at the festival in Tours, and at the beginning of September, he was to perform for the first time in Japan. Richter, who hated flying, had given up the idea of such a long journey, but in August 1970 he traveled by train the long distance from Moscow to Nakhodka and, from there, sailed to Osaka.

People had gathered at the harbor, and he was received like a head of state. But Murakami could not convince the local concert organizers that Richter wanted to play on a Yamaha. Japanese national feeling did not extend far enough for them to believe that the world-famous star would choose a Japanese piano. All of the agreements had been entered into with the Soviet Ministry of Culture; none of those locally responsible knew Richter, and no one was aware of his preferences. There were no fewer than five pianos for Richter to choose from on the stage at the Osaka Festival Hall: two Steinways, one Bösendorfer, and two Yamahas. But Richter—who hated having to choose pianos—threw up his hands with the remark that he just wanted to play on the piano that normally belonged to the hall. That was a Steinway, and Murakami, who would not tune a competing maker's grand piano, listened to Richter play with disappointment. At five o'clock in the morning, however, Nina Dorliak woke up the piano tuner in his hotel room: "Richter wants to play on Murakami-san's piano!" Richter had thought that the hall's piano would have to be a Yamaha. "It is a Japanese piano, isn't it?"

In September and October, Richter gave some twenty concerts in Japan, always on a Yamaha. As mentioned, he developed a great love for Japan and Japanese audiences and returned numerous times to the country. In 1979, when he visited Japan for the third time, he suggested to Murakami that he give a free concert for the piano makers and other craftsmen at the Yamaha factory. This became a tradition every time he visited the country (a tradition he later continued at Yamaha's European factories). Moved by his generosity, Murakami tells of the tremendous impression Richter made on the two hundred employees attending the concert in their work clothes. And Richter complained loudly that the Soviet Union had nothing that could compare with Yamaha's technical academy, an ambitious school where they educated and trained piano tuners.

He signed a contract with Yamaha's division in Paris, and thereafter the firm made piano transport available in Japan and Western Europe pursuant to Richter's needs and desires. He was almost always accompanied by a personal piano technician from Yamaha; for many years this was Segawa, and in his later years the younger Kazuto Osato. In Japan a newly tuned instrument always awaited him at his hotel, even when he was staying only one night.

In certain circles people still wonder at the fact that Richter chose a Yamaha and not a Steinway, "the instrument of the immortals." Richter's own explanation (to his Japanese interpreter Midori Kawashima) was that "Yamaha is a passive instrument. Therefore, it answers with the sound I want to hear." He realized that an instrument's quality does not necessarily have anything to do with the brand; more than anything, it has to do with the intonation and fine adjustments in the mechanism as suits the musician's individual needs and desires. "The most important thing is Yamaha's piano technicians," Richter admitted. "Without them, I might not play on a Yamaha." But he was not alone among the greats; when in 1981 Glenn Gould re-recorded the *Goldberg Variations*, he also chose a Yamaha (his Steinway piano tuner of many years refused to touch the instrument and referred to the recording as the "Yamaha Variations"). The fact that for Richter Yamaha was second to none had made a big impression. At Yamaha showrooms in cities such as Tokyo, Hamburg, and Paris he was received like royalty. But as far as the technology was concerned, Richter, with his prickly attitude to technology in general, was not for a moment interested in what the professionals did to optimize his instruments, to meet his expectations for attack, sonorous pianissimo, perfect evenness, and so on. He was like a motorist who is blissfully ignorant of the mysteries under the hood as long as the automobile works.

His own relationship to cars, by the way, was correspondingly pragmatic. Automobiles, of course, are highly "technological," and Richter never dreamed of learning to drive or getting a driver's license. Throughout his life, he was driven by others—his agents, his friends, his piano technicians, and so on. This did not prevent him from owning a car in Moscow, but he never got behind the wheel of his own car.

Whether Richter's "sensitivity," as Kurt Sanderling called it, is extralarge or not, it is impossible to ignore it as a constant factor in his relationship to his *métier*. Again and again, he spoke of the strain on his nervous system of always having to live up to his own reputation, like an Olympic champion who constantly has to compete against himself! "You can't imagine how it is, at my age, to debut in cities like New York, London, or Paris," he said with a sigh. In October 1961 he played in Paris for the first time, a couple of concerts in the enormous Palais de Chaillot. There were only a few posters, but news spread like wildfire. Almost ten thousand tickets were sold. Afterward, fashion magazines and the sensational weekly press (*Paris Match*, for example) published reports of the event, but the object of attention made himself invisible as soon as possible. He was annoyed with some of the fine points in his performance.

After the concert, a Parisian critic wrote, "He is a great pianist, but not a natural, true pianist." His staid body language, his introverted, brooding stage presence ("as if he'd been sentenced for a crime"), the pained, joyless facial expression, the bowed head "stretched out as if before an executioner," a colossal concentration locked up in an impenetrable cocoon, a magnetic nervousness, all this was the opposite of what the critic viewed as natural.

Most people know that the countless mannerisms accompanying Glenn Gould's playing became part of his myth (the heartless critique of his stage presence was one reason he gave up concerts). Richter would undoubtedly have nodded approvingly to Gould's self-defense: "The whole secret of what I had been doing was to concentrate exclusively on realizing a conception of the music, regardless of how it was physically achieved."

Richter was known for almost storming onto the stage, his back stiff and his head bent slightly to the side, and for hastening directly to the piano with a short, measured nod as the only acknowlegment of the audience. His cool,

Richter's hand drawn by aunt Dagmar at life size (note the ruler). Richter has added, "this is my hand" and also commented on the dirty nails with an arrow and the words "this is dirt."

distant relationship to the listeners, his anything but ingratiating attitude from the stage, the evasive, aloof *noli me tangere* in his presence, all of this was palpable to everyone, whether "true" or not. But it was natural in the simple, obvious sense that this was his nature.

The French pianist Philippe Cassard turned pages for Richter late in his life (and was told, "If you move at all, I will kill you," with an acid smile). Cassard recounted something of the physical aspects of Richter's playing in the periodical *Diapason*: "He places himself high, close to the piano. His always slightly tired gaze suddenly becomes intense, immobile, focused on the score or some distant point. A distinct breathing, slow and strong, puts his whole body into action, like a smith's hammer. I'm on the lookout for the moment he indicates with his head for me to get up, turn the page, and sit down again as quickly and quietly as possible. I watch his left hand, a cathedral arch with his middle finger as the support. At *fortissimo*, his body swings in a colossal movement toward the little finger which one imagines will be beaten to a pulp." From this description, it is easy to understand why so many colleagues envied Richter his physical equipment, and why he sometimes went by the name "the iron man."

When Slava and Nina first visited Schwäbisch Gmünd, Anna Richter and her husband invited a number of their acquaintances to a little get-together, and at one point Richter was encouraged to play for them; the house had an upright piano. On this humble instrument, Richter played Beethoven's D-Minor Sonata (*The Tempest*) and music by Chopin. Paul Moor relates: "It was a unique experience to sit at the end of the keyboard while he played. He seemed, almost literally, possessed. His eyes swelled, his breathing became heavy, and it seemed as if, in a sort of self-hypnosis, he'd forgotten everything in this world except the music and the piano in front of him."

Like most artists, Richter's playing style changed over the years. His musical interests and predilections took him through shifting landscapes, and with his fine antennae, he reacted to changing circumstances, to artistic and human experience, and to insights that gradually accumulated and were assimilated. Yet, to speak of a "development" is another matter. One cannot predict whether artists' work will increase in scope and depth (as with Verdi), or whether, as they grow older, they will look with wonder and perhaps envy at earlier achievements (as with Mendelssohn). And often it is a matter of taste. Perspectives and ideals are replaced, and the stimulants of creativity change. Whether the younger, more powerful, and incredibly spontaneous Richter who opened all the sluices is greater or lesser than the contemplative and at times philosophically introverted older Richter is a question listeners must decide for themselves.

What characterizes the mature Richter more than anything in the 1950s and 1960s is a colossal willingness to take risks. The devil-may-care fearlessness evident in many of the surviving recordings from Russian radio, the sense that he must either sink or swim, that art cannot be reconciled with a safety-first attitude, are an essential part of the almost hypnotic effect he exerted on an audience. His was a mental and artistic fearlessness, which is rare among the star pianists of our day. The price he paid was that his performance could sink. At one point he said, "You start to play and suddenly discover that you're simply incapable of it. Then you begin to get careless, and you suddenly feel indifferent about what comes out."

There are noticeable differences between the two stages in his career, the Soviet pianist and the world-class pianist. But these differences often go hand in hand with his choice of repertoire, which was constantly expanding and increasingly distant from the virtuosity of the Romantic piano repertoire. The always intuitive, often impulsive aspect of his playing, the willingness to trust to inspiration even when it did not arrive, meant that overcast evenings might succeed more stellar moments, that Olympic perfection sometimes arrived side by side with a loss of concentration or control.

Not until the end of his life can one possibly speak of a truly new phase, and this gave rise to some debate among the critics, with some of them hinting that

Richter was no longer Richter. Health problems and illness affected his final years, but he always refused to play if he did not think he was capable of honoring the demands he made on himself, which makes it unreasonable to see the change as the frailty of old age. Rather, it can seem as if this indefinable thing he described simply as "music" took on a new, almost hyperreal significance. Maybe reminiscent of Charles Ives's famous line "What has sound to do with music? What it sounds like may not be what it *is*!" Music is something more than sound. Behind all music, there is silence; music resounds against the stillness, which anyone who has ever silently hummed a melody will know. When music goes beyond this boundary, it does not stop being music. It only stops being sound. Music goes beyond itself and leads beyond itself, out into the world and inward into the mind. The strange, stammering, slightly highbrow organist Kretschmar in Thomas Mann's *Doctor Faustus* makes a similar observation: "Perhaps, it is music's deepest wish not be heard at all, or even seen, nor yet felt; but only—if that were possible—in some Beyond, the other side of sense and sentiment, to be perceived and contemplated as pure mind, pure spirit." That might have been Richter's credo in his final, difficult years, when some people began to speak of a certain "coolness" in his playing. But what some saw as the beginning of his decline can also be read as a new phase, a spiritualization of instrument and sound, perhaps even an aspiration for that place where instrument, music, and life meet in a close embrace. However that may be, it was and remained a perhaps unfulfilled possibility for Richter. No one could go farther down that road; a true heir of Richter simply does not exist among the great pianists of our time.

It is difficult to determine whether Richter had any true role models for his playing or his pianistic self-understanding. His unusual background, his slowly evolving decision to take the path of the piano meant that role models seemed hardly necessary or attractive to him; and Neuhaus was a teacher who certainly did not try to make clones of his students. Richter himself never referred to any role models.

But we do know that one decisive push in that direction occurred when the teenage Richter heard Vsevolod Topilin—who is almost forgotten now and totally unknown in the West—play Chopin in Zhitomir. Topilin, seven years Richter's senior, was highly regarded as David Oistrakh's permanent partner; in 1935–36 the pair created a stir in Western and Eastern Europe. For a time he was part of the student circle that Richter helped organize. As a sight-reader, he was in Richter's class.

Topilin's life story is a tragic, fateful drama: his father fell from his position as a high-ranking officer in the White Russian struggle against the Red Army,

Vsevolod Topilin after the Gulag.

and all his life he had to keep his fall secret. In 1941 Topilin volunteered to fight on the front against the Germans but wound up as a prisoner of war in a German concentration camp. In 1943 he was released and, as an "Eastern worker," was allowed to play the organ in Berlin. But at the end of the war, when he innocently returned to Moscow, he was immediately arrested and later sentenced to death as a collaborator (one remembers Richter's ironic words "just because he was not killed in battle"). However, the sentence was commuted at the last moment to ten years' labor in Siberia. In the Gulag, he worked as a forester and, later, as a medical assistant until 1954. He regained his piano-playing skills after his release, and in the final years of his life, he was a respected teacher at the conservatory in Kiev. He died in 1970.

Another figure—familiar only to a few Westerners—who *may* have been a role model for Richter was Vladimir Sofronitsky (Richter, in vain, tried to hear him in Odessa and later almost worshiped him). In Solomon Volkov's putative autobiography of Shostakovich, the composer describes Sofronitsky as a junkie and an alcoholic ("he might drink a bottle of cognac before a concert and collapse"). But in the final twenty-five years of his life, Sofronitsky was simply "the pianists' pianist" in his homeland, a cult figure whose reputation was growing steadily until he died of cancer in 1961 at the age of sixty. For most of his life, he was plagued by a bad heart and other health problems, and he had a reputation for canceling concerts abruptly. Often the reason was an acute attack of "heart palpitations," but the cancellations fueled rumors of alcoholism.

For forty years, Sofronitsky was in a turbulent marriage with Scriabin's daughter Elena, and as a Scriabin interpreter, he was in a class of his own. At the end of the twenties, the couple lived in Paris for a few years, where a veritable Russian music colony had congregated. Stravinsky, Rachmaninov, and the conductor Serge Koussevitzky were often in town, along with expatriate Russians such as Glazunov, Prokofiev, the pianist and composer Nikolai Medtner, the ballet impresario Diaghilev, and several members of the Scriabin family who resided there. The Parisian press wrote that Sofronitsky played "as if an audience did not exist." And many audience members recounted that onstage he seemed like a medium in a trance, as if a spiritual force he did not control was working through him. Like Richter, he always placed great emphasis on the musical architecture of a piano program.

Sofronitsky was, if such a thing is possible, even more "private" than Richter; his only close musical friend was Heinrich Neuhaus, who introduced Richter to the admired colleague. Rumor has it that the first—and perhaps only—time they met, Sofronitsky exclaimed "Genius," to which Richter could only answer "God!"

Today Sofronitsky can be heard on a large number of CDs playing a wide selection of standard works from the Russian and the international classical repertoire. Unfortunately, on the Arlecchino record label, the sound quality is unacceptably poor (apparently the CDs are crude copies of LPs that were issued by the state company Melodiya); a number of CDs from the Denon label, based on the original tapes, are apparently accessible only in Japan.

The importance of improvisation and inspiration as preconditions for the magic of music, the ability to become one with the music, and the mysterious personality that at once captivates and disappears seem to be common elements for the two great Russians Richter and Sofronitsky. The riddle of Richter can be compared to a phenomenon in quantum physics: things change because we try to measure them and to nail them down. Richter's playing was the very embodiment of what magicians call sleight of hand. Deftly, and with an elegant maneuver, he could make himself and his art appear and disappear again, like a rabbit in a hat. "What are you thinking about when you play?" asked a well-meaning, naïve journalist. Richter replied innocently: "What I'm playing!" An unassailable answer, and yet no answer at all. But this is an indication that Richter was not content with just playing. He *listened*—not to what he was feeling, thinking, or interpreting, but to the piano, to what he was playing. And here may also lie the answer to the question mark Richter left when he explained why he could never work as a conductor: his aversion to "power and analysis." The first is obvious: the conductor exercises a necessary authority— "power," if you will—and for the "different kind of boy" who became Sviatoslav Richter, any power over others was repulsive. But "analysis"? Does Richter's reiterated desire to reach into the deepest secrets of the composer and the music not presume analysis? Yes, undoubtedly. But here the word is linked to the *score*, not to the performance. Here, as elsewhere, Richter tried to preserve the mystery of music; listening to music with the score in hand takes away from the experience of its spontaneity and freshness, the surprise element is lost, and the magic disappears. The word "freshness" is a key recurring concept for Richter. The analysis of a musical work can never represent the work itself, and analysts habitually search for what they know, not for what they do not know. For the phenomenal sight-reader, the man who insisted on the authority of the score, the score was not the music. The notes are dormant music. "I never see the orchestra score for the piano concertos I play. I don't look, I listen. In this way, everything is a surprise for me. I can keep it all in my head and give my imagination free rein."

A recurring approach to the score is his unshakable requirement that the repeat sign always be observed. Many modern musicians find—with some justification—that these repetitions were meaningful at a time when the music was not well known or when it was heard for the first time, but that repetitions in works that are well known can often be superflous and even exhausting. Glenn Gould did not observe all the repetitions in his two legendary recordings of Bach's *Goldberg Variations*, which Richter viewed as an unforgivable artistic betrayal. "Anyone who does not play the repetitions in the final movement of Beethoven's *Appassionata* should be forbidden to play the sonata," he thundered. "The same is true of the first movement of Schubert's Sonata in B-flat Major, even though almost everyone fails to follow the repeat signs. People should *boo* anytime anybody leaves out the repetitions. But no one ever does." Richter recognized that many musicians feared the music would be too long and predictable. But he was certain that both the composer and the audience would feel cheated. "For me, it is simply disgusting and foolish. It shows that these musicians do not understand the music. They do not love it enough. They are afraid it is going to be boring simply because they are unable to sustain the excitement; they are unsure of themselves. So they skip over all the repetitions in Chopin's sonatas. So, I never listen to them anymore."

Richter believed the same is true when it comes to performing classical symphonies; the score is always inviolable. The *Destiny* Symphony is senseless, for example, if the beginning of the last movement is not repeated, he claimed. "People rarely take me seriously when I say that I feel almost robbed when the repetitions are missing. I have come to hear the *whole* work, and I'm cheated of a part of it." This point of view is not as eccentric as it may sound. Without the repetitions, the balance in a work can be affected; for example, the short first movement of the *Destiny* Symphony without the repetition becomes inappropriately short in relation to the middle movement. In Mozart's Sonata in D Major (KV 284), the first movement lasts only around three and a half minutes without repetitions, whereas the variation movement lasts almost twenty minutes, which Richter would have found absurd. He also believed that the use of repetitions took the pressure off the musician. "The first time, I play rather strictly," he told Chemberdzhy, "and with the repetitions I go 'out of myself,' so to speak. . . . With repetition, the artist finds true emotion."

A maybe understandable but also rather odd feature of many solo musicians is that they only reluctantly speak of the job's most obvious and time-consuming activity: working, learning, and *practicing*. At any rate, they speak reluctantly of how much and how long they practice. And finally, here is something that Sviatoslav Richter and Glenn Gould have in common. Both claimed again and again that the piano did not interest them. "I prefer the music," Richter replied if anyone asked him how he felt about the piano as an instrument. And, again, one may consider the difference between a *pianist* and a *musician* who just happens to play the piano. Gould practiced in the recording studio, "on the firm's time," as he claimed. But who can seriously believe that anyone could manage the singing legato that Richter mastered in his Chopin etudes with such dexterity or his tightly controlled pianissimo without spending days, weeks, and months training the convolutions of the brain, finger movements, and muscles?

Several of Gould's colleagues knew him to "practice quite a bit." He claimed, however, that he practically never practiced; for him, it was enough to read the music. Richter insisted that he normally played only three hours a day. "I keep a stop-watch at the piano and try to control how long I practice." But many people, including his companion, Nina Dorliak, remember that Richter sometimes practiced almost around the clock. His friend the pianist Andrei Gavrilov claims that Richter could play the same page of a sonata more than seventy times in a row. And Richter conceded that when pressured under special circumstances—Prokofiev's Seventh Sonata in four days and Rachmaninov's Second Piano Concerto in a week—he put in long hours.

On the other hand, others confirm that he did not touch a piano for weeks. His cousin Fritz Reincke relates that when his mother, Richter's aunt Dagmar (Mary), visited the young conservatory student in Moscow before the war, it worried her that he almost never sat down to practice for a concert until the last moment. Richter confirms this again and again. Reincke also remembers that after days of inactivity, he would suddenly play around the clock, practicing for several hours, sleeping an hour, playing for several hours again, and then an hour's sleep.

Presumably the truth lies somewhere in the middle. Richter's irritation at the myth of his being a workaholic who engaged in marathon practice sessions is yet another expression of his annoyance at anecdotes his admirers told over and over again. One of the recurring stories is that when Richter was dissatisfied with a concert, he would play the whole program once again, after the audience had left the hall. "Nonsense," he says. "It is true that, after my concerts, I have often practiced a new program for the next day. But why should I repeat a program I just played?" (However, to be fair, several witnesses insist that they heard Richter play the whole program again, at a slow tempo, immediately after the concert.)

There is no doubt that Richter felt ambivalent about the tyranny of having to practice. When his Japanese interpreter Midori Kawashima casually asked him one day when he wanted to start practicing, he answered, "Never! I only do it because I have to." And when she hinted that she did not believe that a world-famous pianist would need to practice a lot, he almost shouted: "What? When I was younger I didn't need to practice that much. But when you grow older, it becomes more difficult to keep in form. Now I have to practice twice as much. As a young man, I practiced in the hope of being able to play the works better. Now I'm not sure that it improves the quality. Now it is just necessary."

Perhaps we should remember that the pianist Sviatoslav Richter, to an unusual degree, was a performer who *plays*, not one who practices. As a younger man, he allowed sheer desire to guide him. But many people who were close to him in later years recount that he had a practice book in which he kept careful accounts of how many hours he should have practiced according to his schedule but never actually did. On November 12, 1986, while in Irkutsk, he told Chemberdzhy he "owed" no less than 585 hours! And in March of the same year, he noted in his journal, "When everything is going well, why always this sadness and bad conscience. The eternal theme." Some years later, Andreas Lucewicz remembers him mentioning a deficit of 540 hours.

His attitude to the task of practicing, like his relationship to many other things, is marked by a down-to-earth view of reality: what is easy goes quickly, what is hard takes time! Something is hard in the simple sense that the music is acrobatic, requiring virtuosity; he mentions Scriabin's Fifth Sonata and Liszt's

First "Mephisto" Waltz as examples of the technically most difficult pieces in the repertoire—"devilishly difficult"—and yet these are works he often played but shelved in later years. However, music can be "difficult" in other ways. He found Handel and—perhaps surprisingly—Mozart difficult; not until his sixties did these two composers come to play an important role in his programs.

He worked the way musicians have done for centuries: "I take a page at a time, and don't move on to the next until the first one is under my belt. . . . I never play a piece in its entirety until I've learned each page separately. And if I didn't have the pressure of a forthcoming concert, I'd never force myself to do any work. As a result, it's not unknown for me to play through a whole piece for the first time onstage." This may make some colleagues shake their head in amazement. Of course, Richter read the score before he began to practice. But how did he develop his view of the piece as a whole, of its larger form, with such a linear exercise strategy? The answer is, presumably, if thought-provokingly, he did *not*. His insistence on the element of surprise, the "freshness" he always sought, the free-running imagination, and the willingness to take risks meant that it was important for him to have the sonorous whole simply *arise*, unplanned. Or it exists in advance, in the score.

Practicing can be monotonous, almost like factory work, he admitted. And it does not always provide the desired results. It can feel like "bailing water with a sieve," he said with a sigh again and again. The only cure was to keep on learning new works. "There's nothing I detest more than repeating the same works all the time. I always have to have something new." Throughout his life, Richter retained his interest in the visual arts and painting. But he gave up his own activities as an artist in the 1970s. "I realized that I was always repeating the same thing. It was easy for me, it went fine, but I wasn't developing. It became boring. If you want to do something seriously, it has to develop, and I didn't have time for that."

All his life he avoided scales, exercises, Czerny etudes, and other finger exercises that are the everyday experiences of pianists at every level. The explanation must be found in his self-controlled, autodidactic approach and his consistent refusal to play music he did not care for. (Only a very few performers love scales and finger exercises for purely musical reasons.)

People who were present when Richter practiced describe his methods very differently—so differently, even from his own descriptions, that the idea of a conscious, well-considered method is probably a misrepresentation. Richter spoke to Milstein in detail about his working method:

> One of the problems with working as a concert pianist is the lack of time to concentrate. The reason you sometimes work poorly is that you're not always

able to go into depth. . . . Often there is a lot you must do in a short time. The musician is part of a system. The music cannot exist in itself, on its own power; it is part of the whole. What is important for me is to feel liberated when I work at the instrument. I struggle with emotional strain or distraction. . . . My feeling of security comes from an in-depth study of the score. I study it with care; everything that is important is set out here. . . . What is not revealed at first glance slowly begins to appear, to take shape, to be defined. In a certain sense, everything comes by itself. In a technical sense, I think the help you get from your hands is of great importance—at times, on a purely psychological plane. If you meet with a technical problem in one hand, the other hand's symmetrical movement may help solve it.

The young Richter's most comprehensive attempt to describe his working method is found in an early interview (June 1947) with the musicologist Alexander Vishinsky. Here he is at the age of thirty-two:

Normally, I always begin to practice a new work at a slow tempo. But I have a tendency involuntarily to speed up the tempo. I've discovered how important it is to relax the hands to the greatest extent possible when you play slowly. Which I naturally only do in pieces that are quick or very quick. The slow tempo helps make it easier to remember the movements. And if I have already learned a piece, it provides a pleasant feeling of physical freedom to play it slowly and very precisely and then repeat it at the correct tempo.

When I begin to learn a new piece, I open the score and find the most difficult place and begin to practice. I'm not trying for a particular interpretation. In that way, everything is clear to me right from the beginning. It's all in the score. The slow, problem-free passages I often play only a few days before the concert. And I always play, regardless of tempo, with the full expression of the whole music, as it appears in the notes.

To the question of whether he played from a score or from memory, he answered: "It depends on how long there is to the concert. If it is a short time, I immediately begin to learn it by heart. That is quite exhausting, and what I play from memory on one day, I sometimes forget the next. It is better not to work in that way. In any case, I learn very quickly. But if I use this method, I can easily become disturbed by something. I thought I knew the music by heart, but . . ."

Apparently, his routine of practicing three hours a day came later. "It can happen that I work eleven hours for two or three days and then hardly touch the piano for a week. I cannot work if I'm bored, if I'm working without enthusiasm. When the desire is there, I can sit at the piano for twelve hours. Then I learn very quickly. But without the desire, I can't play a note. It is very difficult to persuade yourself to play two or three hours a day. For me, it doesn't work. I play for a week and then don't for a week."

Vishinsky asked how he kept up his repertoire, whether he always went through the pieces meticulously before each concert. "It depends entirely on the work. It is enough to play Chopin's nocturnes a couple of hours before the concert. But a work like Prokofiev's Seventh Sonata, on the other hand, you have to work very hard on beforehand. Yet, sometimes, repetition is a bad idea. Something troubling might happen, so you become very worried, and then it's like walking to the scaffold. Of course, if you don't play the pieces before the concert, things can go wrong. But you can also play excellently without having played through the pieces beforehand—at any rate, if you put them in the last part of the program. Some of the most virtuoso pieces in my repertoire, I simply *can't* play before the concert."

Was he nervous before concerts? the interviewer asked. Richter replied:

Of course. Sometimes more, sometimes less. It has nothing to do with the audience. But I can be worried about some sort of slipup. You have a sense of where it can happen, and that is why you bungle it instead of feeling completely liberated. And it happens that the feeling of liberation just doesn't come. This feeling at a concert is weird. It can swing between nervous concern and cold, absent indifference.

It is especially in the simplest pieces that I worry about a lapse of memory, pieces with repetitions that have only slight differences. But if you're afraid of forgetting something with the left hand, then you have to concentrate with your whole attention on the right. It almost always works. If you're afraid that the fingers will forget something, you can be sure it will happen. The ear remembers; you have to use your ears and just let the hands play. If you start thinking about the fingers, something even worse happens; then your movements become stiff.

What about disturbances from the outside, coughing from the hall, noise? "It doesn't bother me. I don't think about the audience at all, only my playing. I know that if I play well, then people will be listening and sitting quietly."

During his third (and last) American tour in 1970, almost twenty-five years after this interview, he looked at his work differently. He told his cousin Walter Moskalew that he had learned to practice properly only recently (he was almost fifty-five!) and that he would be able to play far better if he worked with more discipline—if, for example, he practiced three hours a day. During this visit to the United States, Moskalew often heard him practice not new pieces but works in his repertoire—usually as play-throughs and in tempo (or almost

tempo), presumably to refresh his memory. He did not care to have long intervals between concerts. He "kept in form" by playing concerts, he said.

Moskalew relates:

Some remarks [he made] to me in 1970 may summarize his whole attitude. He said that when you practice, you should play expressively and keep
exactly to the dynamic instructions but hold back a little and keep the full
expressive power for the concert. And his *fortissimo* was definitely not what
you heard at his concerts. Presumably, he wanted to make sure there was
room for spontaneity. He always preferred being surprised, and "drilling" a
performance to the last detail was alien to him for the same reason. What he
feared most was apathy. Some of his best concerts, he said, resulted when he
was angry or elated.

His mood also influenced his preparation. In New York in 1970, Nina and
I wanted to go into town, but he stayed home, reluctantly. He had to practice,
even though he didn't want to. He seemed depressed. Unnoticed, I left a tape
recorder running. In an hour, he practiced Beethoven's D-Major Variations
opus 76, and he was clearly frustrated with how it was going. Lots of mistakes, almost as if he had not yet learned the piece or had forgotten it (but a
couple of days later, he played it brilliantly at Carnegie Hall). He kept repeating certain passages again and again, sometimes slowly, most often at concert tempo. When we returned, and Nina asked how it had gone, he made a
face and said that his fingers felt *kak makaroni*, like cooked noodles.

Later in the spring of 1970, when he had recovered from the flu at his aunt
Dagmar in Somerville [Massachusetts], he practiced Beethoven's *Diabelli
Variations*. He said he discovered that he achieved *pianissimo* best by playing
"from the shoulder." I understood by this that the elbow and the wrist were
to be kept steady. Even when he rehearsed, he observed all the repeat signs
(but that is what he was known for). He believed the last variation was the
most difficult, perhaps the most difficult piece in all of Beethoven's oeuvre.
And he was apparently dissatisfied with himself. He never played the *Diabelli
Variations* in the U.S.

It made me recall a similar comment he had made ten years earlier, this
time about the Mozart D-Minor concerto. I asked him why he played the
middle section of the Romanze so slowly. Having been introduced to this
concerto through a recording by Clara Haskil, who plays the middle section
quite tempestuously, I found Richter's slow pace inappropriate, if not per-
verse (I didn't say that, of course). To me it conjured up a storm (I was thinking of Beethoven's *Pastoral* Symphony and Vivaldi's *Summer*). He shrugged
and said, "But what I imagine here is a running brook . . . a waterfall." At

another time, talking about Beethoven's *Appassionata*, he remarked how the last movement becomes progressively more wild and then with the Presto it turns into some kind of dance of witches and devils.

I belive that his playing was always deeply affected by the visual images the music suggested to him, and perhaps it was this capacity for visualizing sound that enabled him to control and balance the larger musical structures so well.

In his conversations with Milstein, Richter spoke of how he visualized Schumann's *Noveletten*: one was about "a hero who wound up on a pirate ship, in the middle of the ocean during a storm." Another was tragic, "with harbingers of catastrophe." At one point, the music made him think of "a sunset, mysteries, like a painting of an old master"; another has "an atmosphere that makes me think of Goya." In Beethoven's *Appassionata*, "everything takes place at night ... the herald of a nocturnal storm, the twinkling of the stars ... and something cosmic in the finale, like voices calling to each other across endless space."

But he told Vishinsky that "when you play, you don't think of images, but of tone, tempo, breathing. It may be that images arise, but they have no impact. They may have an influence when you choose the repertoire. I get images from all the works I play. And a piece may be associated with certain memories. But the memories in themselves have no significance when you are playing. They can create a particular mental state, but to mix them into specific works would only disturb you."

This visual imagination clearly did not turn him in any way into a "program musician." Among Beethoven's works, for example, he esteemed the early, classical ones the most. "I love the first of Beethoven's piano concertos more than all the others. When I hear the orchestral introduction, I can feel a deep emotion overwhelm me as if something light, something wonderful appears to me." The direct, young, courageous, and fresh Beethoven of the early sonatas appealed to him more than the late, Romantic, and dramaturgical, image-creating Beethoven.

A rather unknown side of Richter's relationship to his instrument was his interest in improvisation, a natural outlet for his interest in composing, to which he never gave full expression. His friend Viktor Zelenin tells that he was an excellent improviser and that late in life he even considered giving concerts with improvisations, but he gave up the idea because he was afraid his imagination might run into "dead spots."

In 1981 he decided once and for all to flout the expectation that a pianist play without the score, that is, by heart. The idea had preoccupied him for a long time. He had often played with the score in front of him. But the occasion for this irrevocable decision was a performance of a selection of Liszt's *Transcendental Etudes* at the festival at Grange de Mesley, "a particularly dreadful concert." Why increase the psychological pressure by playing without the score? he asked himself. Was it not a silly convention or empty vanity? And if the audience had this expectation, why did they not have the same expectation when one played chamber music?

He admitted that it required practice to achieve full mental freedom if the notes were right in front of him, but he also discovered advantages. Even though the musical presentation might be particularly intense, the risk in trusting to memory was simply impractical in the long run, he believed. For who would claim to remember every single direction in the composer's hand, every single staccato sign, every single *tenuto*, every single accent, all the dynamics, tempo swings, phrasing or pedal use, all the character designations? With the score in front, one did not risk falling into bad habits or randomness, into *interpretation*. By freeing the brain from this unnecessary waste of time in memorizing all the details of the music, the musician could also avoid performing the same works again and again (and an audience could avoid always hearing the same thing). "I prefer to play twenty Haydn sonatas with the score in front of me rather than limiting myself to playing two from memory."

One of the most often discussed and controversial aspects of Richter's piano playing is his repertoire, his choice of music. He was not attracted to "composite works" and did not play all of the pieces in a collection (Bach's forty-eight "well-tempered" preludes and fugues and the second volume of Debussy's preludes are the most obvious exceptions). The idea of complete works may have seemed like a collector's point of view to him. And the literature's most popular collective works, Schubert's impromptus, Chopin's etudes and preludes, Liszt's *Transcendental Etudes*, and Debussy's etudes, for example, were hardly conceived as formal wholes by the composers. Moreover, he insisted on a completely personal relationship to every single musical work he played, and if something did not appeal to him, he did not play it. He was not interested in adaptations, transcriptions, and piano arrangements of music that were not originally composed for the piano, which implies an aversion (he played only some movements of Prokofiev's ballets, in the composer's own piano versions). He stayed away from certain masterpieces for entirely private reasons—for example, because colleagues such as Neuhaus and Gilels had already interpreted them "definitively."

But it can be difficult to understand, for example, why he was attracted only to the second of three movements, "Le Gibet" (The Gallows), of Maurice

Ravel's *Gaspard de la Nuit*. Here there is undoubtedly a formal whole. But he believed—although this is hardly self-evident—that the famous final movement, "Scarbo," was modeled on Liszt's *Mephisto*: certainly extremely sophisticated but not, like Liszt, displaying a work of genius. Nor is it obvious why he ignored one of Schumann's major works, his *Carnaval*. Nevertheless, he is considered by many one of the greatest Schumann interpreters. And why, of Schumann's three sonatas, did he play only number 2 in G minor? He apparently kept away from Schumann's fabulous *Kreisleriana* out of respect for Neuhaus's interpretation. It is surprising that he did not play some of the greatest piano hits such as Beethoven's Fourth Piano Concerto or his Concerto in B-flat Major (his first concerto, but known as number two), Brahms's First, Rachmaninov's immensely popular Third, or César Franck's "Symphonic Variations," for example. And the fact that he played overlooked concertos by Dvořák, Saint-Saëns, Rimsky-Korsakov, and Glazunov may seem almost eccentric. Richter played Handel, who was almost forgotten as a piano composer, but not the extremely popular Scarlatti. Of course, he played Mozart, but significantly more Haydn. On the other hand, he played overlooked works by Schumann, Chopin, and Liszt, works of whose existence even professionals were almost ignorant.

As he emphasized again and again, he was governed entirely by personal preferences, by a spontaneous, perhaps passing, love for certain works, as when he threw himself into major and demanding works only to play them once or a couple of times. This was true, for example, for Scriabin's complex, secretive Sixth Sonata, Stravinsky's *Capriccio*, Richard Strauss's "Burleske" for Piano and Orchestra, and several Mozart concertos. And it was hardly due to a fear of the technical demands of these works. His recording for Melodiya of the Scriabin sonata, for example, is unsurpassed.

His more recent repertoire—from Brahms to Prokofiev and Britten—was without parallel among world pianists. Strangely, he rarely played music by Stravinsky, and then not until the 1980s. Karol Szymanovski (who, as mentioned, was closely related to Neuhaus) appealed to him in his student days. It is likely that Neuhaus put him on the track of this sonorous and harmonically original piano music. He played Szymanovsky's Second Piano Sonata as early as 1939, and after the war he added several works by this Polish composer to his repertoire. He also advocated a great many of the milestones of modern piano music. He played Bartók's monstrously difficult Second Piano Concerto for the first time in Budapest in 1958, but only a few times, and never his far simpler and far more popular Third. With his friend Anatoli Vedernikov, he recorded Bartók's Sonata for Two Pianos and Percussion. In the mid-1980s, he played Anton Webern's pioneering and strictly dodecaphonic variations for piano some twenty times, and in Moscow he tried his hand at Stravinsky's Webern-inspired "serial" *Movements* of 1959.

New music also interested him, although he did not play it; he believed it often required specialists. But the music of Xenakis fascinated him, and he sometimes listened to composers such as Boulez, Lutosławski, and Berio with interest. Nevertheless, he spoke with skepticism about modern music when it took on the character of a pseudoscience—"I want music that pleases and gives delight." He considered his younger countryman Alfred Schnittke one of the twentieth century's most significant composers (and admitted that he also esteemed him highly because Schnittke had praised his staging of Benjamin Britten's two chamber operas). But he did not play Schnittke's piano music. On the whole, piano music by younger Soviet composers (including internationally known names such as Denissov, Gubaidulina, and Firsova) was absent from his repertoire.

He found Paul Hindemith "much too undervalued" and performed not only his piano concerto from Kammermusik No. 2 some fifty times but also the twelve preludes and fugues that constitute *Ludus Tonalis*, the expansive, powerful Suite "1922," and a couple of his piano sonatas. In addition, he played the piano part in many of Hindemith's other sonatas, several of the violin sonatas, the bassoon sonata, the viola sonata, and the sonata for trumpet. For a long time, he planned to learn Max Reger's rarely performed piano concerto but ultimately gave it up as "too time-consuming." At the age of seventy-eight he even performed George Gershwin's Concerto in F a few times.

The Italian critic Piero Rattalino compared Richter's significance in the development of the piano with such epoch-making pianists as Liszt and Ferruccio Busoni, each appearing at an interval of about fifty years. Liszt became the father of modern piano. Busoni set a new historical standard for the requirements of a pianist. He saw piano music as a refined mirror of the development of Western civilization and distinguished between pianists who threw a spotlight on the music and those who selected from the music to cast a spotlight on themselves.

And in Richter's repertoire, Rattalino saw anything but a random selection from the shelves. He saw a purposeful design, an attempt to show contexts, patterns, and unities, particularly the attempt of French music to free itself from German traditions and habits. An example is the development from César Franck's symbolist *Les Dijons*—a symphonic poem with a piano, not a piano concerto—to two of Saint-Saëns's piano concertos to Ravel and Debussy. When he played Ravel's Concerto for Left Hand but not his Gershwin-like, slightly fashionable Concerto in G Major, it was to show how the Russian tradition from Mussorgsky on gave new French music impulses that liberated it not only from German dominance but also from French academicism, which also explains his hatred of Ravel's orchestral version of *Pictures at an Exhibition*; when the French connoisseur embraced the Russian child of nature, Mussorgsky became a stepchild.

Rimsky-Korsakov, Glazunov, Diaghilev, Stravinsky, Prokofiev, and other Russians in Paris were magnetic fields in the energetic dialogue that lasted for fifty years between these two self-assured, "alternative" music cultures. (For some time, the young Debussy was a piano tutor for the daughters of Tchaikovsky's pen pal Madame von Meck.) The Russian nationalist traits in Richter's self-understanding should not be underestimated just because patriotism is considered tasteless. His love of, for example, Rimsky-Korsakov might well make a Western music lover feel that he must have overlooked something. "If a masterpiece like his opera *The Snow Maiden* disappoints, it is always due to the interpretation. All of Rimsky's music is chamber music, but conductors insist on playing him pompously. He is like a butterfly. If it is not touched with tenderness, its wings lose their dust."

Thus, it is also easy to understand his love of Debussy. "A girder in musical history goes between these points—Mozart, Chopin, and Debussy. Debussy is infinitely varied and elegant, but at the same time incredibly simple. And this simplicity is very difficult to go into and pass along. Ravel is an important composer, very talented and sophisticated. But Debussy is a genius!" His relationship to Stravinsky's vital and original piano music is more difficult to come to terms with, although he always speaks about it in enthusiastic terms. Richter never played Stravinsky's Piano Concerto; for years, he dreamed of playing his 1929 *Capriccio*, but when he finally decided to learn it, he played it only once, in Meslay in the mid-1980s. As mentioned, his intent to perform the work in Copenhagen, where he received the 1986 Sonning Prize, came to naught. He considered the greatest composer of all the arch-German Richard Wagner ("on a level with Shakespeare!"), a seeming paradox, as Wagner did not—or only very sporadically—compose piano music.

A consistent Russian perspective guides Richter's love affair with the piano, and it may be the guiding thread that, through all the seeming randomness, binds his repertoire together into a huge, tightly woven tapestry.

PART IV

The Man behind Invisible Walls

It would be wrong to imagine that the many mysteries surrounding Richter will diminish or be solved by getting closer to the man himself and forgetting everything about the pianist, the musical genius, the intense art lover. For here, too, he is teeming with contradictions. Yet, it is also clear that countless people with whom he was acquainted will see a man of the world like Richter very differently. Some will recall an introverted world-class star, and others will remember a cordial friend or colleague. In his case, the myth-making began long before he left this world behind.

Some of his idiosyncrasies are noticeable everywhere, such as his fierce protection of his privacy in a profession that always entails being in the limelight. He hated being looked at when he was not playing; he did not understand the titillating experience of being "recognized," which some celebrities enjoy. Autograph hounds usually waited in vain outside the concert halls. Richter preferred to disappear out the back exit, even before the applause had died away. His lifelong antipathy toward journalists, TV cameras, and so on, is legendary.

Other idiosyncrasies are anecdotal. For example, for a man who all his life could remember "every note" of an opera he had studied as a teenager, it is surprising to learn that he had no gift for numbers. He had no grasp of mathematics and claimed that he could not remember the number of his apartment or his telephone ("Everyone in Moscow knows my telephone number except me!"). He talked only grudgingly on the telephone, except for Nina Dorliak and sometimes his erotic liaisons. He never answered the phone unless he knew who was calling. The first thing he did in a hotel room was to unplug the phone. The telephone was one of the greatest plagues of the modern world, he maintained. His contact with the outside world was usually limited to postcards, letters, and telegrams.

The man who played the Chopin and Liszt etudes with incredible precision and often at a dizzying tempo always had Dorliak wind his watch, for the task required dexterous fingertips! His irritable and evasive relationship with the recording technology characterized his relation to literally anything having to do with mechanics.

He retained his childhood love of the theater and life's theatrical sides. Even in his student days, and later, he might take it into his head to invite friends to small, improvised theater performances where everyone was given a role. And these masquerades, sketches, and scenes stuck in the minds of everyone who participated. He even took on a film role: the part of Franz Liszt in a Russian feature on Mikhail Glinka, the "father of Russian music," in which Liszt, as a showbiz figure with long, flowing hair, plays showpieces and greets his Russian colleague. *Kompozitor Glinka* was made in 1952, directed by Grigori Aleksandrov.

But in real life as well, Richter liked role-playing and drama to such an extent that it bolstered his image as a complex and enigmatic man. When Kurt Sanderling described Richter as an *enfant terrible*, commenting on his conduct and eccentric choice of repertoire, he added: "*Aber es war vielleicht immer ein bischen Theater* [But perhaps it was always a bit of theater]." His friend the pianist Vladimir Viardo notes that in reality Richter wanted to ignore everything that was mundane or difficult: "He always wanted to play-act, to disguise himself, to play games and wear masks. His 'real' life was in the music. Here, there were no games or masks."

Yet, he hated musicians who were drama queens. Sometimes, however, he found a certain staging necessary, when the music demanded it. Usually he stormed onto the stage and began to play almost before he sat down. But because Liszt's great Sonata in B Minor begins *pianissimo* with some *pizzicato*-like notes in the bass and a slow, quietly descending melody line, he realized that the gloomy, enigmatic opening of this monumental piano work required intense focus by the audience. Therefore, he always used a theatrical trick: he sat down and slowly counted to thirty! This created incredible suspense in the hall; like one big antenna, all of the audience's attention was focused on him and the music.

Richter always examined his appearance with the care of an actor before he went onstage. Pianist Andreas Lucewicz, who often turned pages for him in later years when Richter no longer played from memory, relates that he always made sure his bowtie was perfectly straight and that his shirt was tucked smoothly into his pants. If he was dissatisfied, he would fasten his shirt to his pants with safety pins. He also checked the scores he needed onstage with the greatest care, again and again.

During his first visit to Aldeburgh in 1964, he saw Benjamin Britten's church parable *Curlew River* a few days after its premiere. He immediately fell in love with Britten's music theater and saw it or heard it at every opportunity. In 1983 he came up with the idea of introducing the Moscow audience to Benjamin Britten's two chamber operas *Albert Herring* (according to Richter, "the comic opera of the century") and *The Turn of the Screw* in a staged version. The performances were to take place during his December Nights festival; he collaborated with a director but soon found him incompetent and utterly unimaginative. "We were getting nowhere, sets and costumes were a disaster," he wrote in his notes (published by Monsaingeon). When his collaborator suggested that they abandon the staging for a concert performance, he took matters into his own hands. "I lost no time in concocting a surprise. The audience would think they were attending a concert performance, but they'd be shown a performance they weren't expecting, a sort of improvised charade." Richter had someone announce the performers, but suddenly the orchestra interrupted, and a singer came running through the hall; a staged concert piece had begun. The performance was full of surprising and droll ideas (for example, the audience was given flags, which they waved when a flag was waved onstage). Even in childhood Richter's theatrical imagination had been enormously fertile, and on numerous occasions he was tempted to work as a director. When the young conductor Lorin Maazel suggested that he stage Wagner's *Ring*, a host of images immediately came to his mind, "a rock turning all the time, avenues, horses, and sopranos who remained seated, never moving, while everything around them revolved . . . the whole scene being visible only in flashes, as if in flashes of lightning."

Richter's close friend Viktor Zelenin attests that he jotted down ideas for the staging of numerous operas. One might wonder whether the world lost a great conductor in Richter, but there is no doubt that the pianist stood in the way of a sparkling theatrical mind.

The Italian periodical editor Umberto Massini wrote that "the musician, the artist, the man who greedily gobbled up novels and films had an imagination of which—believe me, dear reader—I have never seen the like. His life was theater, his life was inventiveness every single day; he was continually performing for himself and others. He despised everything that might be the least bit 'routine,' a repetition of things that had already been done or seen. He detested banality."

As mentioned, Richter described his interest in music, art, literature, and theater as "voracious." Opera was and remained his great passion, with Wagner's *Götterdämmerung* highest on his list. But he always insisted that opera should be *seen*. He was amazed that, often, the better the opera was, the worse its staging. He found that opera directors were often self-absorbed and came up with the weirdest ideas simply because they were incapable of creating genuine opera. "Conductors bear some of the blame. They should protest against absurd stagings and refuse to conduct. I would in their place!"

He read writers such as Goethe, Schiller, Racine, Montaigne, Zola, Mann, Balzac, Rilke, Rimbaud, and Proust again and again, always slowly and carefully. As a young man, he read Ibsen's dramas aloud until three in the morning, or put himself in imminent danger when he walked the streets lost in his readings. He knew the great works of Russian literature intimately. Even in childhood, he rated Gogol higher than any other writer, but he also loved Pushkin and Dostoyevsky. He read American authors such as Ernest Hemingway and F. Scott Fitzgerald, but he was especially attracted to French literature, which he knew better than many Frenchmen. Yet, he always read it in Russian translation, even after his French had become fairly good over the years.

Even as a young man in Odessa, when he accompanied silent films, the darkness of the cinema had fascinated him. He would watch a third-rate film just to enjoy the atmosphere in the movie theater. He had an eye for details and objects, landscapes, interiors, and perspectives that most people would miss. His favorite film diva was the celebrated Eleonora Duse, but Marlene Dietrich, Ingrid Bergman, and Anna Magnani were also his idols, and among directors, he was particularly fond of Hitchcock, Kubrick, Polanski, and the Italians Visconti, Fellini, and Pasolini. *Gone with the Wind* made a huge impression on him. He cared less for Ingmar Bergman; he told Chemberdzhy that Bergman's films always "creep in under the skin, like a medical experiment." It seemed natural to him that one could watch a film as often as one listened to a piece of music. He claimed to have seen his favorite films more than thirty times.

Richter the film buff, however, was completely uninterested in television. When he and his friend Jacques Leiser visited Maria Callas (whom Richter admired unreservedly) in her Paris apartment, he wondered aloud why she owned a television set. Leiser says: "I acted as interpreter, and Richter insisted that television was harmful to one's health. He mentioned something about dangerous 'radioactivity'!" Sports such as football, tennis, athletics, cycling, and so on, the special contributions of this medium, had nothing to offer him, not even for the athletic skills that might excite his aesthetic appreciation. He knew that some people ran faster or jumped higher than others, but he could not care less who they were. Moreover, he always despised any form of competition. He loved long walks and sometimes relaxed by swimming or, on rare occasions, bicycling, the closest he came to exercise. Not even chess, the Russian national sport, which close friends such as Prokofiev and Oistrakh played at a high level, interested him.

Richter as a person is described in a confusing variety of ways by numerous observers at different times in his life. Part of the explanation lies in his enigmatically playful and more or less unconscious role-playing, but it is not the only reason. The few living people who knew him in his youth characterize him as a predominantly cheerful, straightforward, and strong man who enjoyed life, with a highly developed appreciation of all the little quirks and wonders of the world. When, after his success in the West, he became a prominent figure on the musical stage, many people increasingly saw him as introverted, self-protective, and unapproachable. In his memoirs, Dietrich Fischer-Dieskau described Richter as an "extremely vulnerable, sensitive person," a man who "found it more difficult than others to reconcile himself to the difficulties of life."

Pianist Andrei Gavrilov's career seriously took off when he performed as a nineteen-year-old at the Salzburg Festival in 1974 after winning the International Tchaikovsky Competition earlier in the year. He was forty years younger than his famous countryman, but in the period before Gavrilov left the Soviet Union in the mid-1980s, the two pianists became close, both musically and personally. In fact, Gavrilov's breakthrough in Salzburg came about because Richter had to cancel there. Richter felt a close pianistic kinship with his young colleague. In the 1970s they divided all of Handel's piano suites between them and, together, gave a series of concerts of this lively, rarely heard Baroque piano music.

In a conversation, Gavrilov describes a great contradiction in Richter's personality: his predilection for theater and masquerade and his aversion to any dissimulation, which the despised Kondratiev and his simulated illness had instilled in him. "Richter had so many masks that he could have worked for the secret service. On the other hand, his honesty when it came to his art was almost insane. Here, he was an impressive role model, and I learned much from him. But our relationship was so close that I also saw his darker sides. He was an incredibly split, contradictory person. For example, he could bear grudges for a long time. He remembered that someone stepped on his toes in a cable car forty years earlier! And his heroes were all avengers." As examples, Gavrilov mentions *The Visit*, Friedrich Dürrenmatt's play about an old and now immensely wealthy woman who returns to her hometown to wreak vengeance for injustices committed in her youth, and Pirandello's *Henry IV*, about a man who pretends to believe he is King Henry but who, after giving up his disguise, commits a revenge killing as if he were still in the past.

Gavrilov relates: "Richter was fearless, and in a physical sense, his fearlessness was almost without limit. But there was a touch of masochism to it. He tormented himself, and it apparently gave him some sort of satisfaction. He was an interesting blend of German pragmatism and pedantry and Russian, Dostoeyevskian self-torture. He reacted with extreme negativity to banality, to life's idiotic sides, and to boring people. This might sound a little strange if you did not know him, but there was no end to how tortuous that sort of thing was for him. Just the word *politics* would make him react like a bull to a red cape."

Gavrilov also provides examples of Richter's fragile, impressionable psyche. "I remember that during one of the mild depressions from which he suffered almost every year in early spring or late fall, he began to talk about the death of his favorite actress, Eleonora Duse, 'beloved above all.' She arrived at a theater in the U.S., but because a trade union had gone on strike, she could not get in. She waited in the rain for several hours, came down with pneumonia, and died. In the middle of his tale, Slava broke down in tears and sobbed: 'Because of a union! What is the sense? How is it possible? How can you go on living after such a thing?'"

Gavrilov comments, with some skepticism, on the notebooks Monsaingeon has published: "Slava did not express himself in words easily. His most honest reactions were best expressed in mime, body language, facial expression, and hand gestures. Moreover, he had a certain difficulty expressing himself in writing—remember that his schooling was deficient. And he censored himself, I think. The spontaneous Richter tried to invent an 'objective' version of himself; an 'authentic' Richter was not what he had in mind."

But there is always more than one Richter. Many people testify that the man who described himself as laconic—and was often viewed as such—could also talk like a waterfall. When, in the early 1960s, Jacques Leiser chauffeured him on his first tour of Italy, Richter talked so eagerly and unceasingly that Leiser was afraid of losing his concentration and refused to drive on the heavily trafficked Autostrada del Sole over the Apennines; he asked the pianist to take the train. Leiser tells: "'*Aber warum?* [But why?]' asked Richter. 'You don't like my company?' I couldn't tell him that he talked too much!" On the videotape that his young apprentice Andreas Lucewicz discreetly made during a rehearsal in Paris, Richter spoke warmly during the breaks and gossiped enthusiastically about whatever occurred to him. However, Yehudi Menuhin experienced a completely different Richter; in his memoirs, he remembers a dinner in London. The conversation flagged despite the violinist's best efforts: "Are you going back to Moscow?" "Yes." "Are you going to perform?" "No, no, I never play in the winter." "Are you going to teach?" "I never teach. I hate it!" "Do you go out much, to the theater or the opera?" "I never go out." Do you prefer to go south, to the Crimea, in the winter?" "I despise the Crimea!"

But gradually, as the evening progressed, it became increasingly difficult to believe that Richter was the misanthrope he pretended to be, Menuhin admits. Richter's desire to talk apparently depended on the situation, on how confident he felt, and on the role he wanted to play in any given situation. The shy, reticent, almost silent Richter Menuhin describes must be taken with more than a grain of salt.

As mentioned, Viktor Zelenin was one of his closest friends for many years. Zelenin rejects the notion that Richter was inclined toward introversion or silence. "Even in childhood, he was in the front ranks when it came to playing theater, dressing up, performances in the woods, or invitations to a carnival. When I was with him, he was engaged in all sorts of things, always talking energetically and with devotion. But, of course, it sometimes happened that we would sit for ten hours without him saying a word. Neuhaus made him aware of how important it was to be able to keep your mouth shut. He could also be quiet when he felt ill, but that was an exception. His disgust for the talkative Sergei Kondratiev, who married his mother, may have played a role. He wanted to avoid looking like a windbag at any price."

The self-protective and, in some respects, self-isolating artistic temperament is clear everywhere after his first tour abroad. When in 1960 and twice later (in 1965 and 1970) Richter toured the United States, he visited his "second" mother, *totya* Meri, and her son Fritz in Boston. After Meri Reincke's death in January 1984, Fritz Reincke wrote several letters to Richter. In a conversation, Reincke says, "I remember that I wrote to him several times. He never answered. He did not want to keep up a connection." Fritz Reincke's only contact with Richter after his mother's death came in the form of an occasional postcard from Nina Dorliak. Reincke shrugs it off, but he is clearly disappointed. At that point, he and Walter Moskalew were the only blood ties Richter had left. "He had room for my mother, but not for Walter and me. Only the three of us were left, but he had no room for us."

This is in glaring contrast to an episode his friend Vera Prokhorova remembers from Richter's youth. At that time, he was an indefatigable and dutiful letter writer. She recalls how he persuaded her to go on a long walk in twenty-two-degree-subzero weather to post a letter before pickup time. He owed someone a reply!

On the question of Richter's relationship to religion, Andreas Lucewicz says that he always thought Richter was a believer. "Not in a traditional sense, not in believing in a particular formal creed, but in the sense that he looked at the world as pervaded by a divine force." For many years Richter wore a Greek

Richter with his Coptic cross.

Orthodox cross around his neck, a gift from Rachmaninov's widow. When it was stolen from a hotel room at the end of the 1980s, he replaced it with an Egyptian Coptic cross. He had no understanding of or sympathy for declared atheists. He gladly visited churches of all affiliations, not to participate in a worship service but simply because the church's architecture and art interested him. He was not content just to look; he liked to sit for a long time in the church, lost in contemplation. Zelenin confirms this. "He liked to visit churches, but I never saw him pray." Lucewicz remembers that before their long car trips, he would insist, in Russian fashion, on one minute of silence. "Then he shook hands and we drove off."

Perhaps as a result of an upbringing marked by poverty and, at times, hunger, Richter's eating habits were incredibly simple. He usually preferred ordinary dishes. Many people agree that his favorite food was potatoes. Zelenin adds that when he traveled abroad and stayed at expensive hotels, it was another matter. He was delighted with elegant desserts and sweets, and ice-cold champagne!

At the end of the 1950s, Richter had designed and built a spartan summer house (a dacha) in the woods outside the city of Tarussa on the Oka River, about sixty miles south of Moscow. The area had a long tradition as a workplace and refuge for authors, artists, and musicians. In the summer and autumn of

Richter and Nina Lvovna in front of their dacha in Nikolina Gora. The dog is a guest.

1935, Prokofiev finished his Second Violin Concerto and wrote part of his ballet, *Romeo and Juliet*, there. Richter bought a cabin used by boatmen, which had four acres of wood around it and was located a hundred yards from the river. He had it torn down and erected a very stolid log house on a foundation of stone.

He was delighted that the place could be reached only by jeep, by boat, or on foot after a hike of several miles through the woods and over wide stretches of fields or along the riverbank. The house was without running water and electricity ("an advantage," according to Richter), and only with great difficulty was he able to have a piano delivered there. The piano had to be hoisted by crane through a window, and Richter had to rent it every time he was there because the instrument would not survive the Russian winter in an unheated house. The dark and solid beam house had a cellar made of boulders, a sort of scullery, and two floors, each approximately 430 square feet. There was a view of the river and the surrounding woods from the little balcony and large windows. On the ground floor were extremely primitive kitchen facilities; Richter himself designed an unusual porthole window that allowed the light to penetrate through the thick wall. Up narrow wooden stairs was Richter's small workroom with a divan and piano, nothing else. Above that was a day room where Nina Lvovna spent her time when she stayed with him.

This workplace, ideal for a man with an incredibly simple lifestyle and a modest need for society and the buzz of people around him, became for a time an important focal point for him. He got up, went swimming, played the piano, went swimming again, and played until the daylight was gone. His simple meals consisted of eggs, potatoes, bread, and perhaps cheese. Drinking water and food had to be fetched on foot from a nearby village, and the selection was very limited. He considered the surrounding landscape "the most beautiful I know in Russia" and was convinced that he always worked better there than anywhere else. He remembers learning Bartók's feared Second Piano Concerto in a couple of months. "And I needed almost two years to get Dvořák's Concerto into my head!"

In the mid-1980s, at a time when he could rarely use the house, his friend Elvira Orlova maintained the place. She often stayed there in the summer with her children. To Richter's concealed annoyance, she had electricity put in. Bubbling over with stories, she showed visitors around the house. She relates:

> Richter was on an extremely good footing with Minister of Culture Furtseva; they respected each other, and she knew that he earned great sums in hard cash for the state when he performed in the West. (As you know, only a diminishing fraction of the artists' fees ended up in their own pockets.) Without Furtseva's help, Richter would hardly have been given permission to build. He loved the place, but as he and Nina grew older, it became more difficult to deal with the primitive housekeeping and the inaccessibility. They were able to find another, far more comfortably furnished dacha in Nikolina Gora, not far from where the Prokofiev family had theirs. Richter disdainfully spoke of it as a dacha for dogs.
>
> At one point, Nina suggested they sell the house. But for Sviatoslav Teofilovich, it was unthinkable, although he realized the house could not just be left empty. He found it inconceivable, but in the winter, due to the remote location, people would steal everything: woodwork, floors, banisters. So, I solemnly promised him that I would take care of his dacha. Without supervision, there would not be a stone left!
>
> In 1992 Richter established a charitable institution, the Richter Foundation, to help and support young musicians and artists, and he conveyed the dacha to the foundation. Colleagues and friends such as Natalia Gutman and Galina Pissarenko also helped financially. The foundation became the basis for the annual Tarussa Festival he established in the Kaluga District.

So even in the illness-plagued 1990s, Richter once again had festival plans, and he got the model from his popular December Nights in Moscow. At the first Tarussa Festival in the summer of 1993, he centered the program around

Edvard Grieg, and the Pushkin Museum showed a series of Scandinavian artworks. This last child of his creativity as a festival creator still lives on, but his brief appearance at the first festival also was his last at Tarussa. His concert calendar took him directly to the Scandinavian capitals, and as fate would have it, he would not see his homeland again until a few weeks before his death in 1997.

At the beginning of the 1970s, Richter and Nina Dorliak moved from their apartment in Neshdanova Street into a high rise in Moscow's student quarter, where they lived until they died. On the sixteenth floor of the Bolshoya Bronnaya, very close to the conservatory and with a direct view of the famous (and hideously ugly) TASS building, which houses the official news bureau, they were able to acquire two top-floor apartments while the building was still under construction. Not only did they get attractive, unusually spacious living quarters for their lives in Moscow, but they had the floor of the apartment soundproofed in order to prevent music from bothering their neighbors below. The high rise is a rather ordinary sandstone building complex, but such high rises are unusual in the center of Moscow. From the huge windows with an eastern exposure and a wide balcony painted white, there is a splendid view of the city's roofs, courtyards, squares, and street life. The two decorated each end of the extensive living area according to their tastes. The apartment had a wealth of built-in closets. Richter filled the walls with a number of the most significant artworks he had collected over the years. He installed two Steinway grand pianos, one an A and the other a B, next to each other in the largest room in the apartment. By decorating in his usual spartan fashion, and with a couple of antique standing lamps that were gifts from the Communist mayor of Florence, he made sure there was enough space to hold chamber music rehearsals and rows of chairs for intimate musical events.

Naturally, there was also space for a record player. The technology-hating pianist listened passionately to records. If he was in Moscow around Christmas or New Year's, he invited friends to celebrate the holidays by listening to music, a tradition he had picked up from Neuhaus. Bach's passions and oratorios were high on the list of repeaters, but the repertoire was unpredictable.

He would put a couple of easy chairs and a sofa in the corner, and often spent the night on the sofa, even though he had his own bedroom. Here, he worked on upcoming concerts, alone or with colleagues and friends such as Natalia Gutman, Oleg Kagan, Yuri Bashmet, and the Borodin Quartet. Occasionally, he and his friends gave private concerts there.

Today, the apartment is, in all essential respects, the same as when Slava and Nina left it, complete with pictures, a huge wall tapestry, books, scores here and there, and even the pianist's concert attire, his coats, hats, and so on. The gilded stopwatch Richter used to keep track of his practice hours is still on the piano. Richter left the most valuable artworks to the Pushkin Museum before his death. The apartment is now owned and managed as a memorial by the museum, and interested pilgrims and Richter fans can visit by prior arrangement.

Here, too, Richter often exhibited paintings, drawings, and watercolors that he he liked for friends, acquaintances, and colleagues. In this way he supported and encouraged younger artists who were not yet recognized in official circles. His extensive art collection consisted primarily of gifts from the artists. Meeting Pablo Picasso at Mougins in 1964 had made an especially profound impression on him. He later wrote, "I will never forget this man with the burning eyes; he was over eighty but younger than all the rest of us. He bolted up the stairs like a young boy, showed us his divinely trashy room, and rejoiced at seeing a plant creeping over the wall. I left this encounter with a gift, a drawing of Frédéric Joliot-Curie created with a uniquely precise pen by a firm, self-assured hand" (Joliot-Curie was a famous French chemist who received the Nobel Prize in 1935 and whose work catapulted France into the nuclear age). In October 1961, in Nice, Richter had performed for Picasso's eightieth birthday.

"I am always rather restless," Richter admitted repeatedly. Many describe him as frequently sitting on the edge of a chair and getting up at the least excuse. He had rapid mood changes and uttered exclamations of joy, melancholy, tension, anger, and calm. Yet he described himself as "laziness and passivity personified," which is another one of the little Schumann-like mysteries in his personality.

A darker aspect of the comparison with Schumann was his fragile psychological makeup, the high price he paid for a life marked by constant psychic pressure, which in Richter's case—especially in his later years—consisted of extended periods of depression. "What costs there are to dedicating one's life to music," he exclaimed. For long stretches of time, he simply stayed in bed, cut off from the outside world. Then he needed help for almost everything.

His personal physician, Irina Voevodskaya, did not believe this to be a clinical depression. Rather, she describes it as melancholy, sadness, apathy, and a lack of desire to work. "But I have never seen the overwhelming spiritual emptiness or despair that marks a depression, nor the periodic recurrence of the symptoms that are characteristic of it." Voevodskaya describes his melancholy as a tremendous feeling of having been wounded, a sort of *Weltschmerz*, but the condition normally lasted less than a week. Dorliak took these symptoms very seriously, and she acquiesced to giving him tranquilizers, particularly before concerts or tours. And sometimes they helped. But Voevodskaya dryly observes

Page from one of Richter's letters to his aunt Dagmar, written in September 1974: "Dear little Dora. As you can see, I am in the mood for writing, It (the lobster) is now in front of me here on my (of course antique) desk. The lobster is quite impressive. I use it to frighten Italians. I pretend it is going to bite them. Now it is my favorite toy. After my illness I need to spoil myself a bit."

that neither medicine nor Dorliak's concern got Richter out of bed. He never sought psychiatric help or treatment (the mere thought of Richter at a psychologist's makes his friend Viktor Zelenin burst into laughter). The pianist may have believed that his inner darkness was simply the price he had to pay for his artistic sensitivity.

In April 1989 he underwent several heart operations in Zurich and canceled his concerts for the rest of the year. A season later, he was once again under a doctor's care, this time at a hospital in Munich. And for the rest of 1990, heart problems rendered him incapable of playing what he wanted, which led to great despondency and, at times, made him lose all desire for anything. But these depressive periods were nothing new. They had plagued him most of his life, and they were often connected with his work.

By the end of 1973, he had begun work on Beethoven's *Hammerklavier* Sonata, and his struggle with this monster showed him his mental limitations, leading to self-deprecation and an extended period of depression (one is again reminded of his "I don't like myself"). It is the longest of Beethoven's sonatas, a work that, to a rare degree, tests the limits of the sonata form, the pianist's ability, and the listener's powers of comprehension. In the middle of January 1974, Richter had a veritable breakdown. He stopped practicing entirely and refused to speak to anyone. For three months he cleared his calendar of concerts, but in April, in Moscow, he played the sonata for the first time. Without any embarrassment, he tells Monsaingeon that he would have been utterly incapable of doing anything during that period without his talisman, a pink plastic lobster he let out of his sight only when he went onstage.

Later on a little woolen sheep replaced the lobster. One may find this droll or even a bit childish, but such childish aspects of Richter's nature turn up again and again. His friend the pianist Vladimir Viardo tells that when Richter visited, he always picked Viardo up to show him how strong he was (sometimes he included Viardo's dog!). "And before every Easter," Viardo goes on, "he spent many, many hours painting Easter eggs, which he then gave to people." If this evokes an indulgent smile, it also reveals "a lack of appreciation of the ability to preserve innocence throughout one's life," according to Andreas Lucewicz. He continues, "It has always fascinated me when you can see the child in adults who have achieved success and self-fulfillment in life. The disappointments of childhood often create a backlash in adults. Despite his complicated relationship with the memory of his mother, the aging Richter always referred to her as 'Mama,' like a child who thinks of his mother."

Vera Prokhorova also connects the darker sides of Richter's life to the loss of his mother. "He was born with the ability to enjoy every moment of life. The core of his being and character was as far from melancholy as can be imagined. But what you are from birth is one thing; what life does to you is something else!"

From 1974 onward, his depression was exacerbated by an unpleasant tinnitus, and for months he suffered from musical hallucinations. "I started to hear a recurrent musical phrase a few bars long, violently rhythmical and rising in pitch. It was based on a diminished seventh chord. In the cold light of day, I tried to work out what it meant, even though the torment was permanent, even telling myself that the phenomenon might be of interest to medical science. But try telling doctors about diminished seventh chords! Sometimes I would lie awake all night to work out what I was hearing—or what I *thought* I was hearing—and tried to work out its pitch," he told Monsaingeon.

In an attempt to help him, his doctor, Irina Voevodskaya, devoured the literature on musical memory and asked him questions. But Richter was not cooperative. "Try to explain how your head hurts if you have a headache," he retorted, annoyed, also at himself. "Everybody has headaches now and then!" However, she dragged it out of him that the hallucinations typically began when he stopped practicing. Once he started work at the piano again, the symptoms disappeared. They also typically appeared when he began working on a new piece. Voevodskaya considered whether the incredible amount of music that had accumulated over the years in Richter's huge musical computer of a brain had begun the fill up his mental "hard disk." Suddenly, he discovered that this tortuous inner music resembled a chord sequence that had made a strong impression on him as a child: Rachmaninov's *Vokalise*, a very popular lied in a song cycle composed in the years shortly before Richter's birth. "The unconscious model of some of my own early compositions," he realized.

However, the tinnitus stopped as suddenly as it arose, but each time he experienced depressive periods, it returned. Later the phenomenon was accompanied by yet another auditory disturbance, which plagued him in his later years. Like many musicians, he had perfect pitch, the ability—often inborn—to hear in the inner ear exact pitches (for example, the "concert pitch"), an ability connected with Richter's phenomenal musical memory. However, he now began to hear tones at a half or whole tone higher or lower, "as if my hearing was out of tune." Voevodskaya recalls that when he returned from Italy, presumably in the fall of 1983, he came down with the mumps and suffered from headaches and burning eyes. "He was forced to remain in a dark room. Light hurt his eyes. No notes on the course of the disease were available. Nina Lvovna had gone home earlier and could say nothing helpful. A few days after his homecoming, the maestro was again depressed. He stopped working, and the new problems with his musical hearing began." But this irksome disturbance was not of recent vintage. When he was thirty-two, he told Alexander Vishinsky that his perfect pitch had begun to give him problems and that he sometimes heard music a half tone higher.

Richter remembered that both Neuhaus and Prokofiev had mentioned similar symptoms when they grew older, but that was no solace to him. The discomfort of playing in one key and hearing it in another is self-evident! The pianist told of humiliating situations where he was playing in A minor, for example, and hearing it as B minor and spontaneously trying to correct it by transposing the music a whole tone downward, only to wind up, without meaning to, in G minor. This was bad enough if it happened during a recital. A different key means a whole new fingering. But with an orchestra, the result is nothing less than a musical disaster. This may explain why Richter, the magician of memory, began to play with a score in front of him. By reading the music, he could more easily separate himself from his insidious, unreliable hearing and the mental tricks it played on him.

His sensitivity to strong light is also the likely explanation for the darkened halls and the single lamp that illuminated his score. This unusual lighting created its own suggestive, theatrical atmosphere, a shadow play that could make him look like a druid or an alchemist conducting magical, esoteric rituals.

Fischer-Dieskau recounts that strong light bothered him during earlier periods as well. "This passionate lover of walking hated sharp light, perhaps, because of his eyes. During a summer festival at the huge barn in Tours, he forbade any spotlight and allowed only small lamps in the hall. I never let him know that I suffered under this gloomy concert lighting, because it made it impossible to draw the audience in as a participant. . . . But how cheerful he could be, how playful, how he laughed with all his heart in the hotel room where the sun did not enter."

His heart problems did not become serious until the mid-1980s. Voevod-skaya diagnosed diabetes and high blood pressure. Richter began to take blood thinners, and the doctor saw the first symptoms of a strain on the heart's arter-ies. Richter was not a good patient. His favorite dishes were potatoes and des-serts, and so he had difficulty sticking to a low-sugar diet.

A major issue in his life was his homosexuality, a terrain that has many rami-fications and must be trod cautiously and with understanding. In biographies of other great artists, this subject would presumably have a prominent place. However, in the case of a Soviet artist, the topic is almost impossible to research, as his circle of friends are taciturn on the subject. Throughout his life, Richter viewed this aspect of his life as a nonissue. It was not a taboo; rather, it simply belonged to the private sphere, something he did not talk about. Richter hated any publicity of his private life. And those closest to him view it as a question of honor to keep this aspect of his life private, a personal matter that he had an obvious right to protect. Whereas Western authors often find it natural to write about this aspect of their lives in their diaries or memoirs, there is no evidence in the entire literature on Richter that he mentioned this subject. And only a very few of the numerous people on whose reminiscences and statements this book is based remember Richter ever raising the topic. Bruno Monsaingeon also avoids this no-man's-land in his conversations with Richter. At any rate, neither his film nor his book contains a single word on Richter's sexual inclina-tion or its effect on his life. But gender and sexuality have a decisive influence on everyone. In his memoirs, the American composer Ned Rorem describes his homosexuality as "a cyclone enveloping my every behavioral viewpoint since infancy."

In the eighteenth century, biographies of prominent people were expected to serve as moral examples. But these days, morality, repugnance, and a dis-like of voyeurism do not justify an avoidance of the subject. In the West, Nina Dorliak always acted like Richter's wife, and no one questioned it. People who were close to Richter—friends, colleagues, coworkers—were aware of the true nature of things, but everyone knew that his sexual identity and inclinations were untouchable. If any of his lovers are still alive, which is more than likely, they have not expressed any desire to make themselves known in connection with this book. And neither chance nor stratagem has made any difference. Whereas the topic of homosexuality has for generations been more or less openly discussed among Western intellectuals, a similar tradition does not exist in the former Soviet Union. Most people there apparently view it the way Richter did. A Western visitor to Russia can easily become the victim of a still vital conception of "them and us," which tends to make Russians screen information that they deem will not be properly perceived and understood in the West.

However, as mentioned earlier, Richter never tried to hide his sexual identity. Of course, a certain discretion was necessary not to discredit Nina Dorliak or their marital status on their travels. Just when Richter became fully conscious of his sexual inclinations is unclear. But nothing indicates that he suffered from feelings of guilt or shame or that, like Leonard Bernstein for instance, he vacillated between homosexuality and heterosexuality. It is clear that Dorliak, his companion of more than fifty years, accepted it. As far as we know, unlike Richter, she never brought her lovers along on their trips together, perhaps out of respect for his career and his public role. The addition of a lover would have threatened their presentation as husband and wife, a status that had been established in the Soviet Union long before they traveled as a couple in the West. In addition, in the Soviet Union erotic love between women was even less visible than that between men.

The difference between the United States and the USSR with respect to sexual "deviations" has less to do with legislation than with the political climate. Until the 1980s, many states in the United States forbade not only homosexual activity but also oral sex and anal intercourse. And the penalty for such offenses, regardless of whether the couple was married or not, varied from three to twenty years in prison! In practice, these laws were considered a dead letter and were rarely, if ever, enforced. By contrast, in the Soviet Union, there are countless examples of moral legislation leading to convictions and prison.

Homosexuality as portrayed in recent Western memoirs is often matter-of-fact and corporeal, with an emphasis on desire. However, there are indications that Richter's understanding of himself as gay was of a different sort in many respects, a natural part of him that preferred to look at all areas of life from an aesthetic perspective. And perhaps this echoed the idea of aestheticism (or symbolism), represented by many European artists in different ways at the beginning of the twentieth century, artists who were more or less openly homosexual

Richter rehearses Max Reger with Andreas Lucewicz, 1994.

(for example, Oscar Wilde, Rainer Maria Rilke, Marcel Proust, Arthur Rimbaud, Paul Verlaine, Jean Cocteau, André Gide, and Sergei Diaghilev). This aestheticism found moving expression in Thomas Mann's novella *Death in Venice*. It was expressed both as a theory of art and an attitude toward life, which put art above everything, even the moral and the social, and allowed homosexual artists an opportunity to come to terms with their sexual identity in veiled language. Richter's predilection for French literature may have some of its roots here.

The young pianist Andreas Lucewicz, who served as Richter's chauffeur and with whom Richter played Reger shortly before illness and death ended his career, is certain that Richter's relationship with him had an erotic element from the beginning.

> When we became acquainted, I was a handsome young man in his eyes. In the ancient sense, a Greek ideal of beauty. In antiquity, older men initiated young men into the mysteries of life. There was nothing strange in an older man's falling in love with a younger man. This is the first time I have ever said this publicly, but I know that he was attracted to me from the beginning. He knew that I was a pianist, but I was much too shy to bring it up. Richter was not only an artist, he was a human being, and then a young man comes to him, a good chauffeur, an interesting interlocutor. We drove four-

teen hours from Vienna via Warsaw to the Russian border at the end of April 1983, and, of course, I felt I was with the Godfather himself. I also felt that he saw me as a young man, as a body. But perhaps because I spent ten years at a boarding school, I am a bit oversensitive to homosexuality. If a man finds me attractive, I immediately go into a defensive posture. But Richter was the most cautious person you could imagine.

In Vienna Richter met a lover, a Greek, whom he kissed in an entirely unmistakable manner. This man could afford to travel. He was the son of a well-to-do merchant, and for a time he was always in Richter's wake. When Nina was not there, he was always there.

In 1993 Richter asked me point-blank what had stopped me from start-ing this sort of relationship with him. We got that cleared up, and we actu-ally became even closer. But he was always a bit hurt about it. He suggested that we say "du" [second person nominative, an informal address] to each other. But I could not imagine that. We each had our own history. I had never dreamed that the Godfather and I would ever address each other informally. The fact that I did not understand this approach also hurt him. He was so cautious, so discreet, so sensitive, and so oblique in his attractions. He let me see he was attracted, but he was not insistent. I clearly noticed that those around him considered his interest in me as purely erotic.

Richter noted in September 1994: "My decision to play with Andreas Luce-wicz gave rise to protests from Nina Dorliak and reservations from Natasha Gutman. But our collaboration has shown that I was right."
Lucewicz recounts:

When he heard a recording of mine I had gathered the courage to put in his hand, he said, "Andreas, I'm jealous. You play Schumann's Second Novelette better than I do!" He also praised my rendering of Beethoven's "Les Adieux" and of Chopin's Scherzo in E Major. He just said, "Yes, you hear my influ-ence." I was so perplexed that I replied, "I don't believe it." And he actually got angry. "When I speak of music, I always mean what I say!"

My mother had an acquaintance, now deceased, Marita Jakobs, who had a female friend who claimed to have been intimate with Richter in the 1970s. Unfortunately, my mother does not remember the woman's name. But Rich-ter may have actually been bisexual for periods of time. I don't think you could preclude it entirely.

One might wonder whether Richter's sexuality—like so much else in his life—can be viewed as part of the tragic tangle of feelings connected with the loss of his mother. In addition to the major devastation he suffered in his unrequited love for a young female dancer (as recounted by Vera Prokhorova), the loss of the feminine magic he associated with his mother, perhaps the loss of women as an ideal, or the concept of *das ewig Weibliche* (the eternal feminine), may have affected him. Nothing indicates that the twenty-two-year-old Richter, who moved from his childhood home in Odessa to Moscow in 1937, was aware of any homosexual inclinations. On the other hand, it was well known among Soviet intellectuals that authorities in Moscow often looked the other way where homosexuality occurred among artists and that Moscow, therefore, offered fewer risks for gay musicians than the cities in the provinces. If Richter acknowledged (or consciously dealt with) a homosexual identity while in Odessa, it may have contributed to his decision to leave his hometown.

The debate about what determines our sexual orientation, whether nature or nurture, genes or learned behavior, went on for most of the twentieth century. Freud believed that overprotective mothers or absent fathers were a contributing factor, and not until 1973 did American psychiatrists remove homosexuality from the list of mental disturbances. But in recent years, a biological explanation has been searched for, and today only a few people adhere to the old theories that connect homosexuality with nurture or the environment. Genetic differences in chromosomes and in the individual's production of sex hormones, for example, to a significant degree determine how homosexuals and heterosexuals react to so-called pheromones, chemical signals that trigger sexual excitement among animals by influencing neurons in the hypothalamus. And many researchers believe that just as influences from sex hormones determine whether an embryo will become a boy or a girl, a similar effect may determine sexual orientation. It may be due to the embryo's position in the womb, its blood supply, or many other random factors totally outside the mother's control. The latest research seems to indicate that our sexual disposition is formed at a very early embryonic stage, while the brain is developing in a masculine or feminine direction.

Almost all researchers now believe that sexual orientation is there from birth (at least, in men; female homosexuality has not been researched to the same extent). However, hardly anyone would deny that developments after birth can play a role as well. Whether little Svetik's gentle, patient nature and his distaste for rough play, violence, and competition are an expression of feminine traits or simply the outcome of his being an only child, no one can determine. Statistically, homosexuality appears more frequently in the same family. Eight to 12 percent of a homosexual's siblings are also homosexual, whereas the percentage among the general population as a whole is 2–4 percent. There is no accessible information that homosexuality appeared anywhere in Richter's immediate family. However, there are myriad examples of a homosexual disposition that is given free rein only in response to some powerful psychological experience.

As mentioned, Richter considered this aspect of his life an entirely private matter. The Western tendency of a homosexual who—perhaps in protest against society's lack of acceptance—flaunts his sexuality has no equivalent in Russia. But there *may* be something to the fact that Richter often included in his repertoire music by composers with a corresponding sexual orientation, even though it was surely not the result of any real, conscious planning. Music by homosexual composers such as Tchaikovsky, Mussorgsky, Saint-Saëns, Szymanovski, Britten, and Poulenc played a large role in his repertoire, but this may be explained in many other ways. Schubert and Handel, composers he focused on at a time when no one else of his stature did, may also have been homosexual, according to several reputable scholars, although there is only circumstantial evidence (the concept itself did not exist in their time, but so-called depravity could be severely punished). We must be allowed to speculate that Sviatoslav Richter, who liked all types of riddles, masks, and masquerades, may unconsciously have hidden a code, a secret message in a bottle in the very choice of his repertoire.

Since the mid-1930s, homosexuality was forbidden under the Soviet penal code and could be punished with five years' imprisonment or hard labor. The introduction of the act (article 121) led to the almost immediate mass arrest of artists, actors, and musicians, among others, not only in Moscow and Leningrad, but also in young Richter's Odessa. Sexual intercourse between people of the same gender was considered not an offense against public morals but a crime against the state, equivalent to espionage and counterrevolutionary activities. Maxim Gorky, the ideological arbiter of cultural life, described article 121 as "a triumph of proletarian humanism," and he believed that homosexuality was at the root of fascism (at the same time, the German Nazis claimed that homosexuality led to communism!).

But under Stalin, the persecution of homosexuals was neither persistent nor consistent. Famous Russian artists, such as film director Sergei Eisenstein, the tenor Sergei Lemeshev, and various male ballet stars were tolerated and acknowledged, despite their sexual orientation, as long as they kept it private and hid their sexual orientation by getting married. The "thaw" under Khrushchev led to a blossoming of jazz clubs and literary cafés, which gave gays and lesbians new opportunities to meet and form social networks; thus a homosexual subculture was born.

There is no apparent sign that Richter's homosexuality created difficulties for him with the Soviet authorities. Of course, the KGB knew everything. But his ostensible marriage to Nina Dorliak ensured that his sexuality would never be public. Despite his position as a national (and international) treasure, he did not threaten general morality or the general sense of justice. This in itself made his relationship with Dorliak an absolute necessity, an unbreachable pact.

It is apparent that he had special status and was given special treatment. And in a way, it makes sense to say that he *demanded* special treatment. The fearlessness that characterized his playing was also indicative of his relationship to the power apparatus. He never became a member of the Communist Party (to which the vast majority of his musical colleagues belonged). In many areas, the commissars looked the other way, or treated him with kid gloves, partly because they knew they could not order him around. If lesser artists did not toe the line, they could be gotten rid of. But not Richter.

If the authorities happened to use force on him, he responded by literally going on strike and refusing to play. Jacques Leiser reports that at the beginning of the 1960s, Richter was invited to a music festival in Athens. "He very much looked forward to seeing the historical sites and to spending a week vacationing near Athens. I was to meet him there, and all the arrangements were made. Then, the Soviet ambassador in Athens got word that the great Russian dancer and defector Nureyev was also performing at the festival. He consulted the Russian authorities, who decided that Richter was not to be on a program together with a persona non grata. A furious Richter went back to Moscow and canceled everything for several months." Of course, anyone nourished by his artistic genius can be grateful that Richter was given special treatment.

Perestroika and Glasnost

In many respects, the second half of the 1970s was a turbulent time in Soviet cultural life and politics. Khrushchev had tolerated the dissident author Alexander Solzhenitsyn, but in the years after Khrushchev's fall, Solzhenitsyn encountered difficulties. In 1970 he was awarded the Nobel Prize for Literature, but fearing banishment, he declined to accept it at the ceremony in Stockholm. His books were now published only in the West; the existence of the Gulag became known in the West only when the first part of his great novel *The Gulag Archipelago* was published in English in 1973. With his realistic novels about the Soviet past and his bitter struggle for artistic and intellectual freedom, he gradually became such a troublesome stone in the shoe of the Soviet government that in February 1974 he was put on a plane to West Germany and, for all practical purposes, banished. Shortly thereafter, his young wife and their two children were granted exit visas, and the family settled in the United States.

Only a month and a half later, the cellist Mstislav Rostropovich and his wife, the soprano Galina Vishnevskaya, wrote an appeal to Leonid Brezhnev, asking for permission "to leave the country with our two children for two years." Rostropovich had defended Solzhenitsyn in numerous ways since 1969, when he let Solzhenitsyn stay in their dacha outside Moscow. Solzhenitsyn later wrote that without his support, he would have been unable to survive. When Solzhenitsyn was awarded the Nobel Prize, a smear campaign was initiated, but Rostropovich defended him in an open letter to the press. Consequently, Rostropovich and Vishnevskaya were increasingly subjected to punitive actions and humiliations. A new recording of *Tosca* was made, but without Vishnevskaya in her starring role. Rostropovich was told that he had "degenerated" as a musician and that he would not be allowed to conduct at the Bolshoi. The two world-famous artists were, for all intents and purposes, put in quarantine. In his memoirs, Yehudi Menuhin writes that in January 1974—shortly before Solzhenitsyn's banishment—Rostropovich was scheduled to perform at a festival in Paris, where Menuhin was playing. When it was announced that the cellist had suffered a heart attack, Menuhin called Vishnevskaya, who told him that Rostropovich was conducting in Georgia and was perfectly fine. Menuhin threatened to leak the story to the Western media, thus ensuring an exit visa for Rostropovich.

The couple's request to depart was granted immediately, and they were given permission "to travel for artistic purposes" for two years. Rostropovich flew to London, followed a few months later by his wife and their two daughters, aged sixteen and eighteen. In a short time, his career exploded. He played and conducted at all the Western metropolises and, three years later, began work as the artistic director of the National Symphony Orchestra in Washington, a post that lasted for many years. Even though Rostropovich told the Western press that he was not inclined to return to the USSR, "until we can play what we want, where and when we want, and with whom we want," the authorities in the USSR did not consider him an emigrant. His exit visa was tacitly renewed several times. Not until 1978, when the cellist requested a further three years' extension, was he told that he and his family's Soviet citizenship had been revoked. The Soviet papers reported that the two artists had systematically harmed their homeland, and this was not compatible with Soviet citizenship. When their recordings were broadcast on Soviet radio, their names were not mentioned. The couple protested, and an extended feud, with accusations and attacks from both sides, began.

In the West, Rostropovich was known as an energetic advocate of human rights and artistic freedom. When, after twelve years in Soviet prisons and psychiatric wards the author and dissident Vladimir Bukovsky was released and banished from the USSR in December 1976, Rostropovich told the Western press that countless other artists were imprisoned or interned in the Soviet Union. "Without freedom, no creativity," he said again and again. In August 1991 he traveled unannounced and without a visa to Moscow to support the revisionist coup attempt. When in April 2007 he died in a Moscow hospital, after a prolonged illness, his position as one of the world's most significant musical personalities was uncontested.

In October 1974 the violinist David Oistrakh died suddenly in the middle of a series of Brahms concerts in Amsterdam. And, on August 9, 1975, the day before he turned sixty-nine, Shostakovich died after several years' infirmity and illness. All over the country, memorial ceremonies were held, a stamp with the composer's portrait was unveiled, and the government released an LP of his "public speeches." Under Brezhnev, he had been decorated like a Christmas tree with medals, prizes, and honors; he was now solidly established as a Communist symbol and a role model in Soviet cultural life. Solomon Volkov's *Testimony*, a book on Soviet cultural life with Shostakovich's ostensible memoirs told in the first person, was published in England and the United States in 1979.

The Cold War was still raging, and the book's colossal success in the West, particularly in the United States, obviously had to do with its criticism of the Soviet Union. In December 1979 the Soviet Union occupied Afghanistan, and President Carter announced the American boycott of the 1980 Olympic Games in Moscow. His successor, Ronald Reagan, further intensified the ideological opposition. In November 1982 Leonid Brezhnev died and was replaced by the Party leader, Yuri Andropov. Shortly thereafter, fighters from the Soviet air force shot down an off-course Korean airliner in the vicinity of Sakhalin Island. Ronald Reagan coined the phrase "the evil empire," and Hollywood produced an assembly-line series of violent anti-Soviet films. The relationship between the superpowers was once again in the deep freeze.

Surprisingly, the earlier heavy-handed KGB head Yuri Andropov put himself in the forefront of a reform process, and in April 1985 his successor Mikhail Gorbachev introduced what has been described as the "second Russian revolution." The watchwords *perestroika* (restructuring) and *glasnost* (publicity, in the sense of openness and transparency) were regularly used. Gorbachev spoke of a "new thinking for our country and the whole world." Soviet artists once again felt the morning air; the days of the old Soviet system were numbered, and changes in art and culture gradually spread. The struggle to break away from isolation and enforced provincialism was visible everywhere. Even the word "Soviet" was difficult to use in the traditional sense (not to mention the dissident "anti-Soviet"). "Socialist realism" made room for completely different aesthetic attitudes; even the concept of avant-garde could be used without negative connotations (although many still viewed the word as an umbrella term for "skeptics, cynics, and nihilists"). The boundaries between "permitted" and "forbidden" in the nation's cultural life became fluid.

A veritable cultural treasure trove was gradually unearthed and made accessible to a broad Soviet audience: novels by Pasternak and Solzhenitsyn (Boris Pasternak's novel of love during the revolution, *Doctor Zhivago*, had been filmed in Hollywood in 1965 to worldwide acclaim, but not until 1988 did the blacklisted novel appear in Russian); plays by Mikhail Bulgakov (whose 1930s novel *The Master and Margarita* was published in 1967); poems by Osip Mandelstam and Anna Akhmatova; and paintings by Kandinsky and Chagall. In music, the upheaval was less obvious. Tikhon Khrennikov, the first secretary of the Composers' Union for many years, may have been described as having a Stalin-like role, a description that, in hindsight, he might not entirely deserve. It is true that he always acted as spokesman and that he had the power to make or break careers. But had he not slavishly followed the cultural guidelines of the Central Committee, he would have been replaced by someone else. And any assessment of him must, at the very least, take into account that during his tenure none of the union's members were arrested or excluded. Although the list of disappearing or executed writers and theatrical people is long, this was not the case for composers. Avant-garde musicians such as Alexander Mosolov and Nicolai Roslavetz ended up as nonexistent people in distant provinces, but they stayed alive.

The Final Years

Characteristically, the collapse of the Soviet Union in 1991 changed nothing in Richter's life. Unlike the friend of his youth Rostropovich, he was in no way drawn into this dramatic sequence of events. During the final period of his life, he lived for a great part of the year in southern Europe, mostly in France and Italy, and his concerts took place predominantly outside Russia. He hardly had any opinion of Boris Yeltsin's Russia. The apartment he and Nina Lvovna kept in Moscow was empty or on loan in the last four years of his life. He complained to Chemberdzhy that Moscow had changed a lot, and "with all these new buildings, it's no longer Moscow."

The Italian magazine editor Umberto Massini, whom Richter had met before Massini's periodical *Musica* was launched in 1976, was the pianist's friend. Shortly after Richter's death, Massini wrote about Richter's trip one night in June 1991 down the tortuous wooded roads through Touraine on the way to the festival at Grange de Mesley. Behind the wheel was Richter's Japanese piano technician Koh Segawa, at his side Richter, and in the back seat Massini. Richter was silent the whole way. Then, he suddenly turned to his friend and said, "I think it's time I retired. The leaf has turned. The book of my life is approaching its end, and I can no longer find any sense in what I'm doing. The world is for the young; they are writing the future, they will play, and music belongs to them." Massini continued, "I did not reply, and I did not immediately say the usual words of comfort that others might have used. The maestro seemed strangely lucid about what he had said. He was peaceful in a way that I had not seen recently. At the last moment, he had canceled his piano recital of the music of Bach and had left the crowd of visitors who had come to hear him with a bitter taste in their mouths once again." Many of them had traveled all the way from the United States and Japan.

At the time when Richter was scheduled to go onstage to play suites by Bach, he was having dinner with a few of his closest friends on the castle terrace of La Tortinière with its view over the park and the valley. At one point, he got wind that a young Parisian pianist had replaced him at the last moment, and he exclaimed, "You see!" He tried to maintain his sense of humor, but those who were present realized that he felt defeated. However, he resumed his work and gave a number of planned concerts in Tours and at La Grange with certain adjustments.

But these gloomy considerations seem almost unreal when one looks at the list of his concert activities in 1991. The average number was eight to ten concerts a month, in Italy, Spain, and Germany. In May he gave six recitals in Moscow, among them memorial concerts for Neuhaus and for the physicist and dissident Andrei Sakharov. He seemed to have no idea that the Soviet Union was a few months away from dissolution. His repertoire, however, indicates that he was conserving his strength. Concerts with orchestras were now gone from his calendar. And until September, Bach (and sometimes Mozart or Beethoven) was dominant in his programs. He kept away from the heavy, physically demanding Romantic repertoire—Liszt, Rachmaninov, Tchaikovsky, Chopin's scherzi, Brahms's sonatas, music by Shostakovich, and, for example, Prokofiev's "War Sonatas" for the rest of his life. Grieg's *Lyric Pieces* began to play a significant role in his programs.

Sviatoslav Richter's declining years were difficult. After his colossal concert tour back and forth across Siberia in 1986, his health began to fail. More than anything else, his illness required him to take things easy. But he had little talent for that. In 1989 he began the year energetically with a tour in Italy and France and continued with strenuous concert performances in London. But by April, things had gone downhill again. He had trouble breathing. To increase the blood flow to his heart, he underwent a bypass operation in Switzerland and canceled all concerts for the rest of the year. The sad story occurred again in 1990: after a confident start with a dozen concerts in Spain and France, he once again needed acute medical treatment at the end of March. And again, his concert calendar remained empty for the rest of the year. His teeth also caused him problems. His favorite dentist was a specialist in Vienna. He had to use reading glasses, and the diabetes he developed in the 1980s exacerbated his vision problems. Eventually, he needed an arsenal of glasses. Diabetes meant that he could no longer eat what he wanted. He encouraged those around him to "keep an eye on him," and in his final years his blood sugar had to be measured regularly. Finally, daily injections of insulin became necessary. He also suffered from insomnia.

But he did not throw in the towel. Gloomy thoughts of having reached the final chapter of his life seem to have been temporary. In fact, the following years were tremendously active for him; he went on countless journeys, often performing two or three concerts a week. His desire to play might look like a dogged protest against the inevitable, reminiscent of Dylan Thomas's poem to his father: "Do not go gentle into that good night, / . . . / Rage, rage against the dying of the light." His programs gradually regained their usual breadth, although concerts with orchestras were still virtually absent, presumably due to his aversion to long-term planning, for which his illness now provided an excuse. The year after his remarks on retiring, he filled his calendar with more than one hundred concerts! One can imagine a retired Sviatoslav Richter only as a thought experiment. In May 1992 he was given an honorary doctorate from Oxford, and for the first time in a long stretch, he played in an English city outside London. He visited the festival in Aldeburgh for the last time and dedicated his piano recital to the memory of his two English friends, Peter Pears, who died in April 1986, and Benjamin Britten, who died ten years before Pears. But he knew, of course, that time goes by and takes all of us with it. The numerous concerts he dedicated to the memory of the deceased in these years—Pasternak, Neuhaus, Sakharov, Kagan, Rubinstein—speak their own melancholy language about getting old. On May 6 Marlene Dietrich died in Paris at the age of ninety, and on the day she was buried in Berlin, he played in Munich. He dedicated his concert to the memory of that "great artist" and sent six hundred roses to her funeral. He also gave a memorial concert for the tenth anniversary of the death of the legendary English record producer Walter Legge, and after the concert, kneeling, he kissed the hand of his widow, Elisabeth Schwarzkopf.

In the early 1990s, Nina Dorliak hired the Russian-speaking Italian Milena Borromeo as Richter's personal agent. She was very important to him in his last years. Dorliak was now over eighty, and her health was not the best. Not only did Borromeo handle the planning of his concert schedule, fee negotiations, and all the practical details of concert tours gently and effectively, but she was with him constantly, helping and supporting him in every way, administering his medicine, and protecting him from the world around him when he needed it. The number of his depressive periods diminished, and thanks to Borromeo, he performed an almost record number of concerts. However, among people close to Richter, some think she may have been too slow in realizing the gravity of his illness.

As the theme for the 1993 festival in Grange de Mesley, Richter had selected "La musique joyeuse," and it motivated the aging master to learn not only George Gershwin's "jazzed" piano concerto but also Saint-Saëns's Second Concerto (and to play Saint-Saëns's Fifth Concerto, long in his repertoire), giving him in May and June the now rare opportunity to work with an orchestra. His voracious appetite for new material was undiminished. Not only did he seize

Grieg's *Lyric Pieces*, he also learned Francis Poulenc's Concerto for Two Pianos and played it several times with his friend Lisa Leonskaya. Even though in the spring of 1993 his heart once again gave him problems and in 1994 he had to have an operation, he filled his healthy periods with a breathtaking number of concerts. As he was approaching his eightieth birthday, he was often surrounded by doctors.

In May 1994 he made yet another excursion into entirely new musical terrain. He began to work on Max Reger's monumental Beethoven variations for two pianos with his young friend and "apprentice" Andreas Lucewicz. As mentioned, Lucewicz had become acquainted with Richter in April 1983, when Richter's long-time friend Johannes Wasmuth asked him to chauffeur the man who hated flying, driving him through Vienna and Russia and, three months later, picking him up again and taking him to Bonn. This was the beginning of a friendship that, ten years later, was to result in an unusual musical collaboration. The young pianist had long been a valued and reliable page-turner for Richter once Richter began consistently to play from the scores. And Lucewitz can actually be heard discreetly assisting in some of Richter's live recordings. Richter ignored the so-called third pedal, which, in contrast to the first, locks the damper on only the keys that are struck. This makes it possible, for example, for the long bass tones to ring on even after the keys have been released. For Richter, this exemplified "technique," and why use a technical trick when a competent pianist was sitting right there with easy access to the bass register? There are several examples of Lucewicz appearing as a ghost player when Richter deemed it appropriate, in Bach, in preludes by Rachmaninov, and, for example, in Brahms's Variations, opus 21.

Originally, Richter believed that Reger's huge, rarely heard work for two pianos would require a year and a half of work. But because of continual touring and his illness, the pair worked for only a month and a half—with breaks, but thoroughly, patiently, and purposefully. In Paris, on June 20, 1994, Lucewicz could not resist the temptation to record—with a hidden camera—one of their long rehearsals, which lasted hours. The tape is a unique document of Richter's method of working.

"Now, it is music," Richter exclaims on Lucewicz's videotape, delighted. "Before it was . . ." He searches for *le mot juste*, and Lucewicz tries to help: "Indifferent? Trivial?" "No . . . Noise!" Richter replies with a Mona Lisa smile. Lucewicz asks, "Aren't we playing it a little down to earth, a little too heavy? Shouldn't it be a bit more flowing?" "First, it has to be down to earth, then it can flow freely," the old master replies. "Otherwise, it becomes unclear."

The tape also provides a lively impression of the colossal physical energy that Richter still possessed when he was not plagued by ill health and provides a rare, authentic insight into his mind. During the short breaks, we see ("finally!" one is tempted to say) the unedited, unsupervised, uncensored Richter speaking straight off the cuff about music, people, and interpretations. Richter was to play Carl Maria von Weber's Third Sonata in a future concert and, when he tries out a sparkling passage in the finale of the piece, Lucewicz hears a Mendelssohnian tone. "No, it is more like opera, more connected to theater," Richter says, "always modulations, something unexpected. In Mendelssohn, everything is just perfect." He speaks warmly about Weber's almost unknown four piano sonatas (of which only the Third, in D minor, was in his repertoire, but clearly he knows all four virtually by heart).

With undisguised annoyance and exhaustion, he speaks of all the people he has to spend time with meeting and visiting in Paris: "Tonight, Madame Rubinstein" (Arthur Rubinstein's widow). He would rather work. But his desire to tell stories is obvious. He first met Aniela Rubinstein in 1970 at a dinner in New York, immediately after the notorious concert with Oistrakh, which was interrupted by an anti-Soviet demonstration. Before his death at ninety-five, Rubinstein suddenly left his wife for a very young English mistress. The rejected Mrs. Rubinstein had confided in Nina Dorliak that her husband "was terrible, horrible, completely intolerable—but I loved him!" Richter the theater man tells the story with a wry grimace that quickly changes into a subtle smile. He appreciated Arthur Rubinstein a great deal—a joyous, funny, and incredibly charming man. "He had such a talent for telling a story," Richter says, "that he almost made us die of laughter!"

His memory of the demonstrations in New York makes the apolitical Richter think of how the conductor Wilhelm Furtwängler was met with insults when he first performed in New York after the war. But, he points out, Furtwängler did not wear the Nazi emblem like, for example, Karajan. Furtwängler tried to protect Jewish musicians; he continued to play "decadent" composers such as Mendelssohn and Hindemith. Karajan was a member of the Nazi Party, both in Germany and in Austria. Nevertheless, Karajan was accepted simply because he propagandized against Furtwängler, Richter believes. "Karajan was an unsympathetic person; he turned his back on those who helped him, but [and again, as if by magic, Richter gives a subtle, ironic smile] . . . of course, he was a great talent."

Lucewicz mentions Maria Callas, and Richter brightens. "I have only heard her on the stage once, it was as Medea in Cherubini's opera. But it was fantastic, entirely unforgettable. And she sang everything, Carmen, Rosina in *The Barber of Seville*. She sang Gilda in *Rigoletto*, Bellini's *La Sonnambula*, Violetta in *La Traviata*, Aida, Mimì in *Bohème*, even *Turandot*. But her first role was, yes, guess: Kundry in Wagner's *Parsifal*!"

Richter's storytelling culminates with a 1970 film he recently saw, *The Night Porter* with Dirk Bogarde and Charlotte Rampling. The film, which is about an ex-Nazi who meets a woman he previously sexually abused in a concentration camp, is hardly a pearl. Some may find its erotic-sadistic plot rather tiresome. Among other things, an intercourse takes place on broken glass. Richter, however, finds the film psychologically interesting, although its ending seemed to him dramaturgically unsatisfactory and unnecessarily banal.

Of their collaboration, Lucewicz tells that Richter never tried to remake him, but that he sometimes simply and discreetly showed Lucewicz how he believed some passage should sound. In the beginning Lucewicz was uncomfortable having to play with his idol. "Suddenly I saw Richter look at me and forget his entrance. 'What's happening?' he asked me. 'It sounds completely new!' And I knew why. I wasn't afraid anymore. I was no longer walking on eggshells."

In the Lucewicz videotape, no one can notice that the vibrant, cheerful, talkative, and hard-working pianist is ill, although his heart problems came and went. At the end of January 1994 he had written to Lucewicz from Japan: "Unfortunately, I was not at all well in December (Moscow), and when I flew to Japan, I had to subject myself to the treatment of Japanese doctors and follow their recommendation: two months without playing. Not until now am I slowly beginning to work, and it's still rather hard going." Shortly after, however, he toured Japan, performing in more than twenty concerts. He traveled on to South Korea for more playing, and at the end of April returned to Europe. At Pinneberg, a Hamburg suburb with a hotel he liked that was only a few miles from Yamaha's European headquarters at Rellingen, he went through a battery of health tests under the supervision of a German doctor. This did not prevent him from mounting a concert tour of Germany and Switzerland. In June, shortly after rehearsals with Lucewicz, he once again visited his beloved Grange de Mesley in order to perform with the Borodin Quartet. This was to be his last performance in the converted barn.

In 1990, at the picturesque little spa of Wildbad Kreuth southwest of Munich, Richter's close friends Natalia Gutman and Oleg Kagan had organized a recurring summer festival *à la* Richter in La Grange. Only forty-three years old, Kagan died immediately after the first festival, which has since carried on in his name. (In January and February of the following year, Richter dedicated all the concerts in which he played Bach "to the memory of this great musician"). At the great hall of the spa, Richter and Lucewicz performed Reger's Variations in July 1994. Bayerische Rundfunk recorded the performance, and the German record company Live Classics issued it on a CD. By then Richter was once again under the surgical knife and had to stay away from the piano for a couple of months. Already in September and October, however, he gave a dozen concerts in Italy and Germany, often with demanding programs that included all of Chopin's ballades and several sonatas by Beethoven. He felt weak and tired. On December 5 he wrote to Lucewicz from the northern Italian mountain town of Asolo ("a paradise!") that he did not have the energy to give concerts. "It hurts me so much! Although there are many signs of improvement and a little 'temporary' interest in music." After about ten days, he had strength enough to realize an old dream. As a boy he had read a story that took place in Chioggia, the picturesque mini-Venice at the lagoon south of the famous city of canals. He had always wanted to play there, but no one had been able to provide a suitable hall. And then it finally happened. On December 15 he played Chopin's ballades and Carl Maria von Weber's Sonata in D Minor, and he was delighted. He suggested on a Christmas card to Lucewicz that they resume working on the Reger in January.

Once again he seems to have improved. In January he was in form and on the go. He gave concerts in Spain, Portugal, Austria, and Germany, often with Chopin's physically demanding ballades and etudes on the program. In the beginning of March, he played, for the first time in almost twenty years, in the Great Hall of the Vienna Konzerthaus, and the audience cheered him with a standing ovation for a quarter of an hour. On March 13, in the same hall, he played Haydn sonatas in the concert's first half and then Reger with Lucewicz. The next day they repeated the program at a concert for the staff at the local Yamaha center and in the following days played the same program at the Rolandseck railway station in Bonn and at a concert in Bremen.

Richter had to add another sad frailty to his list of afflictions. A tall, solidly built man, he fell onto his knees and broke a kneecap. Despite a knee operation, he could no longer support the leg properly and had difficulty walking. He required help from others or a cane. Another chapter in his life was over. Richter the hiker was no more. For some periods he was, in fact, an invalid, dependent on a wheelchair to navigate longer stretches, especially at railway stations and airports. Gradually his knee improved, however, and he was once again able to get about on his own power.

Then he had to endure an eye operation after an attack of inflammation. Surgery, medications, convalescence, and frailty had become part of his life, but only a feeling of incompetence could keep a warhorse like Richter away from the battlefield. His final concert, a closed event for music students in Lübeck where he once again played the Haydn-Reger program with Lucewicz, was no farewell concert. It took place in March 1995, and no one, least of all Richter himself, had any idea that it would be his last. Nothing indicated that he was tired or weak. After the Reger, he even turned to the audience and suggested that he and Lucewicz play the long, physically demanding piece again, which naturally was received with enthusiasm.

But the writing was on the wall in neon. Once again, heart problems put a stopper to his endeavors, and although he felt reasonably well for periods of time and never gave up the hope of continuing, illness led to prolonged enforced physical inactivity and isolation. The result was predictable: a lack of *joie de vivre* and clear symptoms of depression. What is a Sviatoslav Richter who is unable to play, after all?

In collaboration with his friend Dietrich Fischer-Dieskau, Richter planned a huge venture at the festival in La Grange focusing on music by Hindemith. Together with Dieskau's wife, the soprano Julia Varady, he wanted to perform Hindemith's *Marienlieder*, and with Fischer-Dieskau as conductor, he looked forward to a performance of Hindemith's piano concerto from Kammermusik No. 2. But he did not have the strength. He suggested that Lucewicz study the work and perform in his place. Unfortunately, Dietrich Fischer-Dieskau had already entered into another agreement.

In a state of apathy, watched over by nurses and constantly attended by Nina Dorliak and Milena Borromeo, Richter spent the months in the spring and early summer of 1995 isolated like a monk in modest accommodations at the Hotel Majestic in Paris. Here, Bruno Monsaingeon first introduced him to the idea of doing a portrait film. Originally Richter had suggested that Monsaingeon write his biography, but the musically trained film director immediately saw the project would be beyond his abilities.

Richter was often too weak even to indulge in his desire to read. "Nothing interests me anymore." As a self-help aid, he suggested with characteristic irony and wryness: "Brush your teeth thoroughly in the morning and the evening and read a bit of Proust or Thomas Mann every day!"

Monsaingeon describes an immensely animated face that quickly could swing from overwhelming sadness to something almost cheerful or comic, and he adds: "The poetry of his silences and the gestures that accompanied them . . . only a camera could have captured these." Some outside Richter's circle of friends have criticized Monsaingeon's use of a deathly ill artist as the focus of a documentary, an understandable point of view. Yet if the film and the comprehensive interview with Richter had not been made, we would all be the poorer for it.

A magnificent Japanese tour was planned for October 1995 to January 1996. Richter had not touched the piano in six months, it was a long way to Japan,

Richter and Nina Lvovna in Moscow.

and he did not have the strength to repeat his trip from Moscow through Siberia to Japan and back again. He considered canceling, but the idea of escaping the isolation of the hotel appealed to this restless, somewhat incapacitated nomad. At the end of October, he decided to complete the remaining part of the tour on two conditions. He needed at least a month to get into form again, and he suggested a method that he had used before to eliminate the mental and physical discomfort associated with long plane trips: he would be placed under full anesthesia in his bed in Paris, have himself freighted by ambulance to the airport, and then wake up in his hotel bed in Tokyo. This time, however, the idea only made his doctors shake their heads.

Nevertheless, in mid-November he set off, without narcosis, with the intention of beginning the planned concerts after less than a month's hiatus. Before the month was out, he was back in Europe with a very weak heart. All concerts were canceled. Monsaingeon visited him in a little town on the Italian Riviera. Richter was bedridden most of the day, "the very icon of suffering, both physical and mental."

He had not seen his apartment in Moscow for three years, but he did not want to go to Moscow. Some friends found him a house surrounded by natural beauty in the country near Auvers-sur-Oise, north of Paris. He spent the summer of 1996 there interrupted by brief stays in the hospital; at one point he was taken to the resuscitation ward, which further contributed to his depression. Without the piano, without music or books, without the opportunity to go for long walks, the great Richter did not exist. He was a shadow of himself. His condition made Lucewicz consider the ending of Monsaingeon's film, in which Richter declares, "I don't like myself." Lucewicz says, "People who knew Richter from before, when he was still a healthy and energetic celebrity, would find it inconceivable that he could develop such self-hatred. But he often said to me during this period, 'Look at me. I look like a peasant! I don't like my laughter. I don't like my teeth.' You have to separate the man from the artist."

During the summer, he was to spend some time at a cardiac clinic in Germany, and the prospect of a car trip cheered him. "Valenciennes!" he exclaimed to Monsaingeon at the idea that the trip would take him by the old Flemish city on the way to Brussels, "the city of Zola and his cycle of twenty novels!" And without difficulty, the book lover rattled off all the titles of Zola's cycle of novels in correct chronological order!

In late summer, he went to Vienna. Even though he was bedridden most of the day, he tried every form of novelty available, such as eating in a new restaurant in the evening. Here, too, Monsaingeon met with him to work on the film project. He offered to make available to Richter and company his family's apartment in Antibes, a popular vacation spot between Nice and Cannes on the French Riviera, with a terrace and a view of the sea. Later in the year, Richter accepted the offer, and it was here that Monsaingeon, during February–March 1997, made his historic film recordings of the emaciated, fatally ill, but still resolute pianist. For the young Andreas Lucewicz, Richter's illness was not the only concern. Richter had wanted to give his young colleague's career a leg up. Several concerts with the Reger Beethoven variations had been planned, including at Salzburg and in Finland, and he had suggested that they could tour the work in Russia together. Richter was looking forward to showing his young "apprentice" his homeland. At his own initiative, Lucewicz traveled to Antibes and spent some days with the small circle around Richter. He discreetly attended some of Monsaingeon's takes and departed from his tormented mentor with a sense that this meeting might be his last.

At the end of May 1997, the Richter-Dorliak-Borromeo troika moved back to Paris after having spent some weeks at a cloister in Jouques near Aix-en-Provence—a place Richter liked after having performed there several times. The pianist had regained some of his strength, and they moved him to rooms in the Paris building that sheltered his perhaps favorite author Marcel Proust when he died in 1922. He visited the apple of his eye, the still-active festival at Grange de Mesley, for the last time, and, supported by a walking stick, he attended some concerts. Only the festival's management was informed of his arrival (as early as 1988, he had handed over the management of the festival to René Martin). He arrived unnoticed, after the hall lights had been dimmed, and in the darkness of the back row, only a few people noticed him. At the end of June, he returned to Paris and demanded that a grand piano be made available. He slowly began to practice again. Those around him saw some signs of a miraculous renaissance. Now he wanted to go home. Yet another despised plane trip was in the offing, but a train trip through Berlin would have been too much of a strain. On July 6 he and Nina Lvovna flew to Moscow.

The End

Richter the wanderer, the globe trotter, the eternal nomad, returned home. After almost four years, he once again saw his Moscow and his apartment at the Bolshoya Bronnaya. But the city was baking in the summer heat. After three days, Nina Lvovna and Viktor Zelenin decided to move to the dacha in Nikolina Gora (his beloved dacha at the Oka River was out of the question; it was totally unsuited to a sick old man, and the distance from Moscow's hospitals was too great). More than any other city, Moscow was where he had his roots; here, in over fifty years, he had given more than five hundred concerts. And fate mercifully allowed him to embrace his city again. On the corner sofa in the room, with his piano and an expansive view, he was once again surrounded by the proud monuments of the Russian capital. And in Nikolina Gora, tours by car through Moscow and its suburbs became his favorite pastime.

Upon his homecoming, he was met at the airport by his closest friends and his personal physician, Irina Voevodskaya. The latter describes something resembling a minor state reception at the airport: "The Ministry of Culture had secured permission to drive a car into the landing area, all the way up to the plane's stairway. Our Mercedes was opened up in back, at the stairway, and after a few minutes, the maestro was brought down to the car in a chair carried by two officially dressed men. He was very thin, with a large forehead and thin, sharp knees; his eyes were large and expressive like a child's, attentive and expectant. And then a happy smile."

Richter was very weak physically, but mentally he was clear and resolute. He said that this time, the plane trip had not bothered him. Before, it annoyed him quite a bit to travel without being able to see and experience anything, to be transported in what felt like an upholstered coffin seven miles up in the air. But now he felt no need for new experiences. The plane trip had been tolerable. In a hurry and with the chronic stress that Richter's illness had wrought, Nina had forgotten all of his medical records from the previous years in Paris. Only a few journals from the years up to 1993 were available. It became clear to Voevodskaya that Nina Lvovna's health was not much better than Richter's.

In Nikolina Gora, Richter was continually attended by Nina, Viktor Zelenin, and sometimes friends. He was free of pain, and everyone did what they could to humor him. But Nina Lvovna was visibly frail and probably seriously ill as well. She moved as little as possible; her face was swollen; the veins in her neck were engorged; and at night she had difficulty breathing. But it would take a week to persuade this willful woman to see a doctor. After Richter's death, she was diagnosed with a breast tumor. But in those circumstances, she repeatedly refused to have any treatment as soon as hormones and diuretics made her feel a little better.

Richter's time was spent watching his favorite movies and greeting his close friends and colleagues of many years, such as Natalia Gutman, Eliso Virsaladze, and Yuri Bashmet. Car trips to favorite places in the city, particularly restaurants, were high on his list of pastimes; reading and listening to music also lifted the old master's spirits. On a good day, Richter seemed inexhaustible. Nina Lvovna, however, was too weak to participate in the automobile rides. Zelenin relates that Richter gradually resumed practicing and that he had specific plans for a Schubert program.

On July 29, without Nina but escorted by Voevodskaya, a few of his friends drove to a stately Georgian restaurant in the vicinity—a regional cuisine that Muscovites especially appreciate. Richter was in a good mood; he ate and drank almost like in the old days, joked, and told stories from the past. He was so pleased with the food that the next day he asked Zelenin to get takeout from the same restaurant.

No one could see the signs of the beginning of the end. On July 31, at six o'clock in the morning, he suddenly felt ill; he had pains in his heart and difficulty breathing. Zelenin ascertained that his blood pressure was very low, but the pain gradually subsided. Nevertheless, Voevodskaya was so alarmed that she asked Natalia Gutman to get in touch with the Ministry of Culture. Neither Richter nor Nina Lvovna was registered with any particular hospital. A local ambulance was called. Voevodskaya arrived around two o'clock. She relates, "The doctor who came with the ambulance had done an electrocardiogram. He was sitting with it in his hand at the piano and was rather upset. The maestro was lying down in his small room with blue lips and fingers."

Voevodskaya convinced her colleague that Nina Lvovna was also ill and that both of them had to be taken to the Kremlin Hospital. But Nina refused to be admitted (she may have remembered Richter's negative opinion of this famous hospital after the false rumor that Gilels's death was caused by medical malpractice). Voevodskaya and the others eventually persuaded her, little by little; this was the only hospital in which they would have any chance of being admitted together. Time went by. Richter was given a couple of injections, and then he and Nina were driven away in an ambulance. But Voevodskaya was refused admission into the hospital treatment area. Not until the next morning, after numerous telephone conversations with the administration, was she allowed in. "They were each put in their own rooms," she narrates. "Nina was waiting for an examination. The maestro looked much better. The discoloration was gone, and his breathing was not as strained. He ate with a good appetite, talked, and expressed his sympathy about Nina's poor sleep. A nurse came with a wheelchair to take the maestro to the X-ray department. This was surprising in his condition, as it would have been better to transport him on a gurney. While we discussed that, he exclaimed loudly and clearly that he did not want a gurney, he was fine. He got into the wheelchair, quite satisfied, kept an eye on everything and everyone, making comments."

Richter was subjected to a series of examinations and tests. A doctor requested his medical records, but they were in the apartment at Bolshoya Bronnaya. Voevodskaya did not want to leave him, so someone else had to get the documents. Richter fell asleep, exhausted by the commotion.

Voevodskaya continues:

> While he slept, he got a strange, icy, peaceful expression. I tried to wake him by rubbing his hands and ears, and he woke up, although very unwillingly. His pulse was very weak and unstable. I called the doctor; it turned out that he had almost no blood pressure. People ran to and fro; he received a drop with dopamine, and his blood pressure rose somewhat. So, I decided to get the papers at his apartment. In the confusion and difficulty of finding the documents, I was gone almost half an hour. Just as I was leaving the apartment, the telephone rang.
>
> It was over.

At the hospital, Nina Lvovna was full of self-reproach. She complained loudly at having acquiesced to the Kremlin Hospital, and she believed that she should have had Richter admitted as soon as they arrived in Moscow. Voevodskaya relates: "She would not understand that there was nothing more to do. When she was persuaded to go to the Kremlin Hospital, no one thought that even the best doctors could work a miracle cure there. The only thing that could be done was to create optimal comfortable conditions; real treatment was, unfortunately, no longer possible for anyone."

His death was expected, as they say. Yet, how does one prepare for a living person's suddenly becoming an unmoving, lifeless object? How can anyone prepare for eternal separation? The circle of friends around Richter did not lose a world pianist; they lost an old, sick, frail, emaciated man who had still been wonderfully alive. Spring and summer, sun and moon, are born, die, and return. A human being is born, dies, and does not return.

Postlude

Nina Lvovna Dorliak survived Richter by less than a year. Her last months were plagued by illness, respiratory difficulties, and horrendous back pain. She was bedridden most of the day, and she went out only when it was absolutely necessary. Just a few months before her ninetieth birthday, in May 1998, she died on Richter's corner sofa in the bright room of the Bolshoya Bronnaya apartment with the two grand pianos and the tremendous eastern view of Moscow. Richter had not left a will, so she was not legally entitled to inherit. A few months after Richter's death, however, she had a marriage certificate made out at the Russian embassy in Berlin. Marriage to a deceased person is certainly unusual, and the document's legal validity is still disputed. Richter's friend of many years, the cellist Natalia Gutman explains: "The embassy apparently believed that as his cohabitant for fifty years, she was his de facto marital partner. Therefore, she was also entitled to the status of primary heir. That is not clear under Russian law, but they apparently took it as given at the embassy."

At any rate, Nina Lvovna succeeded in achieving marital status with her lifelong companion, postmortem, and the fact that no Russian court of law questioned it may be ascribed to the random and impenetrable practice of law that characterized the period after the dissolution of the Soviet Union. Based on this marriage certificate, on December 5, 1997, she made out a will in Moscow. The apartment in Bolshoya Bronnaya would be divided so that Richter's share could be conveyed to the Pushkin Museum, and her share would go to her nephew. The nephew later sold this share to the museum.

Among the many byzantine mysteries in the Richter case are his finances during his final, difficult years. When he was too ill to play and, therefore, without an income, he suddenly had no money to pay for his expensive medical treatments. He had a contract with the German record company Live Classics, and its owner and his friend, Michel Beyerle, saw to it that he was covered by German health insurance (how an ill man could be insured is unclear). But it is and remains a mystery why, after furious concert activity even in his last years, he was not a wealthy man. When a pianist at Richter's level performs at more than a hundred concerts a year, his fees must generate a considerable amount—in the millions—not to mention royalties his recordings earned from sales and radio broadcasts all over the world. But throughout his life, Richter was completely uninterested in money; his finances simply had no place in his thoughts. Normally, he carried no money, and others managed his finances, used his credit cards, paid for hotels, restaurants, trips, and so on. Lucewicz reports that he never knew where Richter's fees were deposited or how or by whom his fortune was managed. Natalia Gutman was convinced that "Richter had no idea how much he earned at concerts or in royalties. Nina saw to it that her nephew controlled Richter's accounts, even while he was still alive."

The detective work needed to unravel these mysteries is outside the scope of this book. But it seems that the dying pianist's only asset was his estate in Russia. Shortly before his death, it is said, the friend of his youth, Mstislav Rostropovich, offered to buy him a plane ticket and bring him to the United States, where some of the world's best cardiac specialists might have helped him. But apparently the offer came too late.

Someday the shadier side of Richter's final years may come to light. But in order not to cast unreasonable or groundless aspersions on his circle of friends, some kind of explanation must at least be alluded to even if it constitutes a sad addendum to the story of Richter's life. This means that the person mentioned in this context must remain anonymous, which goes against good practice and the principles of this book. Therefore, since the issue is being litigated at the time of this writing, only two choices remain: to gloss over this aspect of the Richter story or to enlighten another dark side of Richter's life under the cloak of anonymity to avoid the risk of legal repercussions. The latter choice seems consistent with this book's intent.

Nina Dorliak had a brother whom she loved more than anyone. When he suddenly died of typhus in the early war years, she transferred this love to her brother's son and, throughout her life, maintained a maternal and protective relationship with her nephew. People in Richter's circle described this love as a sort of obsession. Since, by necessity, the nephew's identity must remain anonymous, the people interviewed on this topic are also anonymous.

The nephew's personality will not be examined here. It is an established fact, though, that he is a little-known actor with a major alcohol problem and that Richter—to put it mildly—did not care for him. The nephew's frustrated artistic ambitions apparently led him to treat Richter with something that might resemble contempt. It is also clear that Nina Lvovna supported her nephew and his first and second wives generously with funds from Richter's income (funds that she considered as theirs, since they had no legal-financial agreement and their life together was like a marriage). And there is no reason to doubt that Richter tacitly agreed to this financial help.

Nina Lvovna is described almost unanimously as an honorable and admirable person. One source adds: "She was an unusual woman with a strong character, very feminine, in possession of impeccable taste and style in everything in her life, with a beautiful, always youthful charisma. She was incredibly ascetic when it came to herself. She rejected all material goods and any form of extravagance. Nina Lvovna was strong and very open in her relationships with other people. She resolved all problems with authorities or officials diplomatically, but firmly. But she suffered from a severe and chronic disease: her love for X [namely, her nephew]. This love reached the clouds and made her look the other way at everything. And, unfortunately, this meant that X never had a chance to deal with his personal problems himself."

Another anonymous source relates:

Nina worshiped her nephew beyond bounds, and it gradually became a burden for Slava. She did everything, simply everything to promote her nephew's career as an actor, without success. He was an alcoholic. But Nina said to Slava: "He only drinks because no one realizes how talented he is!" Her relationship to X was almost a sort of madness. She believed that everyone was against him. With Slava, she called him "our child." But the nephew often reacted with hateful outbursts against Slava, especially after a successful concert. "You think you're a genius," he might say. "But you're nothing. I am the last Dorliak!" As a rule, Slava reacted with self-control and resignation — for example, by muttering again and again, "The Volga runs into the Caspian Sea." But, of course, it had an effect on him. Nina often asked Slava to legalize their life together by marrying her. But he refused every time. I think he imagined that if they were not married, the state would inherit his estate. Not X. Richter wouldn't discuss it. That is also why he refused to make a will.

In the early 1990s, Richter decided that the most valuable pictures and documents in his Moscow apartment were to be donated to the Pushkin Museum's collection. It was done discreetly, at first, under the guise of a "temporary exhibition." But the museum's director of many years, the powerful and still active Irina Antonova, was, by all accounts, helpful in getting a document drawn up in which Richter conveyed his property permanently to the museum. During the long period he was away from Moscow, his closest friend, Viktor Zelenin, lived in the apartment. Zelenin was entrusted with making sure the valuable art objects were delivered. He relates: "The museum's car broke down. So we simply carried the paintings over to the museum. Everything was packed safely.

His music collection, records, CDs, etc., went to me." When asked whether Nina Lvovna was informed of this, Zelenin replied, "She guessed!"

Several times Richter became the unwilling pawn of Nina Dorliak's love for her nephew. When, in the 1960s, X was arrested for driving under the influence, she adroitly exploited Minister of Culture Furtseva's admiration of Richter by sending him to her to get the charges dismissed. A similar event occurred in the mid-1970s. While under the influence, X was involved in a traffic accident. Nina Lvovna tried to hush up the case with the police. She personally went to the police chief with a proposal to let the matter drop if Richter would consent to give a concert at the policemen's annual gala! Nina Lvovna informed Richter of the agreement only the day before the event. Furious, he locked himself in and refused to speak to her, but he knew that he had no choice but to relent. With a devil-may-care cheerfulness, the world-famous pianist stood as the musical guarantor of a swap with the forces of law and order.

Nina Dorliak's willingness to sacrifice herself for her brother's son created friction between her and Richter in several other respects. But a breakup between them was inconceivable. His dependence on her—emotional, artistic, and practical—was too great. One source relates, "I asked him [Richter], 'But why don't you fight? Say you can't stand it!' And he replied, 'Without her, I would lose the desire to play. Music would lose its meaning for me. And she would cry. She would die!'" There is hardly any doubt that the great Richter was, in many respects, a man without great drive. Nina Dorliak helped and cared for her nephew as generously as she could. At one point, perhaps to prevent his close contact with Richter, she bought (or leased) a house for him and his family in Bonn. Whether this in itself is enough to explain Richter's sudden lack of money in the last years of his life is impossible to say. But today, as Nina Dorliak's only heir, X receives all the income from Richter's substantial royalties. There is an ongoing legal dispute over the extent to which X is entitled to his status as Richter's sole heir. Richter's two cousins, both of whom reside in the United States, are his only living relatives. The case is entangled in the highways and byways of love, loyalty, justice, inheritance law, and cold, hard cash in an unfortunate, impenetrable way.

According to his French attorney, Nina Lvovna's nephew has refused to shed any light on this mystery. The mysteries in the story of Richter the musician— "the messenger of the gods" who created music in a sphere beyond time, fate, and the everyday with a child's innocence and an angel's insight—are no fewer. But these mysteries do not cry out for answers and solutions; they simply call for the willing, searching, hungry, sensitive ears of a listener and for an open, receptive mind ready to infuse intuition, feeling, and intellect. For here "solutions" are not a possibility but a risk.

The Musical Legacy

Once upon a time, a musician's reputation lived on only as a dwindling, vague memory. We know a lot, for example, about Liszt's and Paganini's musicianship, about their incredible dexterity, about the overwhelming significance their playing had for other musicians and composers, and about their influence on the course of music history. But no one living has heard them play. Today, however, sound recordings make it possible for us to immerse ourselves in the music of long-deceased musicians. These recordings constitute an authentic tradition that will always shape a music audience's expectations and listening habits for good or ill: the recordings say that the work is supposed to sound like this; the audience expects it to sound like this; and a new generation of musicians will view the canonized image of classical music like this.

It is an interesting irony of history that in the era of the gramophone and CDs, the concept of "fidelity to the work" has had greater career than ever. There are indications that by establishing examples for posterity, recordings may hamper rather than liberate modern interpreters. In this context there is a clear demarcation between the concert and the recording. A concert lives through risk, improvisation, intimacy, the sensation of the moment; a modern recording often strives for perfection. Therefore, the question is whether the image we have of the "old greats" is authentic, a true picture of their genius, or an image through a glass darkly, a souvenir. Fortunately, many of the greatest pianists—Schnabel, Horowitz, Rubinstein—are also represented in an array of concert recordings.

Richter's discography may be the largest and most comprehensive of any classical musician. Not only is his repertoire immense, his recordings come in many different versions, as "official" studio recordings, as the result of contracts with record companies, as radio transmissions made by dozens of broadcasting services, and as "pirate recordings" of more or less unknown origin. His career in the recording medium lasted almost half a century. It began in 1948 and ended in the mid-1990s. The number of record labels is overwhelming, some, like

EMI/HMV, RCA, DG, CBS/Sony, Decca, and Phillips, are familiar names; many others (Nuova Era, Baton, Electrecord, Parlophone, and so on) have a regional character. Countless recordings produced by Soviet radio and the Soviet state company Melodiya have later been released by different companies in different countries (for example, Le Chant du Monde, Ariola, Victor, Parnassus, and Revelation), and other record labels are shrouded in mystery.

At the end of the 1980s, Richter agreed to record a series of concerts with Live Classics, a Munich-based company that represented friends and colleagues such as violinist Oleg Kagan and cellist Natalia Gutman. This resulted in recordings of Beethoven's two penultimate sonatas and a Bach CD in 1991, *Lyric Pieces* by Grieg in 1993, and the radio-recording issue of Reger's Beethoven variations with Andreas Lucewicz in the following year, as well as the Munich concert in May 1992 on the day Marlene Dietrich was buried. But labels such as Teldec, Phillips, and the Japanese Stradivarius and minor companies such as Aura and Laurel have also issued a number of CDs with recordings from Richter's last active years. The company Revelation (sometimes called "Russian Revelation") no longer exists, but an American millionaire is rumored to have bought the rights to a large number of tapes from the Russian radio archives in the 1990s.

However, even if Richter's discography is enormous, many of his interpretations are, unfortunately, still unobtainable, have not been issued, or are accessible only as "private recordings." His friend the conductor Rudolf Barshai comments: "A lot of the things I've done together with Richter have never been issued. For example, we played all of the Mozart concertos he had in his repertoire at that time. We played Schumann's Concerto at the Great Hall of the conservatory with the Radio Symphony Orchestra. My most beautiful memory may be Beethoven's Third Concerto with an expanded Moscow Chamber Orchestra. I performed all of Bach's concertos with Richter. In particular, I remember we played the piano adaptations of his two violin concertos with the Wiener Kammerorchester. He played unforgettably. But only pirate recordings exist."

Today numerous identical recordings can be found on a wide variety of labels. Here is a characteristic example: Beethoven's *Appassionata*, with Richter playing live in Moscow in 1960, on Bruno (BR), Melodija (Dutch), Napoleon (NLC), Saga (FDY), Westminster (WGM), Victor (VIC), and Vox (PL) labels. A great number have been issued by, for example, RCA, Phillips, EMI, and DG in different countries at different times with up to twelve different catalogue numbers; some have been transferred from wax or vinyl to cassette tapes or CD. Many have been reissued in partly improved versions; most were later digitally remastered; many were often grouped randomly, some unobtainable today. Many versions provide a time and a place for the recording, but some have only approximate dates and places. Some live recordings have been discreetly spliced together from several different concert recordings.

Richter is represented on most of the major (and many minor) companies in the West, and an exhaustive review of this topic would constitute a book in itself. There have been attempts, however. In 1999 the Englishman John Hunt published a comprehensive discography. In 1983 Falk Schwarz and John Berrie put together a well-documented list in the periodical *Recorded Sound*. Paul Geffen's Internet site (trovar.com) also contains a comprehensive discography. However, no discography can claim to be complete.

Discographers like to divide Richter's recording activities into periods. From 1948 to 1956, the state company Melodiya issued more than forty 78s. From 1952 and for the next eight years before Richter's debut in the West, Melodiya issued twenty-three LPs with Richter as a soloist performing the best-known Russian piano concertos and solo works by Tchaikovsky, Mussorgsky, Rachmaninov, Beethoven, Schubert, and Schumann.

The first recordings outside the USSR were made in Prague in 1954. Richter recorded Bach's Concerto in D Minor and Tchaikovsky's and Prokofiev's first piano concertos for the Czech state company Supraphon. But even before Richter's career in the West took off, major Western record companies such as Deutsche Grammophon (DG) began to record Richter; the first recording was made in Warsaw, in September 1958, and included Prokofiev's Fifth and Schumann's Piano Concerto. And after his Carnegie Hall debut in 1960, Richter was virtually pelted with offers. The five concerts in New York were issued (against Richter's wishes) by CBS, and during his tour in the United States, he made studio recordings for, among others, RCA. In London, a year later, he made five recordings, including Liszt's two concertos, for Phillips. Possibly in partial recognition of the fact that Western recording techniques were superior to those in the Soviet Union, he stopped doing studio recordings in the USSR in the 1960s, but his live recordings—usually for Russian radio—continued as before. In September 1962 he recorded Tchaikovsky's popular concerto with Karajan and the Vienna Symphony Orchestra, and it is claimed that DG sold more copies of this recording than any other in the firm's catalogue. When Richter toured all over Italy later that year, DG worked with EMI to record all the concerts. In less than four years, Richter had recorded material for thirty-two LPs, which, at his level, may well be a world record. Then, understandably, he took a break. Not until 1967 did he resume his recording activities, particularly live recordings of the piano recitals he began to give with David Oistrakh and Mstislav Rostropovich.

In September 1969 Richter, Oistrakh, and Rostropovich recorded Beethoven's Triple Concerto with the Berlin Philharmonic under Karajan, and it was one of the recordings Richter looked back on with chagrin. He and Oistrakh disagreed with Karajan's interpretation, especially the tempo. The atmosphere was tense; he tells Monsaingeon with irritation that Rostropovich was hand in glove with Karajan. At one point, Karajan stopped work, remarking that they now had everything they needed. Richter protested, saying he was unhappy with several takes. But Karajan responded dismissively. There was no time, he said, because the press photographs had to be taken. Richter was furious, perhaps also because Karajan had answered his cheerful, ironic remark "I am a German" with a foolishly chauvinistic "Then I am Chinese!" In the photographs, everyone put on a good face and smiled at the photographer. "We're grinning like idiots," Richter mutters to his interviewer. A year later, in Moscow, the three musicians once again recorded the work, this time with Kyril Kondrashin as conductor. Apparently, the atmosphere was more congenial.

If the recording with Karajan still seems the more captivating, it is probably because of the sparks flying between the musicians. Richter generally respected Karajan's musicianship and volubly admired him as a Wagner conductor. But as a person, he and Richter were not on the same wavelength. Richter performed in public only twice with the egocentric maestro.

In 1970 Richter announced a magnificent (and surprising) plan to record his huge solo repertoire in the studio—around fifty LPs. He also announced that he wanted to reduce the number of his engagements drastically the next year. The years 1969 and 1970 had been incredibly busy, with close to a hundred concerts and recordings per year. In the years immediately following, the number of scheduled concerts dropped to around half of what they were. The Soviet Melodiya and German Ariola labels agreed to collaborate, and in the following years Richter recorded enough music for around a dozen LPs, including the two volumes of the preludes and fugues that constitute Bach's *Das wohltemperierte Klavier* (a few months later, he played all forty-eight preludes and fugues at four concerts in Innsbruck, "for the last time in my life!"). But in 1973 he dropped the project without explanation. If we were to speculate about the reason, a qualified guess would be his lifelong discomfort at "soulless" work with technicians as opposed to a performance in front of an audience.

In the 1970s Japan played a decisive role not only in his itinerary but also in a long series of concert recordings. In 1975 Richter took on a dramatic mental test of strength with Beethoven's feared *Hammerklavier* Sonata, opus 106. For the first time outside the USSR, he played it in Japan, then a dozen times in Europe; and in London he approved the concert recording (issued on the

Rococo label, later on Stradivarius) that afterward prompted him to write "I don't like myself" in his notebook. He never played the work again.

In 1977 he recorded yet again Chopin's four scherzi in a Munich studio, and, as mentioned, the same year he recorded Alban Berg's Chamber Concerto in Paris with his friend Oleg Kagan in connection with his unique learning project on this atonal heavyweight. But after the 1970s, studio recordings gradually disappeared, and his catalogue was dominated almost entirely by concert recordings, not least from his Fêtes Musicales en Touraine.

Richter is also comprehensively represented in the catalogues as a chamber musician and lied accompanist. Piano quintets by Brahms, Dvořák, and Franck exist in Moscow recordings with, respectively, the Borodin and Bolshoi Quartets from the last half of the 1950s and Schubert's "Forelle" Quintet—again with members of the Borodin Quartet—from 1980. The collaboration with the two world-famous friends, Oistrakh and Rostropovich, resulted in several evergreens: concert recordings of Beethoven's cello sonatas (and cello sonatas by Brahms, Grieg, and Prokofiev) and violin sonatas by Schubert, Brahms, Dvořák, Shostakovich, Bartók, and Prokofiev.

Enduring collectors' items also came out of his amicable collaboration with Benjamin Britten, particularly their versions of Schubert's two masterworks for four hands, the Fantasy in F Minor and the "Gran duo" in C major (both recorded in concert in 1965 at Britten's festival in Aldeburgh). And the energetic collaboration with Dietrich Fischer-Dieskau resulted in unique concert recordings of Brahms's "Magelone" Romances, Hugo Wolf's "Mörike-Lieder," and sixteen Schubert lieder, the latter recorded at Granges de Mesley in 1977.

His collaboration with Nina Dorliak may also be heard in concert recordings, most often from Moscow and primarily from the years 1953–56, including songs and lieder by Russian composers such as Mussorgsky, Glazunov, Rachmaninov, and Dargomijsky, but also Mozart and Schubert. There is also a concert recording with Dorliak of Schumann's *Dichterliebe*, a cycle of poems that are clearly narrated by a man; many female singers, however, followed Lotte Lehmann's example and performed this classic without such a petty consideration as gender identification. Richter's very first recording may be with Nina Dorliak, a song by Glinka and Mozart's "Das Veilchen," recorded in 1948.

It is hardly possible to identify the high points of Richter's recordings of the solo repertoire. The selection would have to take into account far too many facets: artistic interpretation, recording technique, choice of pianos, acoustics, and so on, not to mention the differences in taste and experience that are part of any artistic assessment. And even though it may seem a bit disrespectful, one is forced to draw attention to recordings that Richter himself renounced (or just hated). It is often extremely difficult to understand what he was dissatisfied with (among the countless examples are his famous version of Brahms's Second Piano Concerto with Erich Leinsdorf and the Chicago Symphony Orchestra; Beethoven's Triple Concerto with Oistrakh, Rostropovich, and Karajan; and the powerful, captivating London recording of Beethoven's *Hammerklavier* Sonata).

There is also significant agreement (including his own, one would assume) about some recordings, for example, the Beethoven sonatas he played throughout his career, the last (in D major) of the three sonatas from opus 10, the sonatas in A-sharp minor (no. 12, opus 26) and in D minor (no. 17, called *The Tempest*), and Beethoven's penultimate, opus 110 (which Neuhaus almost had to force him to play in his student years). In his recorded versions of Schubert's *Wanderer Fantasy* or Schubert's sonatas—for example, the sonatas in A minor and B-flat major, the so-called posthumous Sonata in C Minor and the unfinished Sonata in C Major—he achieved more dramaturgical breadth and depth than almost anyone, perhaps even more than Schnabel or Brendel. And many would find his recordings of, for example, Schumann's Sonata in G Minor, his Fantasy in C Major, and the concert recording of Schumann's Toccata from Budapest in 1958 second to none. This is also the case with the London recording of Brahms's two first sonatas, composed when he was twenty, in which Richter fully realizes the music's youthful stormy romanticism.

In Richter's Liszt repertoire, his by turns powerfully dramatic and almost meditative interpretation of the two piano concertos (with Kyril Kondrashin and a highly charged London Symphony Orchestra) still sets the standard for many. And with respect to the Liszt Sonata in B Minor from a concert in Carnegie Hall and in some of Liszt's *Transcendental Etudes* (for example, "Feux follets"), possibly only Horowitz can challenge him. In a recording from Budapest at the end of the 1950s, he plays, with phenomenal energy and unique control, a Liszt work most people would view as an absolute rarity, the "Scherzo and March." Grieg's Piano Concerto with Bergen's symphony orchestra and his friend David Oistrakh as conductor still stands out (countless other recordings of it exist, several with Richter). As a Debussy interpreter, many hold up the legendary Walter Gieseking or point out the crystalline perfection of Michelangeli, but Richter's ability to re-create Debussy's flickering shadow play is unique. Debussy's foggy dream world and feathery melancholy have a kinship with one side of Richter's temperament, and in Richter it is not felt as personal but as an expression of "the unbearable lightness of being." For example, his recordings of "Estampes" and "Suite Bergamasque," of movements from "Images" and from the preludes have a cool poetic tone and a floating sense of time that can make him seem like a Debussy interpreter par excellence.

With Scriabin, he invokes—at times better than anyone—the special atmosphere the composer must have had in mind when he imagined his music "flowing like water" (at least, if one ignores the uneven, difficult-to-procure, but unforgettably dreamy Scriabin recordings of his admired colleague Vladimir Sofronitsky). In the Russian repertoire—Tchaikovsky, Prokofiev, Rachmaninov, Shostakovich, and especially Mussorgsky's *Pictures at an Exhibition*—many of his recordings are thought to set the standard (and of Mussorgsky, this is true whether one prefers the Sofia recording from 1958 with its cult status, the Prague recording from 1956, or the recordings from Moscow in 1952 and 1958; six different Richter recordings of the work exist).

With respect to the rarely heard works Richter included in his repertoire, his recordings can never be ignored—works such as Saint-Saëns's Concertos no. 2 and no. 5, Glazunov's Concerto in F Minor, and Dvořák's Piano Concerto. This is also true of a rarity such as Carl Maria von Weber's passionate and original Sonata in D Minor (no. 3), a Richter specialty such as Tchaikovsky's Grand Sonata, and a number of Handel's piano suites. Richter's preoccupation—especially in old age—with music most people still view as modern has led to stellar moments. He sets the introverted microcosm of Anton Webern's piano variations from 1936 into a melancholy twilight that will make most people forget everything about twelve-tone music, and his recording of Alban Berg's chamber concerto with Oleg Kagan and the wind ensemble from the Moscow Conservatory is stringent and moving, although some may find the sound of the brass somewhat sharp and "Russian" at times. The interpretation takes its time to breathe; it indulges the work's richness of tone and the Romantic swing in Berg's melodies (and, as previously mentioned, Richter had more than one reason to say, "It is this recording I'm most proud of!"). His deep understanding of Berg's language makes one regret that he never recorded Berg's early piano sonata. Listening to his Berg, one feels more than ever that what Stravinsky said of Berg's music is to the point and not a wisecrack ("it makes me think of a woman of whom you say, 'How beautiful she must have been when she was young!'"). As a part of this unique conservatory project, he also recorded Hindemith's piano concerto, Kammermusik No. 2; and his version of Hindemith's *Ludus Tonalis* (from Grange de Mesley, 1985) is worth mentioning. Again with conductor Yuri Nikolaievsky, the late Stravinsky's Webern-influenced Movements for Piano and Orchestra may be found in a Moscow recording from 1984.

There is undoubtedly more to discuss about his Bach. Some find his approach to this strict, self-enclosed music—a music that, so to speak, "expresses itself"—more dynamic and searching for expression than its historical stylistic foundation allows. But Richter was not interested in being "historically correct" or to imitate the harpsichord or clavichord for which Bach wrote the music—by, for example, playing without a pedal or without crescendo and diminuendo, like many of his colleagues. His temperament was not suited to that sort of compromise. And after three hundred years of technological transformation, Bach's spirit and music live on in many different forms; his genius is not bound to history's "great tale"; his capaciousness is without limits. Richter's approach to Bach is, thus, entirely pianistic. He uses the pedal without scruples, the slow tempos and his dense legato can create a sense of religious depth, and the quick movements burst with rhythmic vitality. His versions (studio as well as concert recordings) of *The Well-Tempered Clavier* are on the shelves of collectors all over the world. And in the lively suites by Handel, he gives this more extroverted, simple, and robust Baroque music motoric energy and an array of color; here everyone but a pedant forgets that the music was originally conceived for the harpsichord.

In Haydn he takes himself above the slightly dry academic tradition of interpretation without for a moment forgetting his fidelity to the score. And he ferrets out a richness of color, originality, and humor that many have probably forgotten in "Papa Haydn." But his Mozart splits both connoisseurs and "lay" listeners. Even though today Mozart is played with a multitude of stylistic, tonal, and attitudinal differences, many prefer the easy simplicity and hominess of such pianists as Wilhelm Backhaus, Alfred Brendel, and Christoph Eschenbach or the singing tone and naturally breathing phrasing of Daniel Barenboim or Murray Perahia. But Richter had a special understanding of the operatic gestures in Mozart, an understanding of the side of Mozart that Glenn Gould called "hedonism" and that he tried to squelch in his recording of Mozart's sonatas by putting the music under an operating-room lamp, by performing it with such a clinical overinterpretation that many listeners saw only an X-ray of it. Richter made room for Mozart's theatrical dramaturgy, for gesture, scene shifts, lines, and pauses. He magically produced small tableaux like an imaginary puppet theater. This was hardly an everyman's Mozart, but it was Richter's own.

Precisely because of Richter's huge repertoire, the expressive span of his musical legacy is open, like a huge botanical garden, to everyone's personal desires, fascinations, or predilections. Richter's restless curiosity, his unshakable confidence in intuition, his reliance on the moment, the constant wooing of the unknown muses we call inspiration (which he usually described as "freshness"), transform him from a historical-mythical figure to a speaking fellow human when one listens to his recordings. And they also emphasize the life-affirming fact that a musical performance is always both spirit and life, both soul and body. Again and again, the unique physical presence in Richter's music keeps him wonderfully alive, in every sense of the word, even when he speaks to us through the fragile memory of an antiquated technology.

Afterword

This book is not meant to be a musicological endeavor. Scholars may search, in vain, for traditional academic documentation, extensive references to sources, footnotes, and the like. I am a composer and writer. The inspiration for the book derives solely from my fascination with a great pianist, with his personality and music. My intent is not dutifully, authoritatively, or exhaustively to map out a corner of music history, but simply to satisfy my desire to place this fascination within a historical-musical framework and share it with the reading, listening public. The book is based on a large amount of unsorted data, sources, material, and information, all of it obtained partly through personal contacts and references.

The sources for the book consist, for the most part, of books, periodicals, documents, unpublished notes, writings, memoirs, and personal conversations with a great many people who were close to Richter. My research has put to rest many of the anecdotes and tales surrounding the Richter mystique. But I cannot guarantee that I inadvertently did not introduce new inaccuracies. No one's memory is perfect, and no study can claim to be definitive. It is almost impossible for me to cross check the massive amount of data, information, and sources I used in this book. Richter's life and deeds span many corners of the globe, and it stands to reason that readers with detailed knowledge of aspects of this assignment may find mistakes, omissions, or misunderstandings despite my efforts. I beg the reader's understanding and forbearance, and I hope that this book will lead to others that will expand, put into perspective, and clarify its contents.

An understandable, but hardly alarming, worry is my lack of knowledge of the Russian language. All I can say is that Richter's music and person belong to the entire world. And whoever succeeds in getting to the bottom of his life and deeds or the existing literature about him could be criticized for not mastering other languages such as Japanese, Hungarian, Finnish, Dutch, and Czech, in addition to Italian, German, French, Spanish, and English (languages in which

Antti Sairanen and
Natalya Gutman.

I have a solid background). Composers such as Tchaikovsky or Shostakovich,
for example, were quintessential Russian personalities, but hardly anyone can
claim that only a Russian-speaking writer is qualified to deal with their lives
and music.

Nevertheless, any deep exploration of Richter's personal life story and early
artistic development would be impossible without some knowledge of his
native tongue. And that this drawback did not bother me is due to the background for the genesis of this book. In 2001–4, I was engaged in a close collaboration with the Danish-resident Finnish musician and "cultural entrepreneur"
Antti Sairanen. He initiated my reconstruction of two major forgotten works by
Franz Schubert. Almost by accident, I discovered that Richter's cousins Fritz
Reincke and Walter Moskalew (Richter's only living immediate relatives, now
residing in the United States) had designated Sairanen their representative in
connection with a dispute about Richter's inheritance (see my chapter "Post-
lude"). On numerous occasions, Sairanen had discussed with them the possibility of having a thoroughly researched biography of the pianist written in
a Western language. In an unguarded moment, I mentioned that I might be
attracted to such a project on the condition that Sairanen be willing to help
with the research as an equal partner. Sairanen speaks fluent Russian and has
been interested in Richter's life and art for many years. When the cousins,
approached by Sairanen, reported that the idea seemed interesting and acceptable to them and that they were willing to cooperate by giving advice and pro-
viding access to documents, I agreed to take on the task.

Without their cooperation, this book would never have been written. And
without Sairanen's large network of prominent people in Russia and around the

world, without his inexhaustible legwork—making arrangements, obtaining access to otherwise neglected sources, documents, and recordings of Richter, translating Russian sources and texts, and, particularly, securing fundamental Russian sympathy and help for this project—I would never have been able to take on, much less carry out, this project. Based on my interests and questions, Sairanen took over some of the conversations that constitute important source material for this book and recorded them on videotape. Without having written a single word, he has had a significance for this book that cannot be overestimated.

Of the considerable number of books I have read with interest during my research, the most important are listed in the bibliography. Moreover, many other articles, reviews, published interviews, and so on, have been incorporated into my work.

The sources for the countless quotes by Richter in the book are often mentioned in the text. However, documenting these throughout the work would interrupt the flow. When not clearly identified, these quotes stem from a limited number of sources: Bruno Monsaingeon's *Sviatoslav Richter: Notebooks and Conversations*, based on conversations with the eighty-two-year-old Richter, and Richter's notes on music over a period of more than twenty-five years; Yakov Milstein's conversations with him in *O Svyatoslave Richtere* (About Sviatoslav Richter); Valentina Chemberdzhy's *V puteshestvii so Sviatoslavom Rikhterom* (On Tour with Sviatoslav Richter); Jürgen Meyer-Josten's *Musiker im Gespräch: Sviatoslav Richter* (Musicians in Conversation: Sviatoslav Richter); and Alexander Vishinsky's interview with him in *Besedi s pianistami* (Conversations with Pianists). When people associated with Richter are quoted without identification, the source is almost exclusively Richter in Bruno Monsaingeon's conversations with him. As to cultural politics, conditions, and events in the Soviet Union, Boris Schwarz's *Music and Musical Life in Soviet Russia, 1917–1970* has been an inexhaustible source. The main sources for the chapters on Prokofiev and Shostakovich are listed in the bibliography.

Many people have willingly and generously given their time and effort, advice and aid to this project, often because of their respect and affection for the book's protagonist. Among the most important who deserve thanks are (in alphabetical order): Irina Antonova, Rudolf Barshai, Shuyler Chapin, Grigori Fried, Andrei Gavrilov, Lars Grunth, Natalia Gutman, Jacques Leiser, Alina Loginova, Andreas Lucewicz, Umberto Massini, Paul Moor, Sergei Musaelyan, Elvira Orlova, Vera Prokhorova, Fritz Reincke, Kurt Sanderling, Haruko Takagi, Vladimir Viardo, Irina Voevodskaya, and Viktor Zelenin.

Special thanks go to Walter Moskalew for his help with and the right to use unpublished photos from the family archives, and to foundations that financed the research for this project: the Beckett Foundation, the Gangsted Foundation, the L. F. Foght Foundation, Politiken's Foundation, and the Royal Academy of Music, Aarhus. In addition, I would like to thank the librarian Birthe Heien for her invaluable assistance in helping to procure source materials and Dalia Geffen for her immense care and understanding when line editing the English translation.

KARL AAGE RASMUSSEN

RECORDINGS BY SVIATOSLAV RICHTER
Recommendations by Andreas Lucewicz

The recordings mentioned here are, for me, representative of Sviatoslav Richter's art as a pianist, bearing witness in a unique way to his skill as an interpreter; they can be deemed "recordings of the century."

ANDREAS LUCEWICZ, November 2005

JOHANN SEBASTIAN BACH
The Well-Tempered Clavier I and II
Melodia Eurodisc 610 276-234

French Suites Nos. 2, 4, and 6 (C-minor, E-flat major, E-major)
Capriccio B-flat major
Live Classics LCL 401

LUDWIG VAN BEETHOVEN
Piano Sonatas nos. 9 and 10, op. 14, 1 and 2 (E-major, G-major)
Piano Sonata no. 11, op. 22 (B-flat major)
Piano Sonatas nos. 19 and 20, op. 49, 1 and 2 (G-minor, G-major)
Philips 412 379-2

Piano Sonata no. 17, op. 31, 2 (D-minor)
EMI CDM 7 69032-2

Piano Sonata no. 29, op. 106, "Hammerklavier"
Stradivarius STR-33313

Piano Concerto no. 1, op. 15
Boston Symphony Orchestra/Charles Munch
In addition, Piano Sonata no. 12, op. 26 (A-flat major) and Piano Sonata no. 22, op. 54 (F-major)
RCA Victor GD86804
BMG France 74321 846 052 (2 CDs)

Piano Concerto no. 3, op. 37 (C-minor)
Wiener Symphoniker/Kurt Sanderling
Also Schumann Piano Concerto in A-minor, op. 54

Warsaw National Philharmonic/Witold Rowicki
Deutsche Grammophon DG 427 198-2

Concerto for Piano, Violin, Cello, and Orchestra, op. 56, "Triple Concerto"
Berliner Philharmoniker/Herbert von Karajan
Piano Sonata no. 17, op. 31, 2 (D-minor)
EMI CDM 7 69032-2

Sonatas for Piano and Cello, op. 5, 1 and 2; op. 69; op. 102, 1 and 2
With Mstislav Rostropovich
Philips 412 256-2 (2 CDs)

FRANZ SCHUBERT
Piano Sonatas no. 9, D575, and no. 11, D625 (B-major, F-minor)
JVC/Melodia VDC-524

Piano Sonatas no. 13, D664, and no. 14, D784 (A-major, A-minor)
JVC/Melodia VDC-520

Piano Sonata no. 19, D958 (C-minor)
Also Impromptu in A-flat major, op. 142, 2
JVC/Melodia VDC-1020

Piano Sonata no. 21, D960 (B-flat major)
JVC/Melodia VDC-1021

BEETHOVEN/SCHUBERT/LISZT
Piano Sonatas
Beethoven: Sonatas, op. 2, no. 3, op. 7, op. 31, nos. 2 and 3, op. 90, op. 109, op. 110,
    op. 111
Schubert: Piano Sonatas, D575 (B-major), D960 (B-flat major)
Liszt: Sonata (B-minor)
Brilliant Classics 92229, 5 CDs

ROBERT SCHUMANN
Concerto for Piano and Orchestra, op. 54 (A-minor)
"Introduction and Allegro Appassionato," op. 92 (G-major)
Warsaw National Philharmonic, Witold Rowicki (op. 54), Stanislaw Wislocki
    (op. 92)
Novellette, op. 21, no. 1 (F-major)
Toccata, op. 7 (C-major)
Waldszenen, op. 82
Deutsche Grammophon DG 447 440-2

Symphonic Etudes op. 13
With Beethoven: Sonata No. 27, op. 90 (E-minor)
JVC VDC-1025

Fantasiestücke, op. 12, nos. 1, 2, 3, 5, 7, 8
Marsch, op. 76, no. 2 (G-minor)
Waldszenen, op. 82
Novellette, op. 21, no. 1 (F-major)
Toccata, op.7 (C-major)
ABEGG-variations, op. 1
DG 435 751-2, "Dokumente" 1956–62

FRANZ LISZT
Piano Concertos 1 (E-flat major) and 2 (A-major)
London Symphony Orchestra/Kiril Kondrashin
Philips 412 006-2

FRÉDÉRIC CHOPIN
Four Scherzi for piano
Eurodisc 610 128-231

MUSSORGSKY/LISZT
Mussorgsky: Pictures at an Exhibition (Sofia, February 1958)
Schubert: Moment Musical, op. 94, no. 1 (C-major)
Impromptus in E-flat major and A-flat major, op. 90, nos. 2 and 4
Liszt: Valse oubliée no. 1 (F-sharp major), Valse oubliée no. 2 (A-flat major)
Etudes d'exécution transcendante no. 5 (B-flat major), "Feux follets," and no. 11
    (D-flat major), "Harmonies du soir"
Also Chopin: Etude, op. 10, no. 3 (E-major)
Philips 420 774-2

ANTONIN DVOŘÁK
Piano Quintets, op. 5 and op. 81 (with Borodin Quartet)
Philips 412 429-2

Piano Concerto, op. 33
Bayrisches Staatsorchester München/Carlos Kleiber
With Schubert: Fantasie in C-major, D760, "Wanderer"
EMI CDC 7 47967-2

JOHANNES BRAHMS

Piano Concerto no. 2, op. 83
Chicago Symphony Orchestra/Erich Leinsdorf
With Beethoven: Sonata no. 23 in F-minor, op. 57, "Appassionata"
RCA GD86518
BMG France 74321 846 052 (2 CDs)

Violin Sonata, op. 100 (A-major)
Prokofiev: Violin Sonata, op. 80 (F-minor)
With David Oistrakh
Salzburg 20.8.1972
ORFEO C 489 981 B

PETER TCHAIKOVSKY

Piano Pieces
Regis RRC 1093

Piano Concerto no. 1, op. 23 (B-flat minor)
Rachmaninov Piano Concerto no. 2, op. 18 (C-minor)
Tchaikovsky: Wiener Symphoniker/Herbert von Karajan
Rachmaninov: Warsaw Philharmonic Orchestra/Stanislaw Wislocki
Deutsche Grammophon DG 447 420-2

ALEXANDER SCRIABIN

Piano Sonata no. 2, op. 19 (G-sharp minor); no. 5, op. 53 (F-sharp major);
   no. 9, "Black Mass"
From Préludes, op. 11, op. 13, op. 37 op. 59, op. 74
From Etudes, op. 42, nos. 2, 3, 4, 5, 6, 8
Poème, op. 52, no. 1
Music & Arts CD-878

CAMILLE SAINT-SAËNS/GEORGE GERSHWIN

Saint-Saëns: Piano Concerto no. 5, op. 103 (F-major), the "Egyptian"
Gershwin: Concerto in F
Radio-Sinfonieorchester Stuttgart/Christoph Eschenbach
SDR MAS 294

HUGO WOLF

18 Lieder nach Gedichten von Eduard Mörike
Live at Innsbruck, October 1973, with Dietrich Fischer-Dieskau
Deutsche Grammophon DG 457 898-2

RICHTER AT BBC
16 JUNE 1967, 20 OCTOBER 1968, 8 OCTOBER 1969
Haydn: Sonata in E-major, Hob. XVI:22
Chopin: Nocturne in E-minor, op. 72, no. 1
Beethoven: Sonata no. 11, op. 22 (B-flat major); "Eroica" Variations, op. 35
Schumann: Symphonic Etudes, op. 13
Chopin: Nocturne, op. 15, no. 1 (F-major)
Rachmaninov: 12 Préludes from op. 23 and op. 32
BBC Legends BBCL 4090-2 (2 CDs)

RICHTER REDISCOVERED
Haydn: Sonata in C-major, Hob.XVI:50
Chopin: Scherzo no. 4, op. 54 (E-major); Ballade no. 3, op. 47 (A-flat major)
Rachmaninov: 4 Préludes from op. 23 and 32
Ravel: Jeux d'Eau and La Vallée des Cloches (Miroirs)
Prokofiev: Sonata no. 6, op. 82 (A-major); Gavotte, op. 95, no. 2
Debussy: Les Collines d'Anacapri
Chopin: Etudes, op. 10, no. 10, and op. 10, no. 12; Mazurka, op. 24, no. 2 (C-major)
RCA BMG 09026-63844-2 (2 CDs)

SVIATOSLAV RICHTER PLAYS
Scriabin: Sonata no. 5, op. 53 (F-sharp major)
Debussy: Estampes from Préludes I, nos. 2, 3, 5
Prokofiev: Sonata no. 8, op. 84 (B-flat major)
With nos. 3, 6, 9 from Visions fugitives
Deutsche Grammophon DG 423 573-2

SVIATOSLAV RICHTER IN MEMORIAM
Bach: Preludes and fugues, WTC I, nos. 1, 4, 5, 6, 8
Haydn: Sonata in G-minor, Hob.XVI:44
Chopin: Ballade no. 3, op. 47 (A-flat major); Ballade no. 4, op. 52 (F-minor)
Polonaise-Fantaisie, op. 61 (A-flat major), Etudes op. 10, no. 1 and op. 10, no. 12
Schubert: Allegretto in C-minor, D915, and from Ländler, D366, nos. 1, 3, 4, 5
Schumann: ABEGG Variations, op. 1
Debussy: Estampes from Préludes I, nos. 2, 3, 5
Rachmaninov: Préludes, op. 23, nos. 3, 5, 6, 7, and op. 32, nos. 1, 2, 12
Prokofiev: Visions fugitives, op. 22, nos. 3, 6, 9
Deutsche Grammophon DG 457 667-2 (2 CDs)

SVIATOSLAV RICHTER IN SALZBURG (26 AUGUST 1977)

Beethoven: Andante favori, WoO57

Chopin: Valse, op. 34, no. 1 (A-flat major); op. 34, no. 2 (A-minor); op. 34, no. 3 (F-major)

Scherzo, op. 31 (B-flat minor); Barcarolle, op. 60 (F-sharp major)

Debussy: Suite Bergamasque, Estampes

ORFEO C 491 981 B

EDITION SVIATOSLAV RICHTER

Recordings 1952–1995, primarily from the 1950s and 1960s

Melodia 74321 29461-2 to 74321 29470-2 (10 CDs)

RICHTER IN PRAGUE

Recordings 1954–1988

Harmonia Mundi 354 001 to 354 015 (15 CDs)

Beethoven: Diabelli Variations, Piano Concertos nos. 1 and 3, various sonatas, including "Appassionata"

Schumann: Symphonic Etudes

Brahms: Sonatas, op. 1 and 2

Mussorgsky: Pictures at an Exhibition

Mozart: 6 sonatas

Chopin: Etudes and Ballades

Plus works by Liszt, Haydn, and Rachmaninov

SVIATOSLAV RICHTER VOLS. I–V

Works by Haydn, Schumann, Brahms, Prokofiev, Stravinsky, Shostakovich, Webern, Bartok, Szymanowski, and Hindemith

Decca 436 451-2 and 436 454-2 to 436 457-2

SVIATOSLAV RICHTER: UN PORTRAIT

CD 1: Beethoven: Sonatas, op. 2, no. 1, op. 10, no. 3, op. 31, no.2; Andante favori

CD 2: Schubert: Sonata A-Dur, D 644; Wanderer-Fantasie
Schumann: Fantasie C-Dur, op. 17

CD 3: Schumann: Sonata no. 2, op. 22; Papillons, op. 2; Faschingsschwank, op. 26

CD 4: Prokofiev: Piano Concerto no. 5

London Symphony Orchestra/Lorin Maazel

Berg: Kammerkonzert for Piano, Violin, and Wind Instruments

Sviatoslav Richter and Oleg Kagan/An ensemble from the Moscow Conservatory/ Yuri Nikolaievsky

EMI CLASSICS 7 64429-2 (4 CDs)

Numerous high-quality, live recordings from the final years of Richter's life, solo and with other instrumentalists, can be found on the Live Classics label.

Many of the recordings mentioned here are marketed under the Regis record label, particularly recordings on JVC. Some of the recordings may be found on other record labels in other groupings.

DVD RECORDINGS

Richter: The Enigma (L'Insoumis, Der Unbeugsame)
Film by Bruno Monsaingeon
Warner Music Vision 3984-23029-2

Richter/Rostropovich
EMI Classic Archive DVB 7243 4 928489 0
Beethoven's 5 cello sonatas
Live from Edinburgh, 31 August 1964
Also Mendelssohn: Variations sérieuses, op. 54

SELECT BIBLIOGRAPHY

Brown, Malcolm Hamrick, ed. *Russian and Soviet Music: Essays for Boris Schwarz*. Ann Arbor, Mich.: UMI Research Press, 1984.

Chapin, Schuyler. *Musical Chairs*. New York: G. P. Putman Sons, 1978.

Chemberdzhy, Valentina. *Swjatoslaw Richter: Eine Reise durch Sibirien*. Vienna: Residenz Verlag, 1992.

Danuser, Hermann, et al. *Sowjetische Musik im Licht der Perestroika*. Laaber: Laaber Verlag, 1990.

delle Mura, Sergio. *Testimone del tempo*. Naples: Pagan, 1988.

Dubal, David. *The Art of the Piano*. Cambridge. Mass.: Amadeus Press, 1989, 2004.

Dubal, David. *Reflections from the Keyboard*. New York: Schirmer Trade Books, 1997.

Egert, Georg. *Swjatoslaw Richter*. Berlin: Rembrandt Verlag, 1966.

Fischer-Dieskau, Dietrich. *Nachklang*. Stuttgart: Deutsche Verlans-Anstalt, 1988.

Geffen, Paul. *A Tribute to Sviatoslav Richter* (Biography, Discography, Chronology, and Essays). Available online at http://trovar.com (site last updated 1 December 2006).

Graffman, Gary. *I Really Should Be Practicing*. New York: Doubleday, 1981.

Grun-Grshimailo, Tamara. *Die sowjetische Musik*. Moscow: Apn Verlag, 1985.

Hamrick Brown, Malcolm, ed. *A Shostakovich Casebook*. Bloomington: Indiana University Press, 2004.

Ho, Allan B., and Dmitry Feofanov. *Shostakovich Reconsidered*. Toccata Press, 1998.

Jusefowitsch, Viktor. *David Oistrach: Gespräche mit Igor Oistrach*. Stuttgart: Deutsche Verlags-Anstalt, 1977.

Kennedy, Michael. *Britten*. Oxford: Oxford University Press, 1983.

Khrennikov, Thikon (with V. Rubtesova). *Thikon Khrennikov o vremini i o sebe*. Moscow: Erindringer, 1994.

Mach, Elyse. *Great Pianists Speak for Themselves*. London: Robson Books, 1981.

Maestro Richter's World. Photographs by Toru Konda. Minato-ku, Tokyo: Tokyo Shimbun Press, 1987. (Text in Japanese. Includes Midori Kawashima's interview with Richter and her essay "The Richter I Knew." Translated from Japanese for use in this book by Haruko Takagi.)

Malko, Nicolai. *A Certain Art*. New York: Georg Malko, 1966.

Masini, Umberto, et al. "Sviatoslav Richter: Appunti per un libro." *Musica* 104 (June–September 1997).

Menuhin, Yehudi. *Unfinished Journey*. London: Futura Publications, 1978.

Meyer-Josten, Jürgen. "Musiker im Gespräch: Sviatoslav Richter 1982." In *Conversations*. Paris: Editions Van de Velde, 1989.

Milstein, Jacov. *Sviatoslav Richter, genio e regolatezza*. Naples: Tolmino, 1998.

Monsaingeon, Bruno. *David Oistrakh, Artist of the People*. Film, NVC Arts, 1994.

Monsaingeon, Bruno. *Richter: The Enigma (Richter, l'Insoumis)*. Film, NVC Arts, 1998.

Monsaingeon, Bruno. *Sviatoslav Richter, Notebooks and Conversations*. London: Faber & Faber, 2001.

Murakami, Teruhisa. *What Good Sound Is*. Tokyo: Chopin, 2001. (Text in Japanese. Section on Richter translated from Japanese for use in this book by Haruko Takagi.)

Nestjew, I. *Prokofjew*. Berlin: Henschel Verlag, 1962.

Neuhaus, Heinrich. *The Art of Piano Playing*. London: Barrie & Jenkins, 1973.

Papp, Márta. *Szvjatoszlav Richter*. Budapest: Zenemükiadó, 1976.

Prokofiev, Sergei. *Dokumente, Briefe, Erinnerungen*. Leipzig: Verlag für Musik, 1961.

Raj Grubb, Suvi. *Music Makers on Record*. London: H. Hamilton, 1986.

Reincke, Dagmar. *Hanspeters Waldtraum*. Rødding: Sacontala Publishers, forthcoming.

Reincke, Dagmar. "A Very Different Kind of Boy." Rødding: Sacontala Publishers, 2010.

Richter, Anna. *The Memoirs of Anna Richter*. Rødding: Sacontala Publishers, 2010.

Robinson, Harlow. *Prokofiev*. New York: Viking Penguin, 1987.

Roloff-Momin, Ulrich. *Andere machten Geschichte, ich machte Musik: Kurt Sanderling in Gesprächen und Dokumenten*. Berlin: Parthas Verlag, 2002.

Samuel, Claude. *Prokofiev*. London: Marion Boyars, 1971.

Schwarz, Boris. *Music and Musical Life in Soviet Russia, 1917–1970*. London: Barrie & Jenkins, 1972.

Vishinsky, Alexander. "Besedi s pianistami." *Klassika* 21 (2004).

Vishnevskaya, Galina. *Galina: A Russian Story*. New York: Harcourt Brace Jovanovich, 1984.

Volkov, Solomon. *Shostakovich and Stalin*. New York: Alfred A. Knopf, 2004.

Volkov, Solomon. *Testimony: The Memoirs of Dmitri Shostakovich*. New York: Harper & Row, 1979.

Wahrhaftig, Artyom. *Tchaikovsky Competition: Look from Inside*. Film, Russian Season, 2002.

Wernli, Andreas. *Dmitrij Schostakowitsch*. Zürich: Rüffer+Rub Sachbuchverlag, 2004.

ILLUSTRATION CREDITS

Image on page 236 courtesy of Andreas Lucewicz.

Images on pages 54, 61, 64, 75, 94, 118, 180, 203, and 274 courtesy of Antti Sairanen.

Images on pages 63 and 83 © Lebrecht Music & Arts.

Images on pages 15, 176, 179, 182, 226, 227, and 253 © Toru Konda.

Images on pages 5, 29, 30, 33, 35, 36, 38, 44, 45, 46, 47, 50, 51, 136, 138, 143, 145, 147, 155, 160, 161, 162, 169, 200, and 231 courtesy of Walter Moskalew.

INDEX

Sonata No. 6 in A Major (op. 82), 100; Piano Sonata No. 7 in B-flat Major (op. 83), 103, 206, 211; Piano Sonata No. 8 in B-flat Major (op. 84), 6, 103; Piano Sonata No. 9 in C Major (op. 103), 104; piano sonatas, 103, 172; *Romeo and Juliet*, 97, 227; *Sarcasmes*, 95; *Scythian Suite*, 102; *Semyon Kotko*, 100, 149; *Sleeping Beauty*, 103; Sonata for Cello and Piano in C Major (op. 119), 113; *Symphonie Classique*, 95, 102; Symphony-Concerto for Cello and Orchestra (op. 125), 99, 112–14, 172; Symphony No. 2 in D Minor, 97; Symphony No. 3 in C Minor, 97, 99; Symphony No. 7 in C-sharp Minor, 115; unfinished works, 116; Violin Concerto No. 1 in D Major, 95, 99; Violin Concerto No. 2 in G Minor, 227; Violin Sonata in F Minor (op. 80), 169–70; *War and Peace*, 65, 97; *Zdravitsa*, 108

proletkult, 96

Pushkin, Alexander, 222

Pushkin Museum (Moscow), 173, 178–79, 229–30, 260, 262–63; December Nights, 178–79, 221, 228

Rachmaninov, Sergei, 93, 110, 204; Piano Concerto No. 2, 206; Piano Concerto No. 3, 89, 214; Prelude in G Minor (op. 23, no. 5), 80; preludes, 73, 248; *Vokalise*, 233; works for piano and orchestra, 101

Rattalino, Piero, 215–16

Ravel, Maurice, 85–86, 101, 216; *Bolero*, 95; Concerto for the Left Hand, 215; Concerto in G Major, 216; *Gaspard de la Nuit*, 214; *Pictures at an Exhibition* (orchestration), 216; *Valses nobles et sentimentales*, 60; violin sonata, 183

RCA Victor, 158–59, 163

Reagan, President Ronald, 243

Reger, Max: piano concerto, 215; Variations and Fugue on a Theme of Beethoven, for two pianos (op. 86), 12, 248, 250–51, 254

Reincke, Elisabeth von (maternal grandmother), 27, 34

Reincke, Miroslav (Friedrich/Fritz; cousin), 34, 75, 131, 157–58, 206–7, 225, 274

Reincke, Nikolai (uncle and godfather), 31, 34

Reincke, Tamara (Dagmar, Meri; maternal aunt), 31, 33–35, 37, 76, 206–7, 211; death of, 225; "Hanspeters Waldtraum," 34–35

Reiner, Fritz, 153

repetitions, musical, 205–6

Revelation recording company, 265

Richter, Anna (mother), 26–27, 37, 76, 200–201; death of, 146, 148; invited to visit USSR, 164; marriage to Kondratiev, 138; relationship with son, 135–42; return to Odessa, 32–33; return to Zhitomir, 31–32; reunion with son, 142–44; unpublished memoirs, 27, 135, 137; visits with son in Germany, 144–48

Richter, Daniel (paternal grandfather), 25

Richter, Sergius. *See* Kondratiev, Sergei

Richter, Sviatoslav Teofilovich: as accompanist for lieder, 268; as accompanist for silent films, 43; appreciation of his recordings, 268–72; attends mother's funeral, 148; birth of, 28; career phases, 201–2; Caucasus tour (1943–44), 76–80; as chamber musician, 169–70, 268; character and personality, 1–3, 18–19, 219–20,

223–24; as composer, 40–41; and concert culture, 191–96; concerts with Dorliak, 149, 268; as conductor, 113–14; as conservatory student, 56; "cool" playing, 59; death of, 20–21; discography, 264–72, 277–83; dislike for advance planning, 195–96; early life, 28–35; episode of broken finger, 113–14; essay "On Prokofiev," 98–99, 117; estate issues, 260–63; experience with tinnitus, 232–33; family background, 7, 25–28; final concert, 251–52; final return to Moscow, 256; finances in later life, 260–63; first piano recital, 48–49; foreign travel, 150; and "German" identity, 81, 146; and Gould, 19–20; hands, 2; health issues, 179–81, 187–88, 230–34, 246–47, 251–55; and homosexuality, 84–85, 148, 165, 234–40; and importance of listening, 204–5; interest in film, 37, 43, 220, 222; interest in French culture, 168, 222; interest in improvisation, 212–13; interest in literature, 222, 254; interest in nature, 38; interest in opera, 37, 40–41, 44, 184, 221–22; interest in theater, 37, 44–45, 168, 220–21; as international flagship, 168; as interpreter of music, 3–5; as jury member for International Tchaikovsky Competition, 152; and La Grange de Mesley, 175–78; life in Odessa, 42–49; linguistic background, 39; love of Italy, 168; love of walking, 75, 222; and loyalty to Soviet Union, 156; and Lucewicz's videotaped rehearsal, 248–50; mental health, 230–31; move to Moscow highrise, 229–30; musical legacy, 264–72; musical memory, 2–3, 182, 209–10,

213; myth of, 2–3, 6–7, 16–17, 39, 182, 207, 219, 273; nicknames, 30, 36, 43; as only child, 35–36; opinion of United States, 157; and People's Artist prize, 149; and perfect pitch, 233; performs at Stalin's funeral, 16–17, 117; piano education, 39–40; posture at piano, 57; practice book, 207; and Prokofiev, 97–104; public image, 17–18; receives honorary doctorate from Oxford University, 247; recordings, 150, 158–59, 166, 183, 185, 266–72, 277–83; relationship with Dorliak, 82–89, 263; relationship with mother, 135–42, 200–201, 237–38; relationship with stepfather, 138; and religion, 225–26; reluctance to teach, 40; repertoire, 2–3, 213–16 (*See also separate entry*: Richter, Sviatoslav Teofilovich, works for piano played and mentioned in the text); and retirement, 245–46; reunion with mother, 142–44; and role models, 202–4; schooling, 39; self-criticism, 5; Siberian tour (1986), 184; and Sonning Prize, 186–87, 216; and Soviet culture, 10–12; and Soviet politics, 7–10, 45; stage demeanor, 199–200; and Stalin Prize, 149; as student in Moscow, 60–73; studies with Neuhaus, 52, 54–58; summer home (dacha), 226–28; and surveillance by NKVD, 79–80; technique, 5–6; temperament, 11–13, 15–16; as theater director, 173; tour of Finland (1960), 154–56; tours in Western Europe, 165–66, 168; tours of Japan, 181–82; tours of United States, 142–44, 156–64, 179, 225; visits to mother in Germany, 144–48; willingness to take risk, 201, 208; working methods, 206–12, 248–50; and World War II, 74–75, 77–81; and Yamaha Corporation, 197–99

Richter, Sviatoslav Teofilovich, works for piano played and mentioned in the text: Bach, Double Concerto in C Major, 62; Bach, Piano Concerto in D Minor (slow movement), 117; Bach, *Well-Tempered Clavier* (*Das wohltemperierte Klavier*) (books I and II), 77–79, 213, 267, 271; Bartók, Piano Concerto No. 2, 150, 214, 228; Bartók, Piano Sonata No. 1, 170; Bartók, Sonata for Two Pianos and Percussion, 214; Beethoven, Choral Fantasy, 114; Beethoven, Piano Concerto No. 1 in C Major (op. 15), 164; Beethoven, Piano Concerto No. 3 in C Minor (op. 37), 166; Beethoven, Piano Sonata No. 6 in C Minor (*Pathétique*) (op. 13), 73, 117; Beethoven, Piano Sonata No. 11 in E-flat Major (*Marcia funebre*) (op. 26), 47; Beethoven, Piano Sonata No. 17 in D Minor (*The Tempest*) (op. 31, no. 2), 166, 201; Beethoven, Piano Sonata No. 23 in F Minor (*Appassionata*) (op. 57), 78–79, 160, 265; Beethoven, Piano Sonata No. 26 in E-flat Major (*Les Adieux*) (op. 81a), 237; Beethoven, Piano Sonata No. 28 in A Major (op. 101), 185; Beethoven, Piano Sonata No. 29 in B-flat Major (*Hammerklavier*) (op. 106), 18, 52, 231–32, 267–68; Beethoven, Piano Sonata No. 31 in A-flat Major (op. 110), 57; Beethoven, sonatas, 40, 251; Beethoven, Triple Concerto (op. 56), 267; Beethoven, Variations and Fugue in E-flat Major (*Eroica*) (op. 35), 211; Beethoven, Variations on a Waltz by Diabelli (op. 120), 185, 211;

Berg, Chamber Concerto, 182–84; Borodin, *Prince Igor* (Polovetsian dances), 43; Brahms, *Die schöne Magelone*, 171; Brahms, Piano Concerto No. 2, 163–64; Brahms, Piano Sonata in F-sharp Minor (op. 5), 13; Brahms, Piano Sonatas No. 1 and No. 2, 185; Brahms, Variations (op. 21), 248; Britten, Piano Concerto, 173; Chopin, Ballade in F Minor, 48; Chopin, ballades, 185, 251; Chopin, etudes, 185; Chopin, etudes (op. 10), 48; Chopin, *Polonaise-Fantaisie*, 48, 185; Chopin, Scherzo in E Major, 48, 237; Debussy, preludes, 60; Dvořak, Piano Concerto, 144, 163–64; Gershwin, Concerto in F, 215; Glazunov, *Raymonda* (piano solo), 46; Grieg, Piano Concerto, 170, 192–93; Haydn, sonatas, 251; Hindemith, Kammermusik No. 2 (piano concerto), 215; Hindemith, *Ludus Tonalis*, 215; Hindemith, Suite "1922," 215; Liszt, Concerto in A Major, 163; Liszt, *Les Préludes*, 68; Liszt, Piano Concertos Nos. 1 and 2, 144; Liszt, Sonata in B Minor, 12, 172, 220; Liszt, *Transcendental Etudes*, 213; Mozart, Piano Concerto No. 20 in D Minor (KV 466), 76; Mozart, Piano Concerto No. 22 in E-flat Major (KV 482), 173; Mozart, Piano Concerto No. 27 in B-flat Major (KV595), 171; Mozart, Sonata in D Major for Two Pianos (KV 448), 172; Mussorgsky, *Boris Godunov* (Coronation scene), 43; Mussorgsky, *Pictures at an Exhibition*, 3, 67; Poulenc, Concerto for Two Pianos, 248; Prokofiev, Piano Concerto No. 5 in G Major (op. 55), 73, 102, 152, 196; Prokofiev, Piano

Russell, Ken, 17
Russian civil war, 31–32
Russian culture, 9; and homosexuality, 86–87; "*sudba takaya*," 10. *See also* Soviet culture
Russian Revolution, 6–7, 31

Saint Petersburg conservatory, 94
Saint-Saëns, Camille: Piano Concerto No. 2 in G Minor (op. 22), 247, 270; Piano Concerto No. 5 in F Major (op. 103), 247, 270; Variations for two pianos on theme by Beethoven, 69
Sairanen, Antti, 274–75
Sakharov, Andrei, 128, 246
Salzburg, 254
Salzburg Festival, 147–48, 223
Sanderling, Kurt, 4, 62–64, 70–71, 74, 114, 120, 123, 129, 163, 193–94, 199, 220
scales, musical, 208
Schnabel, Arthur, 88, 264
Schnittke, Alfred, 59, 215
Schönberg, Arnold, 94
Schonberg, Harold C., 161
Schreier, Peter, 174–75
Schreker, Franz, 95; *Der ferne Klang* (opera), 25–26
Schubert, Franz, 86, 88–89; Duo in A Major, 170; Fantasy in F Minor, 171; Grand Duo, 171; Piano Sonata No. 17 in D Major (D. 850), 88; Piano Sonata No. 21 in B-flat Major, 4–5, 20, 172; *Wanderer* Fantasy, 60, 73, 75, 148, 166
Schumann, Robert, 78, 86, 172, 230; *Blumenstück*, 185; *Carnaval*, 214; Fantasy in C Major, 60, 144, 166; *Introduction and Allegro Appassionato*, 171; *Kreisleriana*, 55, 214; *Noveletten*, 212; Piano Concerto in A Minor (op.

54), 43–44, 186; Piano Sonata No. 2 in G Minor, 214; Second Novelette, 237; Toccata, 185
Schwäbisch Gmünd, 34, 139, 144–48, 200–201
Schwarz, Boris, 130, 152
Schwarz, Falk, 266
Schwarzkopf, Elisabeth, 247
Scriabin, Alexander: Piano Sonata No. 5, 207–8; Piano Sonata No. 6, 214; piano sonatas, 166, 172; *Poème de l'extase*, 45
"secretaries," for Soviet artists, 157
Segawa, Koh, 181, 197–98, 245
Semyonov sisters, 43
Serkin, Rudolf, 164
Shepilov, Dmitri, 151
Shostakovich, Dmitri, 65, 87–88, 93, 95, 103, 116–31, 170, 172, 186; and *Boris Godunov*, 110; death of, 242; denunciation of, 107, 121–22; disputed autobiography, 127–30; as "dissident," 128; and formalism, 104, 106, 120–22; as leader of Soviet music, 123–24, 127; place in contemporary orchestral repertoire, 126; and Prokofiev, 117–18; and Stalin Prize, 109; and symphonic genre, 125–26
Shostakovich, Dmitri, works: Concerto for Piano No. 1 (op. 35), 119, 125; Concerto for Violin No. 1 (op. 77), 124; *From Jewish Folk Poetry* (song cycle), 124–25; *Golden Age* (ballet), 125; *Katarina Izmailova*, 125; *Lady Macbeth of the Mtsensk District* (opera), 120–21, 125, 149; *Nose, The* (opera), 125; Piano Quintet in G Minor, 109; Piano Sonata No. 1 (op. 12), 125; Piano Trio No. 2 in E Minor (op. 67), 126; Preludes and Fugues, 126; Sonata for Viola and Piano (op.

Wolf, Hugo, 86
World War I, 27–31
World War II, 7, 74–75, 102, 106
Writers' Congress (1934), 107

Xenakis, Iannis, 215

Yalta Conference, 106
Yamaha Corporation, piano division, 181, 197–99
Yeltsin, Boris, 245
Yevtushenko, Yevgeni, 126, 129, 150

Yudina, Maria, 74, 78, 131
Yusefovitch, Victor, 169

Zak, Yakov, 48, 53, 74
Zelenin, Viktor Gerasimovitch, 185, 212, 221, 225–26, 256–57, 262–63
Zhdanov, Andrei, 104–12, 121, 124, 127; assassination of, 110. *See also* formalism
Zhitomir, Ukraine, 25, 28–29, 48, 202; evacuation from (1916), 29; typhus epidemic, 31